GERMAN CINEMA
SINCE UNIFICATION

The New Germany in Context

Series editors: Jonathan Grix (Birmingham), Paul Cooke (University of Leeds) and Lothar Funk (University of Trier)

The New Germany in Context provides a forum for original research into the state of post-unity German society from a wide range of disciplinary perspectives. Since unification, Germany, and its place in the world, has undergone a period of rapid development and change. This series brings together academics from political science, economics, history and cultural studies in order to explore the legacies and debates which shape the new Federal Republic.

Other titles in the series include:

German cinema
since unification

Edited by
David Clarke

continuum

CONTINUUM
The Tower Building   80 Maiden Lane
11 York Road   Suite 704
London SE1 7NX   New York, NY 10038

Published in association with University of Birmingham Press
Copyright © David Clarke and Contributors 2006

ISBN 0-8264-9106-5 (HB)
     0-8264-8145-0 (PB)

British Library Cataloguing in Publication data
A CIP catalogue record for this book is available from the British Library

Typeset by Echelon Typesetting, Shaftesbury, Dorset, UK
Printed and bound in the UK by MPG Books Ltd, Bodmin, Cornwall

Contents

Contributors

SEÁN ALLAN is Senior Lecturer at the University of Warwick. He has published a number of articles on aspects of the cinema of the GDR and, with John Sandford, is co-editor of *DEFA. East German Cinema, 1946–1992* (1999). He has also worked on aspects of eighteenth and nineteenth-century German literature and is the author of *The Plays of Heinrich von Kleist: Ideals and Illusions* (1996) and *The Stories of Heinrich von Kleist: Fictions of Security* (2001).

DANIELA BERGHAHN is Principal Lecturer in Film Studies and German Studies at Oxford Brookes University. Her research focuses on the cinema and cultural history of East and West Germany. She has published essays on film censorship, cinematic adaptations of literature and Wim Wenders. She is co-editor of *Unity and Diversity in the New Europe* (2000) and *Millennial Essays on Film and Other German Studies* (2001). Her most recent book is *Hollywood behind the Wall: The Cinema of East Germany* (2004).

ROB BURNS is Professor of German Studies at the University of Warwick. His publications include: *Arbeiterkulturbewegung in der Weimarer Republik* (2 vols, 1982), *Protest and Democracy in West Germany* (1988) and the edited volume *German Cultural Studies* (1995).

DAVID CLARKE is Lecturer in German at the University of Bath. His research interests include contemporary German film, the literature of East Germany and contemporary German literature. He is the author of *'Diese merkwürdige Kleinigkeit einer Vision': Christoph Hein's Social Critique in Transition* (2002).

DICKON COPSEY completed his MA and PhD at Glasgow University in the Department of German. His doctoral research focused primarily on the German cinema of the 1990s. It included separate investigations into the representation of gender within the mainstream romantic comedies of the early 1990s, and representations of the former GDR and of ethnic minority voices in Turkish–German cinema.

JOHN E. DAVIDSON is Associate Professor of Germanic Languages and Literatures at The Ohio State University, where he teaches film, literature and cultural theory. He is author of *Deterritorializing the New German Cinema* (1999) and is currently working on a book entitled 'Crossing Over: German Cinema from 1924 to 1954'. He is also co-editor of the forthcoming *German Cinema of the 1950s* (with Sabine Hake).

RANDALL HALLE is Associate Professor of German and Film Studies at the University of Rochester. He co-edited the special double issue of *Camera Obscura* on 'Marginality and Alterity in Contemporary European Cinema' and *Light Motives: German Popular Film in Perspective* (2003). In addition to numerous essays he authored *Queer Social Philosophy: Critical Readings from Kant to Adorno* (2004). He is currently researching and presenting his work for *Frames of Belonging: German Film from National to Transnational Productions*.

RACHEL PALFREYMAN is Lecturer in German Studies at the University of Nottingham. She has published a monograph on Edgar Reitz's *Heimat* (2000) and, with Elizabeth Boa, a study of the *Heimat* genre 1890–1990 (2000).

German cinema
since unification

David Clarke

The issue of commercialism has frequently dominated discussions of German film in the 1990s. Since unification, a new generation of young German directors has demonstrated that it is possible to produce commercially viable German-language films which look to the models provided by Hollywood genre cinema rather than a European art-house tradition. This new mentality has, however, brought with it an apparent rejection of the highly personal and often political attitude to filmmaking adopted by the generation of directors that dominated German filmmaking in the 1970s. Young directors now frequently emphasize the necessity for a teamwork-based approach to filmmaking and their own professionalism. The director is thereby downgraded from the status of auteur (*Autor*) to that of a skilled technician, who keeps a close eye on the marketability of his or her product.[1]

This development has broadly elicited two kinds of response from commentators on the German film industry. The first, represented by the critics Eric Rentschler, Georg Seeßlen and Fernand Jung,[2] for example, has tended to mourn this distinct commercial turn, which is compared unfavourably with the achievements of the directors of the New German Cinema. For these critics, it is not just the alleged tedious conventionality of the films presented by this new generation that offends, but also the perceived absence of any critical impulse within these works. The second, represented, for instance, by *Der bewegte Film*, a book sponsored by the commercial television channel ProSieben, points to a legacy of popular German film and applauds emerging filmmakers who are able to produce quality entertainment products which can appeal to large domestic audiences and perhaps also find distributors abroad.[3]

In many ways, the charges levelled against German film since unification by critics like Rentschler, Seeßeln and Jung would be hard to refute, even if it were the declared aim of this volume to do so. The directors of the New German Cinema (including Rainer Werner Fassbinder, Werner Herzog, Wim Wenders, Helma Sanders-Brahms, Alexander Kluge and Margarethe von Trotta) very often engaged with contemporary German society from the point of view of its victims.[4] They also intervened directly in contemporary social and political debates[5] and grappled with the legacies of Germany's history in the twentieth century.[6] In addition, these filmmakers fought for their financial independence from the mainstream cinema industry and attempted to develop the highly personal directorial styles that lent their work the epithet of auteurist cinema (*Autorenkino*). The 1990s, by contrast, were dominated by a tendency whose origins Hans-Günther Pflaum and Hans Helmut Prinzler had already noted in the films of younger directors in the 1980s: namely, a 'cinema of affluence'. In this the conventions of commercial cinema and the privileging of technical competence over critical subject matter were significant factors.[7] The cinema of the 1990s can also be regarded as a cinema of affluence in other ways. Those represented in many of the most commercially successful German films of the period are middle-class and financially secure, consequently they have plenty of time to concentrate on their personal lives and their career worries (which, however, do not, as Seeßeln and Jung note, include the very real possibility of unemployment[8]). This trend has been most frequently observed in a wave of highly successful relationship comedies of the 1990s, such as Rainer Kaufmann's *Talk of the Town* (*Stadtgespräch*, 1995) and Katja von Garnier's *Making Up* (*Abgeschminkt*, 1993). However, it can still be found in more recent films such as Thomas Huettner's *Moonlight Tariff* (*Mondscheintarif*, 2000), or in a number of popular youth films that concentrate on the trials and tribulations of middle-class youngsters in search of a little (but not too much) independence from parents,[9] their first sexual experience[10] or the ultimate sexual experience.[11] Where adversity is presented in the lives of young people – for example in Caroline Link's surprise hit *Beyond Silence* (*Jenseits der Stille*, 1996), in which the daughter of a deaf couple realizes her dream of becoming a violinist – conflicts with the parental generation are resolved with relative ease. In Rentschler's words, this is also very much a 'cinema of consensus'. The possibility of changing the status quo is no longer one that is entertained by many successful filmmakers even if they felt it to be desirable or, indeed, possible. As Thomas Elsaesser puts it, the 'new wave' of the 1990s is 'cockily mainstream, brazenly commercial' and 'wants no truck with the former quality label "art-cinema"'.[12]

This highly pessimistic reading of recent developments in German cinema must, however, be seen in the context of the German film industry in which young directors now work. The state funding of film production in the postwar Federal Republic was never entirely divorced from commercial considerations.[13] However, the coming to power of Helmut Kohl's Christian Democrat–Liberal coalition in 1982 saw the politicians responsible for the film industry actively proclaiming the need for a cinema of popular (and thus consensual) entertainment rather than elitist (and critical) art.[14] This stance has largely been reflected in film funding policy ever since. The rise of commercial television satellite television stations such as ProSieben, Sat.1 and RTL since the mid-1980s, all of whom produce their own TV movies,[15] as well as the renewed interest of Hollywood studios in investing in home-grown German films in the 1990s,[16] has brought about 'a dramatic transition from a state-subsidized model of film production that was free of anxiety about profit and commercial appeal to a mode dominated by private interest and big capital' in the course of the last decade.[17] Many young directors have recognized that this new situation offers them the opportunity to gather valuable practical experience if they are willing to work in a commercial context. As the interviews contained in Frederik Steiner's recent volume demonstrate, the first step on the road to the eventual realization of a personal project which might be compared to the products of the New German Cinema is often a commission to direct a made-for-TV film for a private broadcaster. This is then followed by further commissions to direct already-existent, commercially oriented scripts for the cinema.[18] A career trajectory of this kind can be seen in the case of Hans-Christian Schmid, who has directed commercially successful youth films such as *Crazy* (2001) and *It's a Jungle Out There* (*Nach 5 im Urwald*, 1995), but who has more recently co-written and directed *Lights* (*Lichter*, 2003). *Lights* is an episodic, realist film which examines the struggles of illegal immigrants, petty criminals, failed entrepreneurs, the unemployed and struggling workers on both sides of the German–Polish border. Another example would be Esther Gronenborn, who used a successful career in directing promotional videos for pop music as a springboard into directing her first feature, *Alaska.de* (2000). This film deals with the lives of teenagers on a run-down high-rise estate on the outskirts of Berlin. The work of these young directors clearly shows how the division between commercial forms of filmmaking and the author's cinema may be beginning to break down, although directors who cut their teeth on commercial projects clearly run the risk of never realizing the more personal and more critical films they might ideally like to make. It should also be noted, of course, that many filmmakers in the 1990s and beyond have no ambitions beyond the commercial genre cinema.

The division between the auteurist film (*Autorenfilm*) and commercial cinema is further eroded by a director like Tom Tykwer, whose box-office success with *Run Lola Run* (*Lola rennt*, 1998), one of the most internationally renowned German films of the last ten years, must be seen in the context of a career producing idiosyncratic, non-mainstream films. These films include his début *Deadly Maria* (*Die tödliche Maria*, 1993), *Winter Sleepers* (*Winterschläfer*, 1996) which is a postmodern reworking of the German mountain film (*Bergfilm*) tradition and his most recent work *Heaven* (2002), an elegiac rendering of a script by the late Polish director Krzysztof Kieslowski. Indeed, *Run Lola Run* itself has recently been re-read in the context of the *Autorenfilm* tradition.[19] It should also be noted that Tykwer was a founder of the independent production company X-Filme Creative Pool, a collaboration between producer Stefan Arndt and directors Tykwer, Wolfgang Becker and Dani Levy, which followed the model of United Artists in the US. The aims of this company are threefold: firstly, to improve the working relationship between producers, writers and filmmakers by integrating them into a cooperative structure that is both critical and supportive; secondly, to take risks and produce demanding, individual, yet enter-taining German films that will reach sizable audiences; and, thirdly, to improve the control of artists over the finished film product.[20] Reminiscent of the Filmverlag der Autoren (the production company founded in 1971 by a group of New German Cinema filmmakers including Fassbinder and Wenders), yet with distinctly more commercial sensibilities, X-Filme seeks to bridge the gap between popular cinema and intelligent and original filmmaking. So far this strategy seems to be paying off, given the phenomenal success not only of *Run Lola Run*, but also more recently with Becker's *Goodbye, Lenin!* (2003), and the less spectacular but nonetheless healthy audience figures for many of its other films.

Another problem with the dismissal of post-unification German cinema as consensual, conventional and commercial is that it tends to focus on the (relatively) large number of domestic popular successes that have characterized the 1990s. Although they have been unable to secure the international recognition which the New German Cinema achieved, a number of directors continue to make highly personal and often critical films set in the contemporary Federal Republic. Even if these films do not pull in large cinema audiences, the funding which state television supplies on a regional and national level for their production ensures them a television screening and, through this medium, perhaps a larger audience than they could hope for with a cinema release. As Marc Silberman argues, the increasing prominence of television as a means of exhibition provides at least the potential for films that are not beholden to the conventions of the commercial cinema, and which can present a critical view of German society in the 1990s. This recalls the opportunities that television provided for the New German Cinema in the 1970s.[21] In this context, any number of films might be mentioned, but works by directors such as Thomas Arslan, Michael Klier or Christian Petzold[22] have all been screened on television following limited theatrical releases. These films have dealt with topics such as poverty, crime, the experiences of second-generation immigrants, the consequences of German unification for individual biographies and the legacy of left-wing terrorism.

Including the work of these and other directors in a survey of German cinema in the 1990s clearly challenges the perception that we are only dealing with a cinema of consensus. As Daniela Berghahn argues in her chapter in this volume, a continuing tradition of the critical auteurist film has been enriched by the legacy of the East German DEFA studios, most prominently represented by the critical realism of former DEFA directors Andreas Kleinert and Andreas

Dresen. We should also not forget the work of provocative, low-budget *enfants terribles* such as Christoph Schlingensief and Rosa von Praunheim. Von Praunheim's work since unification is examined by Randall Halle in his contribution to this volume. Also, whilst Rob Burns' chapter on German–Turkish cinema argues that the films of younger directors such as Fatih Akin shows a worrying tendency to play down the very real tensions of Germany's multi-ethnic society, he also points to the example of Kutlug Ataman's impressive *Lola + Bilidikid* (1998). This film does not shy away from depicting the sense of alienation felt by Berlin's Turkish community, whilst at the same time critically examining notions of masculinity both within that community and amongst young Germans.[23] In John Davidson's examination of coming to terms with the past (*Vergangenheitsbewältigung*) in German films of the 1990s, we see how a justified criticism of the spreading of 'anti-memory' in relation to Germany's fascist past in popular films such as Max Fäberböck's *Aimée and Jaguar* (*Aimée und Jaguar*, 1999) must be seen in relation to works which do not shy away from a confrontation with the role of ordinary people in fascism. Such films include Volker Schlöndorff's *The Ogre* (*Der Unhold*, 1996) and Gordian Maugg's *The Olympic Summer* (*Der olympische Sommer*, 1993). Clearly, alongside the mainstream 'cinema of consensus', there is much more to be discovered.

This volume is presented in such a way as to be of interest to students and film scholars working both within and outside of German studies.[24] The continued relevance of the study of German cinema at university level is amply demonstrated by the many German films made since unification which can be found on undergraduate syllabuses both in the UK and the US. These films feature next to 'classics' of both the Weimar Republic and the New German Cinema. As the contributions to this volume demonstrate, just as films of the New German Cinema can be used as a means of engaging with issues of national significance in the Federal Republic before 1990, German film in the 1990s does not limit itself to a comfortable preoccupation with the personal lives of the middle-classes. It also addresses issues of contemporary relevance such as the post-unification legacy of left-wing extremism, as can be seen in Rachel Palfreyman's chapter. Equally, in David Clarke's examination of representations of Berlin, we can see how recent film has used the new capital city as a metaphor for the conditions of postmodern social existence in post-unification Germany.

This volume also contributes to the welcome reassessment of popular genres of German cinema that has characterized important recent scholarship in the field of German film.[25] Dickon Copsey, for example, uses the reception-oriented theories of cultural studies as the basis for a rereading of the much maligned relationship comedies of the 1990s and argues against their dismissal as a mere affirmation of the status quo. In his chapter on reunification comedies, Seán Allan demonstrates how a number of highly popular, and (in some cases) apparently trivial, comic representations of the integration of East and West Germany can be read as contributions to a 'coming to terms' with the former GDR's socialist past and the consequences of the unification process. Whilst many of the films discussed in these chapters may not be integrated into the canon of world cinema in the long term, as some products of the German Expressionism and the New German Cinema have been, they never-theless provide a fascinating means of examining the ways in which Germans attempted to address significant social and political change at the end of the twentieth century and the beginning of the twenty-first. As will be clear from the above, and also from the research presented in this volume, the often-expressed pessimism as to the state and future of German film does not disqualify German cinema since 1990 as a fruitful object of study for either researchers or students. This volume hopes to serve as a useful tool for such study.

* * *

The editor would like to thank the contributors for their hard work and patience during the preparation of this volume and the series editors for providing us with the opportunity to publish this material.

Notes

1   'Das Lachen macht's', *Der Spiegel*, 16 September 1996, pp. 214–25 (p. 220).

2   Eric Rentschler, 'From New German Cinema to the Post-Wall Cinema of Consensus' in Mette Hjort and Scott Mackenzie (eds.), *Cinema and Nation* (London: Routledge, 2000), pp. 260–77; Georg Seeßlen and Fernand Jung, 'Das Kino der Autoren ist tot: Glauben wir an ein neues? Eine Polemik zum deutschen Film', *epd Film*, 9 (1997), 18–21.

3   Heike Amend and Michael Bütow (eds.), *Der bewegte Film* (Berlin: Vistas, 1997). The title of this book refers to Sönke Wortmann's 1994 hit *Maybe, Maybe Not* (*Der bewegte Mann*).

4   For example in Alexander Kluge's *Yesterday Girl* (*Abschied von Gestern*, 1966), Rainer Werner Fassbinder's *Fear Eats the Soul* (*Angst essen Seele auf*, 1974) and *In a Year of Thirteen Moons* (*In einem Jahr mit dreizehn Monden*, 1978), or Werner Herzog's *The Enigma of Kaspar Hauser* (*Jeder für sich und Gott gegen alle*, 1974).

5   Most famously in the collective film *Germany in Autumn* (*Deutschland im Herbst*, 1977) which addressed the climate of political repression around the time of the murder of industrialist Hanns Martin Schleyer in 1977 and the subsequent suicide of the imprisoned leaders of the Red Army Faction (*Rote Armee Fraktion* or RAF).

6   See Anton Kaes, *From Hitler to Heimat: The Return of History as Film* (Cambridge, Mass. and London: Harvard University Press, 1989).

7   Hans Günther Pflaum and Hans Helmut Prinzler, *Film in der Bundesrepublik: der neue deutsche Film von den Anfängen bis zur Gegenwart mit einem Exkurs über das Kino der DDR: ein Handbuch* (Stuttgart: Hanser, 1992), p. 143. Pflaum and Prinzler's original term is 'Wohlstandswerke' ('works of affluence'), which I adapt here.

8   Seeßlen and Jung, 'Das Kino der Autoren ist tot', p. 20.

9   See Hans-Christian Schmid's *It's a Jungle Out There* (*Nach 5 im Urwald*, 1995).

10 For example, Hans-Christian Schmid's *Crazy* (2001).

11 In Dennis Gansel's *Girls on Top* (*Mädchen Mädchen*, 2001).

12 Thomas Elsaesser, 'Introduction: German Cinema in the 1990s' in Elsaesser and Michael Wedel (eds.), *The BFI Companion to German Cinema* (London: BFI, 1999), pp. 3–16 (p. 3).

13 On film funding in Germany see Thomas Elsaesser, *New German Cinema: A History* (London: BFI, 1992), pp. 20–35; John Sandford, *The New German Cinema* (London: Wolff, 1980), pp. 13–16.

14 Eric Rentschler, 'Die achtziger Jahre: Endzeitspiele und Zeitgeistszenarien' in Wolfgang Jacobsen et al. (eds.), *Die Geschichte des deutschen Films* (Stuttgart: Metzler, 1993), pp. 285–322 (p. 288).

15 A number of the commercial successes of the 1990s were in fact 'amphibian films', originally produced for television, but then given a theatrical release: for example, Sönke Wortmann's *Alone Amongst Women* (*Allein unter Frauen*, 1991) and Kaufmann's *Talk of the Town* (*Stadtgespräch*, 1995). Michael Bütow, 'Großer Bruder Fernsehen' in Amend and Bütow (eds.), *Der bewegte Film*, pp. 49–56 (p. 51).

16 Elsaesser, 'Introduction', p. 3.

17 Randall Halle, 'German Film: *Aufgehoben*', *New German Critique*, 37 (2002), 7–46 (p. 11).

18 Frederick Steiner, *Stepping out: Von der Filmhochschule zum Spielfilm: Junge Regisseure erzählen* (Marburg: Schüren, 2003).

19 Ian Garwood, 'The *Autorenfilm* in Contemporary German Cinema' in Tim Bergfelder, Erica Carter and Deniz Göktürk (eds.), *The German Cinema Book* (London: BFI, 2002), pp. 202–10.

20 See 'Eins, zwei, drei... x Filme' in Michael Töteberg (ed.), *Szenenwechsel: Momentauf-nahmen des jungen deutschen Films* (Reinbek bei Hamburg: Rowohlt Taschenbuch, 1999), pp. 40–3; Jörg Magenau, 'Großes Kino: Von Berlin in die Welt: X-Filme versteht sich als Manufaktur fürs Kino und setzt dabei auf Niveau und Publikumsnähe', *Deutschland Magazin*, 4 (2003), http://www.magazin-deutschland.de/content/archiv/archiv-ger/03-04/art9.html; http://www.xfilme.de/html/philosophie.html.

21 Marc Silberman, 'European Cinema in the 90s: Whither Germany?' in Gerhard Fischer and David Roberts (eds.), *Schreiben nach der Wende: Ein Jahrzehnt deutscher Literatur 1989–1999* (Tübingen: Stauffenburg, 2001), pp. 317–30 (p. 326).

22 Petzold has in fact worked more frequently in the field of the television film, to great critical acclaim.

23 For a much less sympathetic reading of *Lola + Bilidikid* from a Turkish–German perspective, see Feridun Zaigmolu, 'KanakSüperStar' in Töteberg (ed.), *Szenenwechsel*, pp. 207–18.

24 For this reason, this volume gives quotations and film titles first in English, with the original German in parentheses or notes.

25 For recent examples, see Part One of Bergfelder, Carter and Göktürk (eds.), *The German Cinema Book*; Randall Halle and Margaret McCarthy, *Light Motives: German Popular Film in Perspective* (Detroit, Mich.: Wayne State University Press, 2003); Sabine Hake, *Popular Cinema of the Third Reich* (Austin, Texas: University of Texas, 2001); and the discussion of the 1950s and 1960s *Heimatfilm* in Elisabeth Boa and Rachel Palfreyman, *Heimat: A German Dream: Regional Loyalties and National Identity in German Culture, 1890–1990* (Cambridge: CUP, 2000).

Chapter 1

The fourth generation: legacies of violence as quest for identity in post-unification terrorism films

Rachel Palfreyman

The Baader–Meinhof Group, later known as the Red Army Faction (*Rote Armee Fraktion* or RAF), rocked the seemingly fragile West German democracy of the 1970s with a series of attacks on targets identified by the group as representing capitalism and American imperialism. The leading members of the RAF – Andreas Baader, Gudrun Ensslin, Ulrike Meinhof, Jan-Carl Raspe and Holger Meins – were arrested in 1972 but their harsh treatment in prison gave rise to concern among left-wing intellectuals and arguably contributed to an escalation of violence in a new generation of terrorists. In 1977, West Germany experienced its worst terrorist crisis, the notorious German Autumn. Hanns Martin Schleyer, the president of the German employers' association, was kidnapped by the RAF in September in an attempt to secure the release of their imprisoned comrades. After a Lufthansa plane, hijacked by a Palestinian group in support of the RAF, was stormed by German special troops, the RAF prisoners Andreas Baader, Gudrun Ensslin and Jan-Carl Raspe apparently committed suicide on 18 October in Stammheim prison. Schleyer was murdered by his captors. Doubts remain over the Stammheim deaths, with some curious details (such as the fact that Baader and Raspe each had a gun hidden in their high-security cells) giving rise to speculation that the prisoners might have been murdered. Terrorist attacks continued sporadically into the 1980s and early 1990s before the RAF announced that it was disbanding in 1998.

Artists and intellectuals, respected as key social commentators in West Germany, were crucial in articulating a critical response to the crisis. Margarethe von Trotta, Rainer Werner Fassbinder and Volker Schlöndorff used film to examine connections between terrorist violence, state authoritarianism, the 'terror' of domestic repression in the 1950s and the postwar response to National Socialism. The way these and other filmmakers reflected on the German Autumn can be seen as a defining moment in the development of the New German Cinema. However, in a striking and audacious turn, filmmakers of the late 1990s and the new millennium – including, interestingly, Schlöndorff again – are returning to the issue of left-wing terrorism in their films. In this chapter, I will discuss four examples of this tendency: the feature films *The State I Am In* (*Die innere Sicherheit*, Christian Petzold, 2000) and *The Legends of Rita* (*Die Stille nach dem Schuss*, Volker Schlöndorff, 2000), the feature documentary *Black Box FRG* (*Black Box BRD*, Andres Veiel, 2000);[1] and the fictionalized biopic *Baader* (Christopher Roth, 2002). Of course historical narratives are also interventions in the present, and in every case discussed below the look back to West German history is an attempt to consider the meaning of this period of West German history for a unified Germany. To assert power over historical meaning is also to stake a claim relating not just to the past, but to the present and to the future as well. Though the films discussed below have West German terrorism in common as a central theme, they do not all adopt the same position but use their engagement with the past to suggest subtly different analyses of post-unification Germany and different visions of its future.[2]

In exploring contemporary German identity via the West German past, the new films allude to the cinematic tradition of the New German Cinema both by taking up the genre of the terrorism film and by consciously alluding to the aesthetics and politics of the earlier generation of films. In this double move there is a clear effort to identify the new cinema of the Berlin Republic as belonging generically and aesthetically to a cinematic tradition, while at the same time demonstrating that the aesthetic and political project of the 1970s and 1980s art cinema cannot simply be repeated. Again, there is no particular aesthetic conformity in these films so there is no single position on how the post-unification cinema should relate to the New German Cinema. Schlöndorff's allusions to DEFA[3] as a further cinematic tradition imply that the new films are not only interested in the New German Cinema but in how filmmakers in the Berlin Republic might acknowledge both East and West German cinemas yet function within a broader international film landscape. The unmistakable gesture back to the terrorism films of the 1970s and 1980s indicates that both the history and the *film* history of the Bonn Republic form a framework to investigate questions of contemporary Germany and the relationship of cinema both to its own past and to its current political context.

UNIFICATION AND CINEMATIC LEGACIES

The unification of Germany promised new directions in cinema. Certainly there seemed to be no going back to older modes of film funding.[4] Filmmakers needed the collaboration of TV companies and there seemed to be an increasing desire to abandon the project of the New German Cinema and produce German genre films that would please audiences, fit on the small screen, be funny and romantic but have a quirky German flavour. While these films could unkindly be described as middlebrow, a 'cinema of consensus' as Eric Rentschler put it,[5] the highbrow end of the market was concerned with unearthing and rediscovering the forgotten or suppressed DEFA classics which had been deprived of attention during the time of division. In the second half of the 1990s, however, there were signs that German filmmakers were returning to specifically German issues, though they were using popular idioms to explore crucial issues of identity.[6] Among the most well-documented are films which investigate the legacy of East German identity, such as *Sonnenallee* (1999) and *Goodbye, Lenin!* (2002).[7] But there is a marked and apparently analogous tendency to look back at West German history in a veritable wave of films considering the RAF and the crisis of the West German state as it sought to respond to the threat of terrorist violence in the 1970s and 1980s. In addition to the four films under discussion in this chapter, feature documentaries such as *Starbuck – Holger Meins* (Gerd Conradt, 2002), *Greater Freedom – Lesser Freedom* (*Große Freiheit – Kleine Freiheit*, Kristina Konrad, 2000), the TV documentaries *Deadly Game* (*Todesspiel*, Heinrich Breloer, 1997) and *Germany and the RAF: In Our Sights* (*Im Fadenkreuz: Deutschland und die RAF*, Christian Berg and Cordt Schnibben, 1997), and the comedy feature *What to Do in Case of Fire?* (*Was tun, wenn's brennt?*, Gregor Schnitzler, 2001) all deal more or less directly with West German terrorism and its legacy.[8]

Such films explode the notion that while east Germans are grappling with seismic changes to everyday life, political structures, job markets and popular cultures, it is a case of 'as you were' for the west. While east Germans' engagement with their experience of the GDR has led to the opening of State Security Service (*Stasi* or *Staatssicherheit*) files and then to a nostalgia for certain aspects of life in East Germany (*Ostalgie*, literally, 'eastalgia'), the west German experience of unification has supposedly been underwhelming (were it not for higher taxes and economic problems). The notion that unification was an exclusively east German experience acknowledges the unequal nature of the political process and the greater upheavals that east Germans faced. However, the logic of this attitude might suggest that were west Germans to look back to the Bonn Republic, they would see unfailing prosperity and stability punctuated by various steps on the road to a more or less successful reckoning with the past (*Aufarbeitung der Vergangenheit*). In fact, the examination of 1970s and 1980s terrorism functions as an important corrective to such a view in that it focuses on the biggest crisis in legitimacy that the Bonn Republic suffered. In addition the films' persistent quest for a usable identity suggests that more changed in the west with unification than might at first be supposed. West German terrorism appeared to push the state to the point of implosion: a stratified, top-down, authoritarian democracy indicated a return of the National Socialist repressed for a critical younger generation. In turn, their violent political struggle was vilified and demonized as a threat to democracy by state and media. An evocation of West Germany as nervous, vulnerable and dominated by entrenched ideological groups and interests is an interesting proposition as *Westalgie* (literally, 'westalgia'),[9] though it is true that a sober look back is sometimes undercut by a clear fascination for the glamour and excitement of terrorism in a grey and bland society.

The films considered in this chapter engage with a moment in West German history and the reckoning with a West German perspective on violence, the hated authoritarian state, division and unification. In addition, they also represent a reckoning with the mighty shadow of the New German Cinema, the film history of the Bonn Republic. At once artistically revered and at the same time in danger of becoming a millstone round the necks of younger filmmakers, the New German Cinema famously became a cultural site for the critical exploration of terrorism in the 1970s and 1980s. Films like *Germany in Autumn* (*Deutschland im Herbst*, 1977), von Trotta's *The German Sisters* (*Die bleierne Zeit*, 1981),[10] Schlöndorff's and von Trotta's *The Lost Honour of Katharina Blum* (*Die verlorene Ehre der Katherina Blum*, 1975) and Reinhard Hauff's *Stammheim* (1985) were crucial spaces of resistance in an otherwise conservative, self-censoring media landscape. The recent terrorist films are certainly exploring the question of how the legacy of the Bonn Republic can be understood in the political climate of the Berlin Republic. A key concern is how a west German identity might, through reckoning with the West German past but also with east–west relations, become a pan-German identity. But they also suggest that parallel developments in the cinema need to take place too: namely a reckoning with the international classics of the New German Cinema, but at the same time an engagement with the critical realist canon of DEFA. *The Legends of Rita* in particular, where Schlöndorff collaborates with the renowned east German scriptwriter Wolfgang Kohlhaase, acknowledges a debt to the DEFA tradition, with characters fleeing to the east instead of the west,[11] and attempts to negotiate a hybrid identity. In addition, German cinemas in both the east and west must come to terms with the changed financial and institutional circumstances that prevail both nationally and globally. Is it possible for cinema to be the space of resistance that it once was? Is it possible or even desirable to attempt to occupy the artistic high ground of the New German Cinema and appropriate the defamiliarizing narrative techniques and strategies for spectatorial autonomy that became the internationally recognized signature of the German cinema in the 1970s? Or might the critical realist legacy of DEFA offer a usable model? Would a hybrid mutation, a synthesis, be possible? What space might German cinema occupy in a new global cinematic climate? The new films do not give definitive answers to these questions, nor can they be said by any stretch of the imagination to sit neatly alongside each other in a show of political unity, but they demonstrate a clear appetite for the labour of constructing German political and cinematic identity. They are emphatically not an attempt to reproduce what Hollywood offers, nor are they necessarily intended to work as middlebrow European TV co-productions. Instead they evince elements of a critical socialist aesthetic which in contrast to the New German Cinema uses estrangement techniques only sparingly.

THE STATE I AM IN

Arguably the most significant New German Cinema film resonating through the current generation of terrorism films is *The German Sisters*, Margarethe von Trotta's film based on the life of the left-wing terrorist Gudrun Ensslin and her sister Christiane. Criticized in some quarters for not being feminist or political enough, or sufficiently critical of the terrorists or of the state, von Trotta's film was by no means universally celebrated.[12] *The German Sisters* looked at the intersections of the personal and the political in the German Autumn, suggesting that the radicalism of the 1970s was born of the leaden repression of the 1950s where moral authoritarianism is enlivened only by puritanical zeal of the Protestant pastor. His children are drilled to be good girls but radicalized by (amongst other things) a school screening of Alain Resnais's Holocaust film *Night and Fog* (*Nuit et brouillard*, 1955). The sister most rebellious in adolescence, Juliane, becomes a liberal feminist seeking legal reform and campaigns for a feminist agenda in the radical press. Marianne, apparently a more conformist child, becomes a terrorist, leaving her young son Jan with her partner, Werner, whose suicide leaves the boy in foster care. When Marianne is imprisoned, Juliane begins a gradual process of overcoming the bitter tensions between them to reach a point where she radically identifies with her sister's suffering and attempts to prove that the inconsistencies of her apparent suicide demand full investigation. At the end of the film she takes on parental responsibility for Jan who has suffered a violent attack in foster care. When the embittered boy demands answers, she tries to tell a sympathetic version of his mother's story.

In Christian Petzold's *The State I Am In*, the story of a terrorist family whose personal relationships are complicated by a radical, criminalizing political position is brought forward to post-unification Germany. The legacy of their violent struggle against a state which no longer exists in the same form is now complicated by the fact that this underground couple did not leave their child in foster care but have somehow evaded capture with their daughter Jeanne, now a teenager, in tow. In *The German Sisters*, Jan ends the film by demanding 'Begin!' ('Fang an!') – Juliane should begin the story of his mother's life. Jeanne, on the other hand – a kind of younger sister to Jan – has not been deprived of her parents in the way that Jan has, but has seemingly been deprived of everything else: every kind of normality from school and friends to clothes and music. At the end of the film Jeanne's parents' bitter warnings about any form of personal contact appear to be borne out. Forced to return to Germany from Portugal, the outlaw family are brought to their knees when Jeanne's first love apparently betrays them. The car they are trying to escape in is forced off the road and though Jeanne is thrown clear, the prospects for her parents seem bleak. Paradoxically, this might finally free Jeanne from her lonely exile.

The State I Am In seems to inhabit a parallel world to *The German Sisters*, imagining what might have happened had Marianne remained at liberty and taken her son with her. Von Trotta approaches her examination of the politics of family and the emergence of radicalism with a sober, almost numb aesthetics, which may have contributed to the film being less prominently received than other works of the time. Scenes between the sisters, which could arguably have yielded a certain kind of glamour, are treated in a careful, desensationalizing and desexualizing manner. When the sisters exchange tops in prison, their brief nakedness recalls a childhood sisterly intimacy which is both defiant and at the same time reveals their essential vulnerability as they are surrounded by hostile surveillance. Similarly, the contemplative length of shots such as that of the car parked in the forest clearing in which Werner has committed suicide, and the extremely restricted colour palette of whites, greys, browns and blues fundamentally undermine the potential for sensation that could have been drawn from the material, and which is arguably exploited by *The Lost Honour of Katharina Blum* and *Stammheim*. *The German Sisters* develops its study of radical politics in the form of a careful and patient search for the identity of Marianne focalized through her sister Juliane. *The State I Am In* echoes these aesthetic techniques, particularly in the scenes of the roads and car parks where meetings with the family's contact are supposed to take place, and of course, in the filming of them being violently forced off the road. These aesthetic references signal that *The State I Am In* is also engaged with a quest for identity; here the young Jeanne struggles to deal with a parental legacy which places her involuntarily in hiding. Trapped in her parents' underground world, it is not safe for her to engage in any kind of conventional teenage search for identity. Jeanne cannot disengage herself from her parents in the way other teenagers can, and her attempts to negotiate divided loyalties between her young lover and her parents fail. The symbolic ending, where the guilty parental generation is literally exploded, departs from *The German Sisters* which suggests a psychological engagement, even radical identification, with the estranged and guilty sister. *The State I Am In*, by contrast, is focalized through Jeanne, the daughter, and her plight – exile and bitter isolation, not only from worldly pleasures but even from her sense of self – is so extreme and so unjust that the presumed death of the parents becomes a grim source of hope, a desperate and slender chance for Jeanne to move forward.

In contrast to *The German Sisters*, *The State I Am In* has no complex structure of flashbacks explicitly connecting adult political struggle with childhood and adolescence. There is no attempt to explore (much less explain) the political background and convictions of Hans and Clara, Jeanne's parents.[13] The film remains in Jeanne's present world, focalized through her experience. However, it does gesture explicitly to political legacies in a key sequence that connects the film both to German history and, through this connection with *The German Sisters*, to German film history. Just as Marianne and Juliane had before her, Jeanne too sees Resnais's *Night and Fog* at a school screening. Her clandestine attempts to connect with a social base of young people lead her directly in the footsteps of Marianne and Juliane, both of whom, it is suggested, were fundamentally changed by the experience. In the two films the extracts from the Resnais's film overlap – both include the end of the film which shows the contemporary reality of Auschwitz. At the very point Jeanne attempts to find a social identity she is confronted with Germany's historical legacy, which, as evidenced by *The German Sisters*, could be what pushed her parents to reject their own social identity and actively try to destroy the state. Such a dreadful cycle, in which young people are somehow compelled to suffer again and again through the generations for the sins of their fathers and mothers, hints obliquely at a connection with the original icon of innocent young suffering, Anne Frank, who was also cut off from ordinary life. Jeanne, we hope, might escape into orphanhood like her boyfriend, who is, of course, socially and psychologically disadvantaged, except when compared to Jeanne, whose situation makes him seem almost fortunate.

The relevance of *Night and Fog* suggests that, to an extent, the issue of historical identity is just as problematic in the new Germany as it was in the old Federal Republic. However, the response of the viewers is quite different. While Marianne and Juliane were physically sickened by their viewing experience, Jeanne and the others do not appear to be directly physically affected. Jeanne is challenged to comment on the film by the teacher and cannot say anything, though whether she is unable to speak about what she has seen, or whether she simply has nothing to say is unclear. Their generation, it seems, will respond differently – but to the same agenda. In addition to the crimes of National Socialism, Jeanne must struggle with the consequences of her parents' crimes against the state, just as they reacted against the crimes of their parents' generation. Jan too bears the consequences of his mother's rebellion in *The German Sisters* – his anger and Jeanne's refusal to stick to the rules of her shadowy existence suggest that again a generational contract has been broken.

Progression from generation to generation is dominated by a connection which might be usefully considered in relation to Marianne Hirsch's concept of postmemory. Though she developed the notion with reference to the children of Holocaust survivors, Hirsch explicitly suggests that it might also be applied to other examples of younger generations dominated by the traumatic memories of older generations:

> Postmemory is distinguished from memory by generational distance and from history by deep personal connection. Post-memory is a powerful and very particular form of memory precisely because its connection to its object or source is mediated not through recollection but through an imaginative investment and creation. This is not to say that memory itself is unmediated, but that it is more directly connected to the past.[14]

As Hirsch argues, postmemory is not merely an absence of memory, a hole in personal history, but can be 'obsessive and relentless' so that the stories of subsequent generations are 'evacuated by the stories of the previous generation'.[15] Beyond the second generation, into the third or even fourth generation (Jeanne as a teenager in 2000 could conceivably have grandparents born during World War II with few if any first-hand memories of the Third Reich), German family history is one of fractured relationships. However, the warring generations cannot seem to break free and the flawed generational bond becomes a generational bind, which is relentless and obsessive, as Hirsch puts it. Younger generations like Marianne, Juliane, Hans and Clara, and then Jan and Jeanne, are condemned to grapple with postmemories of violence and crime that transcend the generations, force families apart and yet chain them together in a hideous, enslaving compulsion to repeat the violence and/or endure desperate estrangement and loss of identity.

Flickering through the story as a nagging, persistent trace is the uneasy sense that Jeanne's apparently failed attempt to negotiate a social identity that will somehow not destroy her isolated family is in some way emblematic of a broader struggle for social identity in the new Germany. Jeanne's story is resolutely, but ultimately disingenuously, fixed on the present, for it is haunted by two troubled past generations which return unbidden to complicate her efforts to find a usable social identity. Although there is no flashback to previous incarnations of Germany, the disorientating effect of Hans and Clara's return to a country they no longer really know is made abundantly clear in the fugitive family's desperate search for funds. Hans digs for buried treasure under the motorway bridge, recalling Gabi Teichert's obsessive 'digging for history' in Alexander Kluge's *The Patriot* (*Die Patriotin*, 1979). He finally finds bundles of old-design Deutschmarks but they are no longer valid. They seem to be entirely cut off from the Germany they once rejected; yet Hans and Clara base their identity on their rejection of the old FRG, and so their sense of self founders on the disappearance of the hated 'other'. Their old comrades in the struggle have come to a sceptical accommodation with the once-hated society and cannot help, especially as they are still (perhaps) under surveillance by state security organizations. An identity crisis looms for such bodies, too, even as they maintain a watchful eye on the terrorist remnant: clearly such superannuated activists are no longer society's major preoccupation. New political problems dominate and people-trafficking appears to be a more pressing concern: when the family stop off at a motorway service station, police arrive in numbers, but it is soon clear that Hans and Clara are not the targets; a crowd of women suddenly fleeing from the toilets into nearby fields indicates the state's priority is illegal immigration. When Hans and Clara's former comrade is on his way to meet them and the police descend it is somewhat unclear at first whether he or the young woman hitchhiker is the target of the surveillance. Whilst the viewer infers all this, ideological questions are largely drained from the film: Hans and Clara, the apparently quintessential terrorist pair, do not discuss politics or ideology. The viewer may or may not be able to supply the missing political context, but there is no direct representation of an ideological struggle in the film text itself. Hans and Clara concentrate on the practical difficulties of surviving undetected and their key quest throughout the film is actually money – far from rocking the state, they seem to be trying to ensure that the family has the bare necessities for survival. Such a concern seems to deny them a political status as left-wing terrorists and reduces them to something more like Bonnie and Clyde: sexy bank robbers in a slightly comic mode whose desire for each other never fails and who finally die together on the run. The emphasis on bank raids as an ancillary terrorist activity also points towards one of the contemporary themes of the film – the gulf between haves and have-nots in post-unification Germany. Jeanne's desire for the right clothes and music is not criticized as such; consumer pleasure itself is less the target of the critique than the social pressures on the poor in such a society. Jeanne's shoplifting is presented as an understandable response to her impossible position, impossible not just because of the political bind she inhabits, but because of her poverty. Her young boyfriend, Heinrich, who appears in some ways to be better off without parents, is not of course. His desire to imagine himself with rich parents undermines any temptation to read the film as a simple critique of the historical mess of the German Autumn which has now been resolved in post-unification Germany – if only Jeanne could become reintegrated into this Germany. It is impossible to ignore the film's clear focus on the now as well as on German history for it remains implacably critical of the unified Germany as a divisive consumer society. Jeanne's only opportunity to re-enter the German social world is as an orphan, which, as we can see by the example of Heinrich, is a fast track to continued poverty and membership of a social underclass, where shoplifting and fantasies of rescue into wealth offer the only balm. In this sense *The State I Am In* is less a film about history than about postmemory, the way second-hand memories and experiences dominate Jeanne's blameless life in a Germany which, too, shows no sign of having resolved the social contradictions that led to terrorist violence, and persists as an unashamedly capitalist consumer society overshadowed by its past incarnations.

This, then, is apparently where *The German Sisters* and *The State I Am In* part: von Trotta is engaged in a quest precisely to understand and even identify with the terrorists as political prisoners and thus to restore the personal, family intimacy that marks Juliane's and Marianne's shared socialization. *The German Sisters* is focalized through Juliane who has her own political intelligence which in turn shapes her quest for Marianne. But *The State I Am In* is focalized through Jeanne, for whom ideological struggle has become a kind of banal reality, something that is obstructing her need to engage with the social reality around her. For her, there is absolutely no sense of self to be found in opposition to a now defunct state. What remains, though, is the complex question of the personal and the political: the original German title *Die innere Sicherheit*, which translates either as 'state security' or 'inner security', demonstrates the interdependence of the political (state security and surveillance) and the psychological (the 'inner' security of a stable identity). What appears to be a film about an especially complex teenage rite of passage is shot through with postmemories of her parents', grandparents' and perhaps even great-grandparents' traumatic past. As such, it comments particularly on Jeanne's contemporary difficulties in finding an identity in a Berlin Republic uncertain of its immediate predecessor and still troubled by National Socialism. Jeanne, like Jan, is apparently orphaned at the end of the film; but the reception of *The German Sisters* indicates a parallel search for a filmic identity, for a German film culture that is not an orphan adrift in a globalized market, but can instead forge meaningful connections back to a German film tradition. Aesthetically spare and sober, *The German Sisters* was less lionized and feted than the works of the great male auteurs and perhaps therefore something of a Cinderella of the New German Cinema. Yet it offers great potential as a usable cinematic model: its feminist sensibility in exploring families, the postmemories of generation upon generation and the personal as political would appear to be more needed now than ever.

THE LEGENDS OF RITA

Like *The State I Am In*, *The Legends of Rita* is a quest for identity. However, this time it is a completely new identity that is sought. Rita Vogt, now disillusioned with terrorism and killing, needs to erase her past self completely and seizes the opportunity to do this with gusto. The *Stasi* broker who offers her the opportunity to cast off her past crimes and live a normal, working life in the GDR sees her as a kind of private project as well as a recognition of their common enemy, the West. He, of course, is an expert at manufacturing identity: Rita knows him as Erwin but also knows that this is not his real name. Rita herself is no stranger to disguise, indeed one might argue that her identity began to unravel the moment she effectively abandoned her citizenship of the Federal Republic. Together they invent not just one, but eventually a second new persona for Rita so that she can have what she imagines to be a peaceful retirement from terrorism. In quiet labour towards the socialist project of Germany's 'better half', she believes herself to be somehow atoning for her crime. However, this attempt to erase the past is rocked by her love, first for Tatjana, then for Jochen. Her desire for family, for love, is the first contradiction in her impossible position because precisely that fundamental component of identity involves the threat of exposure. Since she cannot be known, she cannot know others. Finally her search for normality founders because of the fall of the Wall, which exposes the political subterfuge that allowed terrorists to hide behind the Iron Curtain. At this point both Rita and Erwin realize that they have not been hiding anything from the West but that the whole episode was based on a pragmatic political arrangement. Rita's search for the naïve sincerity of ordinary life in the GDR, as demonstrated for her at Tatjana's family gathering, was impossible because all was not as it seemed; layers of constructed and disingenuously created identities are all exploded as the Cold War status quo collapses. Now on her third persona, and with the knowledge that her secret is already known to her pursuers, Rita flees in what she knows is a hopeless attempt to evade capture. Her death at a road checkpoint recalls the violent end of *The State I Am In* and Alfred Herrhausen's death in a car bomb as told in *Black Box FRG* (which will be discussed later in the chapter). She – like the fictionalized Andreas Baader in *Baader* – dies like a cinema desperado. Unable to use any of her created identities, she must revert to being Rita Vogt, the terrorist on the run, the one identity that she had found impossible to inhabit. Her death is a logical consequence of her impossible position, and in its finality and grim closure, the ending of *The Legends of Rita* stands in marked contrast with the rather open, ambiguous ending of *The State I Am In*. At least Jeanne might finally be able to move on from the generational bind she is in. But Rita's certain death and the final shots of Tatjana trapped by a new set of captors (an invading force, as it were, in Rita's flat) show the political union embodied by these emblematic women characters to be a bitter failure.

Volker Schlöndorff, a key director of the 1970s and 1980s, is in a different position to the younger generation of German filmmakers in that he represents a possible continuity with the work of the New German Cinema. Certainly *The Legends of Rita* does seem to gesture back to his film *The Lost Honour of Katharina Blum*, made with Margarethe von Trotta in 1975. The two films document opposite trajectories: Katharina Blum is an honest, conservative, hard-working woman who is catapulted into the role of national scapegoat and denounced as a 'murderer's whore' ('Mörderbraut') by the gutter press because of her liaison with a presumed terrorist who is wanted by the police. Rita Vogt starts as a terrorist but later seeks a life of mundane routine which appears to be possible as a factory worker in the GDR. The two leading actors, Angela Winkler (Katharina in *Katharina Blum*) and Bibiana Beglau (Rita in *The Legends of Rita*) bear a passing resemblance, particularly in the first of Rita's GDR guises where she wears her hair straight and tied back off her face.

The film does not use the restricted colour palette of von Trotta's *The German Sisters* in any sustained manner, though there are moments when a similar spare approach is deployed. This can be seen particularly towards the end of the film during Rita's desperate attempt to escape capture, which like many of the other key moments of violence in terrorist films new and old, takes place on the road. In addition, the exploration of a relationship between two women gestures to von Trotta's key concern in *The German Sisters*, though the outcome is bleak here, without even the consoling emphasis on Juliane's radical identification with her sister. Both *Katharina Blum* and *The Legends of Rita* use melodrama as an aesthetic mode to explore the interface between personal and political: Rita's frantic search for new, workable identities that will allow her a life which includes both love and political integrity cannot succeed. Just as Katharina Blum is radically stripped of her carefully constructed identity and left no option but to become her gutter-press persona, so too can Rita do nothing in the end but revert to the defining identity of outlaw.

The Lost Honour of Katharina Blum tells the story of how an individual is brutalized by the state and media to the point of using violence. An emblematic individual destiny allows Schlöndorff to analyse and satirize the methods of a gutter press which supports the ideological purposes of the state. The secret complicity of press and police leads to the inevitable and logical conclusion that the liberal democracy of the FRG is fundamentally flawed. Certainly Heinrich Böll's novella, on which the film was based, is more satirical and analytical than Schlöndorff's film, which deploys the cinematic genre of melodrama. The heavy investment in the person of Katharina and the linear plot structure utilize affect and suspense to heighten the anomaly of Katharina's violence, and reveal fundamental flaws in the West German system.

The Legends of Rita examines the GDR through the perspective of a West German 'lefty', for whom it functions as desired other. Rita idealizes the GDR as a space where socialist values might flourish, but to keep the faith she must ignore the reality around her in flagrant denial of everyday unhappiness and tedium as well as larger political failings. She cannot hide her disappointment, though, in her fellow citizens who are much less interested in maintaining a socialist German state. The look back at the attitude of dissatisfied leftist West Germans to an idealized East Germany through Rita's emblematic reaction sets up a framework within which east–west relations now might be examined in the light of East–West hopes and illusions then. Through *The Legends of Rita*,

Kohlhaase and Schlöndorff perhaps lament the loss of a socialist Germany, though they do this in heavily ironized mode since Rita's various paeans to socialism come across as so much West German preaching. Finally the film also exposes the corrupt pragmatism that characterized relations between the two Germanies. The intertextual connection between Rita Vogt and Katharina Blum shows that both states fall far below the standards they set themselves as workers' paradise and liberal democracy respectively.

The Legends of Rita also gestures to a cinematic legacy that Schlöndorff could not engage with as he might have wished to at the time of his celebrated New German Cinema films, namely that of the DEFA studios. Set mainly in the GDR, The Legends of Rita is scripted by Wolfgang Kohlhaase, a key DEFA filmmaker with a CV which includes the screenplay and co-direction of Solo Sunny, an important DEFA film made in 1979 with Konrad Wolf, another of DEFA's most admired directors. In Solo Sunny an unconventional young woman singer struggles to find respect and acceptance in the GDR. A lonely figure, marginalized by a conservative society and sacked by her band, she is pushed to the point of destruction and self-destruction, taking an overdose and hiding a knife in the bed when she sleeps with her faithless lover. Sunny remains defiant at the end of the film and pursues the identity she wishes to create: the glamorous, self-reliant artist, free to express her individuality. The film clearly highlights the plight of someone like Sunny within GDR society who is isolated and under extreme pressure as she attempts to lead an individual, unconventional existence 'in a society which constantly proclaimed that no one was lonely'.[16] The character of Tatjana in The Legends of Rita appears to be a reference to Sunny, an indication that unification, which has such disastrous consequences for Rita, has opened up the question of another cinematic tradition for Schlöndorff in his collaboration with Kohlhaase. Both films are readable as stories about the politics of identity, while The Legends of Rita also explores a cinematic identity which has its own unification issues. The character of Sunny became a cult heroine in the GDR and Tatjana with her striking clothes and hair and boho-style flat appears to be a 1980s acolyte. An alcoholic misfit who longs to leave for the West, she appears initially to be more vulnerable than Sunny and less purposeful, perhaps because she does not have a creative outlet for her individuality and sleepwalks through her job at a textiles factory where she has no friends. Loneliness is a key problem for both Sunny and Tatjana, who both fall in love but are let down. Tatjana's love for Rita, who of course longs to conform, suggests the initial possibility of redemption. As Rita seeks to return to a life of convention and normality she is confronted by Tatjana, who, like Sunny, longs to be able to express an individual identity and cannot abide the strictures of her dull surroundings. However, though Rita tries to help Tatjana develop a stable identity and conquer her addiction to alcohol, she must inevitably flee once she has been connected with her past persona following a TV report. The *Stasi* veto the relationship and Tatjana is left alone. Finally Tatjana is even imprisoned by Rita's *Stasi* protector because she represents a threat to Rita's new identity. The fledgling relationship fails explicitly because of the political situation and Rita's past.

Schlöndorff looks back to his own New German Cinema past in making a film which updates the left-wing terrorist legacy, but seeks also to update the German cinematic tradition. This tradition too might undergo a kind of unification with the critical realist tradition exemplified by DEFA writers and directors. His collaboration with Kohlhaase looks both at the crucial political preoccupation of the Bonn Republic and at the effects of unification. *The Legends of Rita*'s archetypal East German locales, particularly the factory and the summer camp, consciously evoke the *mise-en-scène* of DEFA films. Furthermore, in their gestures towards two of the most celebrated women characters of the New German Cinema and DEFA, Katharina Blum and Sunny, Schlöndorff and Kohlhaase reprise both cinemas' enthusiasm for creating women characters to embody emblematically the body politic.[17] In their intertextual gestures and DEFA *mise-en-scène* they indicate a desire to explore new hybrid constellations as well as cinematic histories. The political and social search for identity which places Rita and Tatjana in an impossible situation is *cinematically* both possible and necessary, it is suggested, if there is to be a German cinema standing in the traditions of both DEFA and the New German Cinema.

BLACK BOX FRG

Black Box FRG also develops the thematic concerns of left-wing terrorism as a careful and painstaking search for identity, but does so in the form of a documentary film about two contrasting biographies. Alfred Herrhausen, chair of Deutsche Bank, was killed in a car bomb attack in 1989 by the Red Army Faction. Wolfgang Grams, wanted for terrorist crimes, was shot dead on Bad Kleinen station in 1993. The circumstances of both deaths are still somewhat obscure: it is not known whether Grams was party to the attack on Herrhausen, and the investigation of the shoot-out at Bad Kleinen, which also resulted in the death of an anti-terrorist squad officer, Michael Newrzella, was flawed and ultimately inconclusive. A mixture of reconstructions, talking-head interviews and contemporary footage, *Black Box FRG* clearly operates with the thesis that an investigation of the personal development of these key players, and their presentation as parallel lives, might illuminate the question of the West German terrorist past. It starts by putting the personal above the political, avoiding obvious moral judgements in its examination of the conflict between two key generations of the Bonn Republic. Herrhausen is representative of the West German industrialist class which sought to overcome the trauma of defeat in World War II with material success and economic power. However, this stance and this generation, educated in the Third Reich, is utterly demonized by young people who became politically active in the squatters' and student movement of the late 1960s and early 1970s, and who could not abide the focus on material success. An irony of the presentation of Alfred Herrhausen's life, given a prominent position in the discussion of his life, is that his career was under threat just before he died because of his ambitious global restructuring plan and his views on Third World debt relief, which were – to Deutsche Bank at least – somewhat radical.[18] Herrhausen, educated in an elite Nazi school and described as lacking 'human warmth' ('menschliche Wärme'), apparently comes to see the injustice (and poor business sense) of keeping the developing world indebted while on a visit to Mexico. In an apparently opposite development, Grams, the sensitive conscientious objector, with perfect pitch, becomes radicalized and brutalized by the treatment of RAF prisoners to the point of bearing arms against the state. The film tentatively suggests in its juxtapositions that the two men need not have necessarily been enemies. Both are presented rather sympathetically as idealists. As Veiel puts it, 'it was fascinating to discover what is left of German idealism and to observe its effects at two entirely different points in German reality'.[19] Ultimately there is a conciliatory note in the detailed exploration of the two biographies. The viewer is invited to consider parallels in the two lives: both, as Veiel says, fight for their convictions; both end their lives isolated from former companions precisely because of their convictions. Perhaps Herrhausen is the father Grams ought to have had; Grams's own father's dreams were modest and material in character. Herrhausen, by contrast, is not just 'The Lord of Money' ('Der Herr des Geldes'), as *Der Spiegel* put it, but a man of big ideas and global visions.[20]

In its emphasis on globalization as a defining characteristic of Herrhausen, but one that ultimately separates him from the rest of his capitalist colleagues, *Black Box FRG* consciously evokes a *current* field of potentially violent conflict. Herrhausen as a senior figure in Deutsche Bank is clearly, and unashamedly, part of the globalizing economic system, even beyond what is palatable to the rest of the board members. However, he also has the ambition to intervene in the globalized economy to limit some of its catastrophic effects. In a film that clearly engages with current questions via the past conflict between capital and terror, the repeated emphasis on Herrhausen as an internationally ambitious, globalizing figure is significant. In the Grams household, by contrast, the issue of now that is implicitly raised amid the cosy familiarity of Grams's parental home is the question of *Heimat*. These homely surroundings – shots of the family having lunch, of his parents recalling Wolfgang's piano practice and of Ruth Grams showing off his cross-stitch – are explicitly and repeatedly set against the sleek, modernist temples of capitalism that Herrhausen inhabited. Even his country villa, though it alludes to vernacular architectural styles, is actually a modern, architect-designed building. Grams's family home comes as a downmarket relief from the anonymous menace of the Frankfurt shots, a comforting *Heimat* set against global capitalism. However, the oppressive aspect of *Heimat* is also gradually revealed as the viewer comes to understand why Grams rejected the petit-bourgeois (*Spießbürger*) narrowness of *Heimat*, which in its own small way is just as materially motivated as the bank. The nurturing home is gradually complicated by hints of authoritarian discipline and the emphasis on finding a 'proper job'. Herrhausen's milieu, in a parallel move, is gradually softened by the mitigating evidence of his enlightened globalization and apparent fall from grace at the bank (material introduced towards the end of the film) as much as his presentation as a caring father. In the painstaking revelation of the two biographies we not only come to understand that Herrhausen and Grams had things in common, but we also see that their loved ones have developed and grown through their experiences, which again has the effect of modulating the apparent sense of opposition. Werner Grams, it is implied, has learnt through the suffering he has had to bear and has reflected on personal, family and political histories. Traudl Herrhausen, too, has suffered and apparently developed through her experience of her husband's murder; her thoughts on background, privilege and political engagement bear witness to an intense and considered reflection. In 1991 Traudl Herrhausen became a CDU representative in the regional parliament of Hessen and speaks for her party on higher education, something not mentioned in the film, though it is implied that her awareness of German politics and the public sphere has grown through her very public bereavement. Its interventions in the now are thus framed by an interest in one of the key current questions of late modernity: is it possible to find a *Heimat*, forge a local identity in an increasingly globalized world? The film seeks to explore these conflicts between globalized capital and the anti-globalization movement through this older battle between government and capital on one side and violent protest and terrorism on the other.

As a documentary film, *Black Box FRG* apparently gestures to *Germany in Autumn* in its use of authentic materials and analytical approaches. It, too, includes scenes of murdered industrialist Hanns Martin Schleyer's funeral that form part of Alexander Kluge's contribution to *Germany in Autumn* and juxtaposes them with a RAF funeral. In *Black Box FRG*, however, the funeral is not that of Raspe, Baader and Ensslin, but the earlier one of Holger Meins in 1974. The appearance of the politician Otto Schily at the head of the procession, and the shot of Joschka Fischer during a violent confrontation with the police establish a direct link between those broadly sympathetic to the critical position of the terrorists and a political generation that chose another route and is now in power. The apparent refusal to take sides, in contrast with *Germany in Autumn*, is compounded by deliberate attempts in the selection and positioning of material to argue that the two polarized positions are less far apart than they might first appear. Like *Germany in Autumn*, *Black Box FRG* is interested in the ideas that underpin the terrorist project and sympathetic to the view that the Bonn Republic was in some way culpable. Veiel's film implies that its blind enthusiasm for capitalism and material recovery almost inevitably led to a principled political opposition, a section of which, however, saw no purpose in engaging with the official political culture of the FRG. The repeated shots of a convoy of three company Mercedes in formation are at once a reminder of the constant threat to Herrhausen's life, a reconstruction of his death and a rather menacing image of corporate West Germany. The cars are a blank, but somehow threatening, vision of status and power expressed through material symbols. The shots of a secretary placing pencils at precise angles on A4 pads for a board meeting, and a veritable army of cleaners hoovering away in preparation for a Deutsche Bank corporate presentation clearly satirize the conservative, exploitative financial empire that Grams so hated. But Herrhausen is somehow spared the brunt of this critique by the emphasis on his maverick tendencies, and his global ambitions are set against the implied parochialism of the rest of the board. Ultimately the viewer is left with the impression that his death was even rather convenient for the board, which may have sacked him shortly afterwards anyway.

Unlike *Germany in Autumn*, however, the examination of the state does not function primarily on an abstract level. In spite of the implied criticism directed at the Federal Republic and the montage which suggests that terrorism might be a consequence of a certain political and economic culture, *Black Box FRG* demonstrates a closer affinity to *The German Sisters* in its dedicated pursuit of Grams's motivation and process of radicalization. It too is engaged in a quest for identity, but this time it is a more multi-faceted, double identity: the ambitious high flyer who does not quite fit into the bland corporate culture of the Bonn Republic, the dissident son who cannot find accommodation within the state in which he lives. Just as the two sisters Marianne and Juliane explore the closeness of their identity from somewhat opposed political positions, so Veiel's film attempts to present Herrhausen and Grams as an estranged father and son who, in implacable opposition, lead parallel lives and, as radical idealists, share a violent end.[21] By revealing the common features of the two men's characters and careers and allowing family members and friends to present their stories without a moderating voice, *Black Box FRG* explores a therapeutic potential in its evaluation of the fractured, violent 'state on the brink'. Perhaps the two positions are not as far apart as imagined. Perhaps both sides are peopled by complex, sympathetic, loved individuals wrestling with their own ideals and how best to achieve them. Indeed, any simple victim–perpetrator binary within the field of terrorist studies is implicitly undermined both by the structure of the film and the content of the interviews. The uncomfortable labour of memory undertaken by the friends and relatives is complicated exponentially by the viewers' knowledge that the interviewees had agreed to participate in a film which would have at its heart a desire to show the other side of the story. In one of the preliminary discussions before filming began, Veiel told Traudl Herrhausen that he visited Grams's partner Birgit Hogefeld regularly in prison.[22] Herrhausen then asked whether Veiel had looked into Hogefeld's eyes and what he had seen. On camera the repeated long close-up shots of the bereaved trying to fight back their tears place individual suffering at the heart of the film, which contributes to the effect of breaking down entrenched positions within the discourse of terrorist studies. This is especially striking with Werner Grams, whose sorrow, bewilderment and honest engagement with his family's trajectory result at one moment in him being unable to speak; he almost gasps for words which, however, completely elude him. The close-up shots of human faces in distress make this film the most open of all the films discussed. Viewers are implicated in the distress of the families and are implicitly challenged to respond to the ordeal that has overwhelmed the witnesses. Such a focus on the unimaginable distress of the bereaved, and the painful difficulty – both in principle and in practice – of even speaking in such a context as *Black Box FRG*, function as a powerful revision to the binary oppositions of terrorist discourse from the 1970s and 1980s. Implicit in this tendency to interrogate binary oppositions is the notion that such approaches might also be applied to other conflicts in the German public domain – the efforts to understand the origins, workings and legacy of the Third Reich for example, and the public debate over the GDR and its legacy.

Traudl Herrhausen and Werner and Ruth Grams are powerful, dignified storytellers, with their careful, touching tales of love at first sight and clandestine meetings, their fears of violence and their treasured memories. Veiel insists that *Black Box FRG* is 'a film about the present' ('ein Film über die Gegenwart'), an attempt to explore wounds that are still open though it may never be possible to open the 'flight recorder' of the Bonn Republic and discover precisely what happened to Herrhausen and Grams. As well as a historical recording device, he also describes the 'black box' of the title as a space for projected emotions.[23] The viewer is thus invited to see it as a kind of therapeutic device which might somehow be able to rescue the FRG, bridge the gulf between state and dissidents, and heal the traumatic divisions. Space is left for the viewer to engage in this therapeutic projection of emotions and identities by the radical removal of any overarching documentary narrator or interviewer figure.[24] What emerges is a tragic story of fathers and sons who are lost to each other, a story that the viewer must patiently weave together from strands of narrative to construct a tableau in which Grams and Herrhausen both appear. The problem then is how to interpret it, as Ruth Grams discovered with the lovely embroidered picture done by her son while on the run. The naïve depiction of exotic creatures is beautiful but ultimately inscrutable, a possible criticism of *Black Box FRG* too, which leaves questions for the most part unanswered. Like *The German Sisters* which ends just as Juliane is to begin her story, the deaths at the end of the film gesture back to its beginning and demand the personal engagement of the viewer in the quest for understanding.

BAADER

Christopher Roth's fictional biography of Andreas Baader is apparently only peripherally interested in providing a truthful record of the person who led the struggle against the West German state. Though the culture of the Baader–Meinhof group was researched with information from those close to the left-wing terrorist scene, many episodes are imagined and have no factual basis. The film version of Baader's death totally contradicts the known facts of the case and is so far from the historical record that there is paradoxically perhaps less danger of Roth being accused of manipulating the truth: *Baader* is a fictional film and confronts the viewer with much more than a biography. Roth takes the historical figure of Andreas Baader and uses some of the known facts about him to explore his leadership role in the RAF, not just in terms of his political intervention against the state but as a mythologized and self-mythologizing star. Roth's uncompromising fictionalization attempts to read history and film history together and explore the connections between them in a way that posits the myth of Baader–Meinhof as a myth of cinema.

The fictional Baader is constructed as a criminal anti-hero; his origins as a car thief and the gangster glamour this lends him are presented as every bit as important as his political reflections on ideological struggle and later theories of revolution. In fact Baader is not only presented in the film as a kind of charismatic, retro-chic 'bit of rough'; he is most significantly shown as carefully developing his own image. Roth's Baader is obsessed by his own persona and by presenting himself in a certain light. He is not only presented as a leader, but also sees himself almost as the arty director of a bohemian film clique. Roth shows Baader filming himself, and the group, in Paris with a super-8 camera; Baader trying on shirts; Baader experimenting with drugs; and Baader explaining how to steal the coolest cars. His absurd demonstration of how the group must wear their guns – pushed into the front centre of the waistband – is supposed to be a constant reminder of the political struggle they are engaged in, but clearly it is also a reminder of the sexual power and allure of the outlaw, which facilitates, even necessitates, the kind of strut more frequently seen in Sergio Leone films.

Whereas the other films examined in this chapter explore Germany's history and troubled search for identity, but ultimately reveal that they are engaged in a search for cinematic identity that is just as significant, *Baader* wears its pursuit of film history on its sleeve. Though *The Legends of Rita* and *The State I Am In* flirt with the notion of the terrorist as fugitive bandit, *Baader* comes closest to representing Ensslin and Baader as Arthur Penn's Bonnie and Clyde. The shoot-out ending where Baader emerges from a lock-up garage to die like a hip Ned Kelly in a defiant 'last stand' is the logical conclusion of this exploration of Baader as a legendary Western icon. Roth is less interested in pursuing the biography of the historical figure Andreas Baader than in exploring the meaning of the myth of Baader. This requires the rewriting of the historical end (itself somewhat shrouded in mystery) to relocate Baader's death. In Roth's film the ambiguous circumstances of Baader's death in prison are transformed into the rather melodramatically staged death of a mythical hero. This allows Baader to display his legendary chutzpah to the end, and preserves his obsession with controlling his own role, his own performance in the struggle against the state. Apparently caught out and trapped by the anti-terrorist arm of the Federal Police (*Bundeskriminalamt* or BKA) he nevertheless finally dies according to his own choreography, by conjuring up a final gun-slinging surprise and obeying his own stage directions for the group: they are only ever caught or killed and never give themselves up.

It is not only American film mythology which is invoked, however. The greatest German film myth of all, Rainer Werner Fassbinder, is ever-present in the film. Frank Giering's Baader not only bears a resemblance to Fassbinder, but his style, his dominant leadership of the troupe, his reliance on a cast of regulars, his tendency to choreograph every movement and direct their struggle like a precisely rehearsed and stylized action film are unmistakeably suggestive of Fassbinder. Indeed, Roth has acknowledged his interest in the figure of Fassbinder in his creation of Baader.[25] The Fassbinder references which allude to the director's self-representation as director recall Fassbinder's section of *Germany in Autumn* where he plays himself in abusive and self-centred mode, alluding to his own myth in a clear acknowledgement of the primacy of performance over documentary record. The notion of terrorism having a motivation beyond ideological struggle is also evident in Fassbinder's *The Third Generation* (*Die dritte Generation*, 1979), where political change is no longer the motivation of the terrorists, indeed they lack 'any motivating idealism or ideology' and, as Imke Lode argues, far from functioning as the enemy of the state, they actually engage in a mutually dependent sadomasochistic relationship with the state authorities.[26] Aesthetically the film looks to Fassbinder films like *Love Is Colder Than Death* (*Liebe ist kälter als der Tod*, 1969) and *The American Soldier* (*Der amerikanische Soldat*, 1970). The film citation in *Baader* of *48 Hours to Acapulco* (*48 Stunden nach Acapulco*, 1967) by Klaus

Lemke could easily have been an extract from a Fassbinder film: Roth considered showing a Fassbinder extract and settled on Klaus Lemke because of a desire to resurrect his neglected oeuvre.[27] Lemke's film also features an adventure-seeking protagonist who models himself on American movie heroes in his gangster career. *Baader* thus unequivocally combines the desire to explore both West German history and West German cinema, as well as suggesting various intersections between the two, but deliberately references Lemke in addition to Fassbinder, a rather unsung German director who was strongly influenced by American cinema and who was critical of the intellectual weightiness of the New German Cinema.[28]

Baader explores German film history by taking a rather grim, authoritarian West Germany and setting it against an aestheticized ideological struggle directed by a cross between Rainer Werner Fassbinder and Che Guevara who then dies in the proverbial blaze of glory, a cult anti-hero in the making. Roth is clearly exploring the film and media landscape that offers an aesthetic legacy for today's German filmmakers. He is also audaciously juxtaposing film history with history in a way that goes beyond the other new terrorism films. Far more than the other films he explores the terrorist phenomenon as a mythologized cinematic discourse. Roth's sustained engagement with Baader as revered retro icon of the 1970s suggests that what the new Germany in the west is looking for is a foundational myth of disenchantment with the old FRG. Baader appears as a glamorous and ruthless warrior against the colourless conservatism of West Germany and stands for resistance against the grey days of ideological division. In the post-unification environment there appears to be a need to reappraise West German society and revise the notion of the powerful, victorious society that swallowed up the GDR. The Baader–Meinhof group is the link back to the tribulations and repression of the West, a counter-balance to the explosion of interest in the aesthetic and social experience of life in the GDR, and the enthusiasm for memory work and engagement with the comparatively recent past represented by the phenomenon of *Ostalgie*.

In its exploration of a fictionalized West Germany a further element is added to *Baader* that is drawn from the American 'outlaw' films that romanticize the gun, a motif that is also common to Fassbinder's emblematic, allegorical German figures. Baader, like all self-respecting outlaws, has a worthy adversary in Kurt Krone, the (fictional) Federal Police chief, a character based on Horst Herold, who became head of the Federal Police in 1971. This potential demon of authoritarian West Germany is explored in some detail as a paradoxical figure. He is himself a 'lefty' and is, as Roth discusses in his DVD interview, way ahead of his time in pursuing the terrorists in that he designs his operation as a computer-supported, intelligence-led, holistic system. As such, he is rather misunderstood and something of a maverick within the system, mirroring Baader as the maverick outlaw. The meeting between Baader and Krone overreaches itself in cliché so beautifully that it dramatizes and deliberately announces the cinematic myths that are both indulged in and reflected on. The two meet like clandestine lovers who long to escape the limits of their respective positions and yet whose bond depends on the mirrored relationship between state and terrorism as posed by Fassbinder in *The Third Generation*. Krone is Baader's lost father figure and the 'blokey' tenderness between them as Krone shows off his state-of-the-art kit hints at both a kind of West German parental responsibility for desperate outlaws, and at once exposes this as a problematic cliché. As Baader finally lies dying, Krone holds him in a kind of West German pietà. The excess of affect here is a direct signal that the cherished myths surrounding the provenance of, and responsibility for, West German terrorism need to be recognized for what they are: a convenient cinematic shorthand that should be interrogated rather than accepted.

Roth's presentation of Baader as a mythological gangster figure, a key avatar of *Westalgie*, demonstrates the allure of the myth (and also indulges in its pleasure), and at the same time exposes it as a construct. The film has at its heart an examination of how Baader became such powerful shorthand for a cluster of critical reflections on West Germany. Andreas Baader as historical figure is deliberately and flagrantly ignored throughout the film, but of course the most audacious departure from the documented biography comes at the end of the film. This ensures that it is impossible to reflect on the film and still remain under any illusion of authenticity. The teasing interweaving of simulated super-8 footage that invokes notions of documentary evidence is finally exploded at the end with the death of Baader in a 'last stand' gunfight. Its fictional status is proudly displayed, even flaunted in increasing measure as the film nears its end. In some ways *Baader* gestures to *Black Box FRG*, which included home-movie footage of Alfred Herrhausen and footage from an experimental film featuring Wolfgang Grams. Here super-8 footage is artfully contrived to show Baader as a narcissistic creative type playing the role of director at the centre of his trusty actor clique. Both films are engaged in an attempt to explore and ultimately explode myths, constructs and cherished binaries that haunt the discourse surrounding terrorism in the FRG. Arguably, though, the 'authentic' footage and conventional documentary mode might potentially contribute more to dubious myth-making processes and the fictionalized, sensationalized, 'wrong' version could ultimately be a more honest treatment. For in flagrantly creating 'untrue' images, *Baader* acknowledges the inherent falsehood of images and thematizes precisely the myth of Baader, not any 'true' or 'real' historical figure. *Black Box FRG* avoids the mythologizing trap of certain documentary treatments by its extreme openness and uncomfortable implication of the viewer in its engagement with historical trauma, but other documentaries such as Ben Lewis's *Baader–Meinhof: In Love with Terror* compare much less favourably.[29] *Baader*, by contrast, not only reads itself against the grain as 'biopic', it also by implication calls into question other, more 'authentic' versions of the RAF story.

HISTORY OR FILM HISTORY?

Filmmakers in Germany have repeatedly grappled with the representation of history, exploring the potential for estrangement as well as identification that the cinema offers. Indeed, it is the interest in examining Germany's history in feature films that has earned the German cinema its international reputation. Yet, there is, as Thomas Elsaesser puts it, 'a suspicion of cinema as fundamentally inadequate for the representation of history, as well as its opposite, a suspicion of cinema's excessive seductiveness'.[30] Certainly there is evidence of scepticism about recent filmic treatments of the RAF and related issues.[31] The films that have been released since the late 1990s are clearly not 'authentic' records of the 1970s and 1980s but look back to the period in a gesture of *Westalgie*, of engagement with a peculiarly

West German past that is emblematic of unease and dissatisfaction with the state. Largely sympathetic in the representation of those in implacable opposition to the state, and seeking to understand the consequences of their violence, *The Legends of Rita* and *The State I Am In* do not look back in fondness for a glamorous, violent past. Rather, these films treat ironically the bizarre plight of the post-Bonn Republic terrorist remnant. A clearly discernible, if somewhat tentative quest for identity in the Berlin Republic emerges from their exploration of West German terrorism and its legacy. *Baader* and *Black Box FRG*, by contrast, both engage in a detailed exploration of the key figures, the 'stars' of this particular struggle, and both could be implicated in the creation of a counter-myth of the identity of the West German state: prosperity and blandness are displaced by paranoia and menace. *Baader* especially glamorizes the urban guerrillas and dark machinations of the state anti-terrorist measures.

By comparison the earlier wave of films on this subject appear sober and analytical, as if deliberately confronting the potential criticism of the mythologizing power of the cinema. *Germany in Autumn* and *The Third Generation* employ aesthetic strategies that undermine any potential for unproblematic viewer identification. *The German Sisters* (*pace* Byg), while adopting some of the conventions of family melodrama, goes out of its way to drain the film of glamour, colour and fast narrative pacing. However, the new wave of terrorism films does not, on the whole, adopt the aesthetic strategies of Kluge and Fassbinder even where they explicitly reference the earlier generation of films. Their deliberate subordination of historical material in favour of a good story and lack of defamiliarizing aesthetics would seem precisely to invite the charge of 'excessive seductiveness' and mythologizing tendencies. Yet an understanding of this deliberate flirtation with the myth of left-wing terrorism only emerges when we look at both the reception of German history and the reception of the New German Cinema 'first generation' films together.

As Elsaesser has rightly identified, the German cinema is a series of problematic intersections between history and film.[32] In a review of Edgar Reitz's *Heimat* (1984), for example, Elsaesser described the film saga as 'not so much a review of German history as a review of German *film* history'.[33] The reception of Schlöndorff, von Trotta, Fassbinder and

Kluge in the latest generation of terrorism films indicates not only a desire to negotiate a cinematic identity between DEFA, the New German Cinema and dominant entertainment cinemas, but an engagement with the historical myth created by cinema. Such a myth has emerged even through the estranged and critical work of Fassbinder and von Trotta as part of a complex visual field incorporating TV documentaries, wanted posters and news bulletins, as well as cinema treatments.[34] The desire to understand the West German terrorist past as a (negative) foundational myth of the new Germany has fuelled interest in new fictional and factual treatments, which, however, resist aesthetic categorization by both indulging in the cinematic pleasure of mythologizing history and at the same time identifying this as a central concern. All four films discussed here place heavy allegorical burdens on their key characters in terms of the quest for a usable identity that is at the heart of each film. But the combined effect of their overdetermined figuration, their overt acknowledgement of cinematic traditions, their sometimes extremely open, uncomfortable exploration of personal distress and their some-times playful evocation of left-wing terrorism as movie adventure is (also) an explicit examination of the mythological construct Baader–Meinhof. As Elsaesser puts it, writing of Weimar cinema's 'historical imaginary', this apparently dubious connection of history and cinema 'should be regarded as a "veritable history of the false" [...] rather than as examples of "false history"'.[35]

Notes

1   The official translation of the title is *Black Box Germany*. However, this appears to me to be fundamentally inaccurate since the word 'Germany' implies the post-unification situation, whereas the German title denotes both pre-unification West Germany and post-unification Germany. If anything, the term *BRD* tends to be associated more with pre-unification West Germany.

2   I am grateful to Elizabeth Boa for her suggestions and for the opportunity to discuss the films in question during the writing of this chapter.

3   DEFA (Deutsche Film Aktiengesellschaft) was the state-run film studio in the German Democratic Republic. For a further discussion of DEFA and its traditions, see Daniela Berghahn's chapter in this volume.

4   Ian Garwood, 'The *Autorenfilm* in Contemporary German Cinema' in Tim Bergfelder, Erica Carter and Deniz Göktürk (eds.), *The German Cinema Book* (London: BFI, 2002), pp. 202–10 (p. 204).

5   Cited in Malte Hagener, 'German Stars of the 1990s' in Bergfelder, Carter and Göktürk (eds.), *The German Cinema Book*, pp. 98–105 (p. 98).

6   See Garwood, 'The *Autorenfilm*', pp. 205–09.

7   For a discussion of these films, see Seán Allan's chapter in this volume.

8   Even Tom Tykwer's international art-house film *Heaven* (2002) based on an unmade script by Krzysztof Kieslowski alludes to terrorism and desperate violence as the catalyst for an exploration of radical, uncompromising love.

9   This term is used to describe nostalgia for the pre-unification Federal Republic amongst westerners which is a counterpart to the *Ostalgie* felt by former citizens of the GDR.

10 In the United States this film is known as *Marianne and Juliane*. The German title *Die bleierne Zeit* translates more closely as *The Leaden Time*.

11 In an oblique way Konrad Wolf's *Divided Heaven* (*Der geteilte Himmel*, 1964) is evoked, for example in the link made between escaping to the West and the betrayal of a lover.

12 See for example Lisa di Caprio, '*Marianne and Juliane/The German Sisters: Baader–Meinhof Fictionalized*' in Terri Ginsberg and Kirsten Moana Thompson (eds.), *Perspectives on German Cinema* (New York: Hall, 1996), pp. 391–402 (p. 401), which criticizes von Trotta for not suggesting any political solutions to the problem she elucidates. Barton Byg criticizes the film's 'acceptance of patriarchal norms' and argues that its 'manipulation of history in service of her narrative is also objectionable'. Byg, 'German History and Cinematic Convention Harmonized in Margarethe von Trotta's *Marianne and Juliane*' in Sandra Frieden *et al.* (eds.), *Gender and German Cinema: Feminist Interventions, Vol. 2, German Film History/German History on Film* (Providence and Oxford: Berg, 1993), pp. 259–71 (p. 264).

13 Christian Hißnauer, 'Nach der Gewalt: Linker Mythos RAF – Linker Mythos BRD', *Testcard: Beiträge zur Popgeschichte*, 12 (Linke Mythen) (2003), 40–5 (p. 42).

14 Marianne Hirsch, *Family Frames: Photography, Narrative and Postmemory* (Cambridge, Mass. and London: Harvard University Press, 1997), pp. 21–3 (p. 22).

15 Hirsch, *Family Frames*, p. 22.

16 Wolfgang Kohlhaase, 'DEFA: A Personal View' in Seán Allan and John Sandford (eds.), *DEFA: East German Cinema 1946–1992* (New York and Oxford: Berghahn, 1999), pp. 117–30 (p. 126).

17 As, for example, in films by Rainer Werner Fassbinder such as *The Marriage of Maria Braun* (*Die Ehe der Maria Braun*, 1979), von Trotta's *The German Sisters*, Helma Sanders-Brahms's *Germany, Pale Mother* (*Deutschland, bleiche Mutter*, 1979), and DEFA films such as Konrad Wolf's *Divided Heaven*.

18 See Herrhausen's text 'Die Zeit ist reif', http://www.black-box-brd.de/diezeitistreif.html.

19 'es war faszinierend zu entdecken, was von diesem deutschen Idealismus bleibt und wie er sich an zwei vollkommen unterschiedlichen Punkten der deutschen Realität auswirkt'. Interview with Andres Veiel, http://www.black-box-brd.de/interview.html.

20 *Der Spiegel*, 11, 13 March 1989.

21 An intriguing variation on *The German Sisters* and *The State I Am In* is the fact that, in this examination of innocent suffering, it is not the children who suffer for the crimes (real and symbolic) of their parents, but the parents who suffer unending pain because of the actions of their son. Werner Grams is a sympathetically considered counterpoint to Marianne's father in *The German Sisters* and Gudrun's father in *Baader*.

22 Hogefeld surrendered at Bad Kleinen and is serving three life sentences, though not specifically in relation to Alfred Herrhausen, the details of whose assassination remain unclear.

23   Interview with Andres Veiel, http://www.black-box-brd.de/interview.html.

24   In the Inter Nationes video release used to prepare this chapter, the titles identifying speakers which appeared in the cinema release are missing. This would appear to be unintentional, but certainly creates an interesting effect as the viewer has to piece together details of the interviewee's relationship with Grams or Herrhausen from what is said. The speakers thus function as representative characters – the widow, the colleague, the bereft mother and father, the brother, the flatmate, the girlfriend. Anyone with this version wishing to check names of speakers should refer to the list on the *Black Box FRG* website, http://www.black-box-brd.de/gespraechspartner.html.

25   Interview with Christopher Roth, Atlas Pictures DVD release of *Baader*.

26   Imke Lode, 'Terrorism, Sadomasochism, and Utopia in Fassbinder's *The Third Generation*' in Ginsberg and Thompson (eds.), *Perspectives on German Cinema*, pp. 415–34 (p. 416).

27   A retrospective of Lemke's work in May 2003 at the Central Kino in Berlin perhaps indicates some success.

28   See http://www.mach-dich-grade.de/retro/filme2.html.

29   Made for BBC4 and screened 8 July 2003 on BBC2.

30   Thomas Elsaesser, 'The New German Cinema's Historical Imaginary' in Bruce A. Murray and Christopher J. Wickham (eds.), *Framing the Past: The Historiography of German Cinema and Television* (Carbondale and Edwardsville: Southern Illinois University Press, 1992), pp. 280–307 (p. 291).

31   See for example Dagmar Brunow's interview with Irmgard Möller, 'Zur Mythenbildung nicht geeignet', *Testcard: Beiträge zur Popgeschichte*, 12 (Linke Mythen) (2003), 60–65 (pp. 62 and 64).

32   See Thomas Elsaesser, *Weimar Cinema and After: German Cinema's Historical Imaginary* (London: Routledge, 2000); Elsaesser, *The New German Cinema: A History* (Basingstoke: Macmillan, 1989); Elsaesser, *Fassbinder's Germany: History, Identity, Subject* (Amsterdam: University of Amsterdam Press, 1996).

33   Thomas Elsaesser, 'Memory, Home and Hollywood' in Miriam Hansen, 'Dossier on *Heimat*', *New German Critique*, 36 (1985), 3–24 (p. 13).

34   See, for example, *Germany and the RAF: In Our Sights* (*Im Fadenkreuz: Deutschland und die RAF*, a documentary series in five parts made for ARD in 1997 (available on Komplett-Media video), and Ben Lewis's *Baader-Meinhof: In Love with Terror* for the BBC. At the time of writing a public debate is taking place over the planned Berliner KunstWerke exhibition 'Mythos RAF' which was due to open in November 2004 but will now be subject to delay. Curators have been forced to alter their controversial original proposal following criticism from politicians and families of RAF victims who have objected to an emphasis on myth, e.g. the perception of the RAF as 'wild' and 'sexy' – words which had formed part of the original proposal. A further example of the complexities of negotiating the mythologized visual field surrounding the RAF is the 1989 cycle of paintings by Gerhard Richter which re-imagine and rework some of the most iconic and notorious photographs of the Baader–Meinhof terrorists and their Stammheim deaths. Richter's blurred, enigmatic images thematize precisely the mythologized quality of the images and the difficulty of finding a perspective from which to satisfactorily view the events of the German Autumn. (Viewers frequently move closer to, and then further away from, the canvases in the vain hope of bringing them into focus.) Sadly (and perhaps significantly) these remarkable and endlessly stimulating paintings have not found a home in Germany but now form part of the permanent collection of the New York Museum of Modern Art, where the resonances of the original press and police photographs are not nearly so powerful and immediate but need to be painstakingly explained in captions.

35   Elsaesser, *Weimar Cinema and After*, p. 420.

Chapter 2

Shades of grey: coming to terms with German film since unification

John E. Davidson

Memory studies have given us many tools and terms with which to assess the range of works attempting to come to terms with the heinous acts committed by Nazi Germany, its allies and fellow-travellers. By 'coming to terms' I mean a process that is never to be completed, composed of a number of strands. Firstly, keeping the memory of the victims alive; secondly, increasing our knowledge of all 'sides' of the historical record both public and private; and thirdly, generating an impact in the present that goes beyond an empathy with those who suffered atrocities perpetrated more than fifty years ago. While striving to do so, we must face the fact that there is no adequate means of fully representing the events and experiences of the Holocaust. Material that contributes to each of these three strands, even when it presents true stories, runs into grey areas that require us to distinguish between moments where it is possible to construct meaningful memory, and those which further what Geoffrey H. Hartman has called 'anti-memory', that is those which steal or falsify the possibility of real cultural memory.[1] The role of documentary in this process of coming to terms seems clear enough, although there has been much debate about what approach and subject matter lend themselves most effectively to the effort. The role of fictional works seems intuitively less clear, but there is an unshaken belief in the intellectual community that art helps give form to 'shapes of memory', and a healthy suspicion that factual history alone does not. My concern in this chapter is to examine cinematic texts to see whether attention to how feature films 'come to terms' formally in their spatial and chromatic components will help us get a better understanding of these grey areas of memory than focusing on the narrative or dialogue.

Hartman formulates one understanding of the 'shapes of memory', the subtitle for his anthology, like this: 'Art constructs, in brief, a cultural memory of its own, in which the struggle of the individual with (and often for) experience – including the collective memory itself – never ceases.'[2] These shapes of memory are thus spaces of contestation, and to enter these spaces critically requires three vital components in my opinion. First, one must recognize as clearly as possible the individual investments directed by personal desire and structural emersion that inform the producers, consumers and interpreters of culture. Second, the analysis employed must be appropriate to the artwork at hand, engaging with the work's intrinsic properties. (In the next section I discuss the particular difficulties raised by film for the methods of memory study that have come to dominate concern with coming to terms.) Finally, one has to resist the urge to monumentalize the text itself. Just as the totalizing impulse of cultures and individuals leads to dangerous dreams of omnipotence, so the totalizing demand that a work fully 'come to terms' stifles the process. Quoting Rilke's modernist insight while describing the difference between monuments and memorial practices, James Young reminds us that public markers reify the potential of art, for there is something about a monument's occupation of space as a shape of memory that makes the memorialized impossible to see.[3] This seems particularly disadvantageous when working with the spatial constructions of a visual medium such as film.

Although projects loosely grouped under memory studies often use film and video, most run into problems with satisfying the second condition listed above in regard to film because their methodologies call on infinite linguistic ambiguities most appropriate to written texts. Film today is, of course, not simply a visual medium, yet the place to begin looking for traces of the excess of yearning that marks the struggle to which Hartman alludes is not with the screenplay, but rather with how things look. Similarly, it is important not to simply follow the story itself, but to look to the melding of sounds and images in the building of the story. If we do that, some of the difficulties that language models – including the linguistic turn in memory studies – pose for film work begin to occur to us. Hartmann offers many examples of the interpretive moment privileged in this turn, as he often evokes visual metaphors to illustrate his points. For example, he describes 'anti-memory' as a process that steals 'the colors of memory' in order to falsify history and foster forgetting.[4] The metaphor of colour becomes difficult when he considers the relations between visual and written texts. Pursuing the 'wealth' Günther Grass found in the '"heart-rending beauty of all the shades of gray (that) was to be celebrated in damaged [post-Holocaust] language,"' Hartmann appends a telling footnote indicating the difficult relationship of these language-based theories to visual representation, most especially narrative film:

> Moshe Kupferman's painterly minimalism also seems to explore those 'shades of gray': here the art of the survivor has chosen a non-figurative mode, works on paper that create a different kind of 'newspaper', that evoke the fragility of paper as it bears its always 'new' constructions without the full palette of painting. Where Adorno can talk of 'damaged life' and Grass of 'damaged language', it is harder to conceive of 'damaged color', which is one reason Grass celebrates gray.[5]

While the attempt to maintain a notion of beauty within the serious engagement with the past seems imminently understandable and vital, we need to differentiate more clearly between visual and written media. Grass' treatment of grey is, of course, mediated by language in a way that Kupferman's is not, although it is interesting to note how Hartmann chooses as his example a visual artwork that essentially becomes (an exploration of) a newspaper, be it figurative or not.[6]

Of particular interest to me here is the way colour, although rhetorically opposed to language, is understood only in the mediation of (written) language, that is, as metaphor. However, by thinking about real, visually perceived colour, one might claim that it is hard to imagine that certain presentations have not damaged colour, or at least left imprints on it that go beyond the metaphoric to become traces of memory themselves. I would recall here specifically the striking effect of Agfa-colour in Nazi films.[7] It is not simply by association, but also by the role of its aesthetic effect in a system of violence, that such colour may be considered damaged by the lasting effect of that processing.

A different, but equally relevant, sort of example can be found by looking back to the liberating use of colour in the expressionist and surrealist paintings of Kandinsky, Marc, Dali and others. Remembering that, it is not difficult to see a kind of damage inflicted on colour by the muted restraint of (bourgeois) realism, a mutation made ascendant again by the National Socialists. Damage is always at hand in an aesthetic of restraint but it is magnified out of all proportion through the destruction of 'degenerate' works and the eradication of those who made them.

The point here is that turning something grey within the spaces constructed by visual modes of representation is not the same as writing it grey, and my aim is to examine closely some films that explore this damage to colour and make muted restraint speak. Films that try to dispense with the naturalness of colour, to draw attention to its unmediated effect signal a need for critical engagement that calls on the history of the form as much as on the story. This is particularly the case given the manner in which the grey areas of the past with which we grapple seem to be expanding rather than contracting. Expectations of objectivity and truth operate differently in regard to feature films than documentaries, but with more and more features from reunified Germany turning to real stories of the past centred on individual experiences, the concern that history will be displaced in its return as film seems more valid now than ever.[8] The remainder of this chapter examines recent attempts at aestheticizations that concentrate on individuals within particular spaces in German history and stress the 'colour' of memory in the cinema to uncover the potentials of various shades of grey.

TO SEE WHAT WE CAN SEE

Some highly publicized and successful films about the Nazi past focusing on individual stories, such as Josef Vilsmaier's *Stalingrad* (1992), *Comedian Harmonists* (1998), and *Leo and Claire* (2001), clearly participate in spreading anti-memory.[9] Reducing complex situations to individual conflicts may be deemed a necessary move in creating a commercial feature film, but those conflicts lose specificity in the larger context when viewed through the lens of generic convention. The reference to, and in some cases re-enactment of, historical events centred around classically realistic modes of narration rarely gets beyond a blunting, rather than enlightening, emotional appeal.[10] In most films of this sort we are confronted, again, with the tension between the psychologized version of coming to terms on the one hand, and the process of individualized rediscovery of the past on the other. My argument with these works would not be that the wrong questions are being posed, but rather that they are being posed in a manner that does not maximize the potential of the medium for evoking productive engagement for the 'relative outsiders' of Nazism and the Holocaust.

A noticeable trend of late requires us to proceed with special caution, since many of the individuals depicted in features are to be aligned with the perpetrators rather than the victims of German history. Max Färberböck's *Aimée and Jaguar* (1999) is perhaps the best known of my examples, compiled from the true story of Lilly Wust.[11] I want to begin here because the film offers an example of the manner in which the seemingly progressive use of time and spatial difference actually aids in the normalization of German history.[12] It employs cinematic conventions of spatial construction in order to structure and encode the areas in which public demands and private desires overlap. In this way it generates a tension between public and private, both now *and* then, and concretizes that tension in its mode of developing relationships between (two) people in public space. Färberböck privileges the conventional cinematic mode of constructing interpersonal spaces, that is, the shot-reverse-shot sequences using 30° camera positions insisting on the 180° rule. This technique generates a private visual conversation for viewers by cutting back and forth between two (or more) figures in a manner that lets viewers have the sense of standing next to each figure in turn, without being gazed at directly or switching over to the space 'behind' the speakers (both of which were once assumed to be disorienting). Färberböck sets these against images taken from a steadily moving camera, or within shots in which many people are shown in constant motion, which indicate more thoroughly public spaces and occurrences. This stylistic division is not absolute, of course, for the classical construction shows itself to be porous and unstable, at times subject to pressures from the state and unable to keep people with ill intent from entering into close proximity with our heroes. What this means is that the cinematic space of intimacy becomes a space of danger in times of trouble – such as the Nazi period. The shot-reverse-shot sequence can thus be said to construct a public kind of intimacy, or an intimacy within a public space in which other elements are at play. It is significant in this regard that the film's one love scene – an absolutely private affair – is shot in two long takes that deploy a slowly moving camera pivoting slightly around the two women, emphasizing the complete (if only momentary) exclusion of anything outside of this intimacy.

These stylistic devices are not unique to this film. However, what makes them particularly significant in this case is the manner in which the film uses them to argue for a radical distinction between an autonomous private space and the public space of history, which should always be elsewhere. What keeps public history at bay is the sense of private history that strings together the moments of happiness, moments of exclusion, into a continuum. The public/private opposition is introduced at the level of the camera and *mise-en-scène*, which are formally similar, although modulated differently for the two different historical periods the film treats – the contemporary Federal Republic (the frame narrative) and the last three years of the Third Reich (the internal narrative and bulk of the movie). Hence, Färberböck's normalization of the Nazi past is not one of forgetting so much as one that envisions its transgressions according to general principles about the relation of the state and its citizens under liberalism. These grey areas, like the metaphoric use of grey to signify age, show us exactly how much this film reflects the mindset of neo-liberalism in relation to the role of the state in enabling freedom, the fetishization of youth, and the urge toward like-minded sub-groups within the body politic.[13]

The shot-reverse-shot construction of intimacy, unstable due to the nature of its montage, presents a problem for this view of the world that the narrative portion of the film, bowing to the necessities of lived history, is unable to solve. However, the film's closing sequence belongs to neither time frame in the strict sense, and thus provides a kind of coda that offers a solution. Far more than an out-take, this final sequence presents an alternate model of intimacy (in form and content) that tenders a resolution to the conflicts within the private sphere of desire, and between that sphere and the arena of public history. Here the slowly shifting camera pivots around one-third of a circle of friends playing cards, setting up an absolutely exclusive space of security that will then house the final shot-reverse-shot suture of intimacy between Aimée (and with her the audience) and Jaguar. This sequence represents a final recuperation of the steadycam, which has previously been the film's vehicle for depicting the uncontrollable flow of historical forces, but also of uncontrollable passion. Finally, it becomes the means of positing a carefully self-regulating private sphere that displaces both public history and space. However, the use of the steadycam reflects the problematic core of this vision of exclusive utopia, of which the film is not aware, since it internalizes the principles of the external sphere. Hence, the cinematic normalization here of the Nazi past resides not only, perhaps only marginally, in any overt relativizing of its crimes. The formal traces of the historical facts in this artistic production indicate that normalization is, as much as anything, a fabric of thought made possible by a combination of contemporary technology and the neo-liberal mindset. Such a combination insists on increasing privatization of all things public – even while relying on non-invasive governmental protection – and celebrates self-stylizing.

It is important to stress that while Färberböck's film deploys the 'greyness' of its central character as a visual reminder of the power of her experience to last over time, it does little to actuate the tensions of this true story in a distanced, cinematic realism. That term is usually used in reference to challenging works such as Claude Lanzmann's *Shoah* (1986), but there are certainly some films that adhere largely to the format of the commercial feature for which this notion is germane and powerful. This of course also means that they are often the subject of controversy, as was Andrej Wajda's *Korczak* (1990), a German–Polish co-production. Wajda chooses a very particular black-and-white imagery, shot by the phenomenal Robbie Müller, to depict the true story of an exceptional man who cared for orphans in the Warsaw ghetto. An internationally renowned pedagogue and paediatrician, the Polish–Jewish doctor Henryk Goldszmit, commonly known as Janusz Korczak, works tirelessly and selflessly to aid 'his' children, maintaining a functioning orphanage under extremely brutal conditions until its 'evacuation' to Treblinka in 1942. On several occasions Korczak frustrates others' attempts to save him and braves confrontations with Germans of all ranks. Wajda understood this story as an indication of a radically humanistic strain in a 'secret' Polish history that needed to be told to a Polish audience by a Polish director.[14]

This well-publicized intention led to one of the two major complaints about the film, which began to surface after its screening at Cannes in 1990: namely, that it shows Poles in too favourable a light and thereby becomes an anti-Semitic film. The much-quoted voice that led the way was Daniele Heymann in *Le Monde*: 'Whom do we see around Korczak [...]? Germans (obviously brutal) and Jews, resigned or collaborating. There are no Poles. The Warsaw ghetto? This is a matter between Jews and Germans. This is what the Pole wants to convince us of.'[15] This objection is largely a matter of subjective interpretation regarding how much the director needs to point to Polish complicity in order to show it properly (or avoid hiding it).[16] This is not the case with the other major complaint, which revolves around the film's final sequence showing the doctor and his assistants accompanying the children to the train station and into the wagon on the 'outing' that they have been promised. After tracking the group (complete with a banner) through the street to the station, the camera picks up the train as it rolls through empty meadows on the way to Treblinka. Suddenly the last car uncouples and slows to a stop. The locked and sealed door simply opens, and the passengers spill out to run joyously in slow motion into a mist that eventually envelops them: a title line then appears over the cloud-filled screen telling of their fate in the camp. 'This final image', wrote one German reviewer, 'is not only kitsch, not only a transgression against the proscription of images [*Bilderverbot*]. It is a Catholic version of salvation, a variation on the Christian ascension.'[17] Unlike the first subjective objection, this objection misinterprets the visual composition of the film.

This final sequence is far less 'Hollywood'[18] than the rest of the film, which shows evil being confronted in an exemplary manner but does not pursue the roots and reasons for that evil's existence. But the bulk of the film departs from a Hollywood-esque presentation in the use of black-and-white film, not simply as a historical marker or mood indicator, but as a gesture to the danger and death that surrounds these Polish Jews. The greyish light in the ghetto and the orphanage grows more prominent as the film progresses, and is only of a different valence than the glaring white that pervades when the Nazis enter the offices of the

Judenrat (Jewish Council) and brutalize the elders. This grey light, then, becomes a presence that infuses every image with an expectancy that in this historical context can best be linked to the audience's foreknowledge of the murderous outcome of such stories. Thus, the luminescent grey mist into which Korczak and the children disappear does not represent an obfuscation of the end met by these people in reality, but rather is consistent with the film's use of a key visual element. The grey presence arises from our knowledge of the exterminationist machinery that structures the ghetto, of which there is never any doubt in this film, and its final occupation of the screen signals nothing but the end for these figures.[19]

No doubt this is a much more peaceful ending than one could imagine for this film if it were to conclude with realistic images of slaughter, but that does not mean Wajda's work proposes an apologetic or revisionist 'narrative' about the Holocaust. Rather, he maintains the film's central problematic by generating an ending that both indicates annihilation and continues the doctor's humanitarian drive to spare the children's suffering. This core tension is introduced quite early on, when Korczak's former charges, while obviously still enthralled by the man, accuse him of having crippled them with his lessons of goodness: they feel they cannot respond adequately to this conjuncture in which fighting back would clearly be justified. The importance of this complaint against his teachings is underscored by its repetition roughly midway through the movie. The film's dilemma, then, is whether Korczak's amazing compassion and toil to alleviate the children's suffering is really a deadly form of quietism in this context. It seems that Wajda clearly wants to come down on the side of Korczak and pure humanitarianism here, but I am not convinced that the film he has produced fully bears him out. At one point the doctor requests not that the authorities end the situation leading to the death of countless children, but rather that they set up 'Houses of Death' (*Sterbehäuser*) where they can die peacefully. Again and again in discussions with his pupils, assistants and admirers it is the cult of personality surrounding the charismatic Korczak that brings the others to act as he wishes.[20] And yet, the historical record allows Korczak only that modest victory, for the end result remains the same, even if the path there was made less intolerable for some children. But since the story as told assumes the evil simply to exist it cannot posit Korczak's response as a solution: would it have been better if everyone in the ghetto had acted as he did? Yes. Would it have changed the situation? No. The final sequence, then, must be seen as one in which the historically true and heroic actions of this great man do not provide a counter-narrative, but rather a necessary greying of the historical record that opens the relative outsiders in the audience to impossibilities they had not previously considered.

The final two films I would like to analyse in detail have been, like *Korczak*, unfairly dismissed as part of a trend which is, if not unremittingly apologist and revisionist, then certainly dangerous in its naïvety. What Volker Schlöndorff's *The Ogre* (*Der Unhold*, 1996) and Gordian Maugg's *The Olympic Summer* (*Der olympische Sommer*, 1993) add, that Wajda excludes, is the vital component of a personal desire that has the power to draw one into the ranks of the perpetrators and bystanders.[21] In different ways these two films invite a questioning of this desire that furthers the project of coming to terms. This invitation stems from specific choices about visual representation on the part of the filmmakers to make grey manifest in the movies themselves. This questioning works at four levels. First, the means of cinematic reproduction should come under scrutiny, a scrutiny begged by the very appearance of the films. Schlöndorff shifts back and forth between black and white, sepia and garishly bright segments, which call for a reckoning with Agfa-colour; Maugg uses a camera contemporary to the age of his story, and uses it to create very particular grey effects. Second, the stylized story construction calls for examination because of tensions between the visual and oral narration: both are journey/rite of passage stories told in voice-over, one in first person (*The Ogre*) and one in the third person (*The Olympic Summer*). Third, the thematic issue of the relationship of National Socialism to certain configurations of individualized sexual desire pervades these films. Finally, following on the specific question of sexual dynamics, these films inquire into the role of the pursuit of personal happiness in the making of history and, by extension, in our (aesthetic) reconstruction of history: each considers the place of the individual in the interrelated spaces of myth, history and historical investigation.[22]

THE HEART OF RADIANCE:
VOLKER SCHLÖNDORFF'S *THE OGRE*

One would be hard pressed to argue that *The Ogre* has no faults, but the absolute refusal of the critics to engage with it, and the absolute disinterest of the public seem to indicate that the general tenor of the times, in relation to this subject matter, may be as much to blame as the shortcomings of the work itself. Having discussed elsewhere the contextual attitude into which this film was thrust,[23] I now want to consider the text itself in light of its aesthetic project. The obvious starting point would seem to be that Schlöndorff's central concern is indeed to further a coming to terms and to break the boundaries of national specificity in regard to the past in doing so. *The Ogre* is adapted from Michel Tournier's book, a Frenchman's novel featuring a French protagonist or, perhaps more accurately, central character, whose 'sinister writings' provide much of the narrative.[24] While my interest here is not to judge the relative value of literary, as opposed to cinematic texts, in the case of Schlöndorff's work we do need to recognize the importance of the literary models themselves for this director, and acknowledge that thorough familiarity with the literary source increases one's viewing pleasure and comprehension. Here it must suffice to highlight two elements from the literary source: Abel Tiffauges' dialectical obsessions with the movement of history, and with absolute stasis. Schlöndorff adapts these to a specifically cinematic presentation that interrogates film representation and the seduction of National Socialism, then and now.

Though translated into English as *The Ogre*, Tournier has taken his original title, *Le Roi des Aulnes*, from what in France is often considered the Ur-German text, Goethe's 'The Erl King' ('Der Erlkönig').[25] This deceivingly straightforward ballad tells of a father and child's night ride, during which the child sees and hears the beckoning of a phantom in the wood. The man cannot sense this presence and explains it away as belonging to the natural sights and sounds of the forest in the dark. The voice heard by the child is cajoling at first, but becomes laced with both desire and the threat of violence and, when the safety of their courtyard is reached, the child is indeed dead. One way of interpreting the poem would be as a Romantic fetishization of the pre-adolescent perfection lost upon entry into the world of adult desires. This seems a particularly relevant reading for an understanding of Abel Tiffauges, given his obsession with children and youth. The poem contains many of the major motifs to be used in the novel: the dynamic between man and child, and the violence latent in their interaction; the dread aroused by the spectre of a figure in the misted woods, seen by the child but unnoticed by the adult; the attempt to constrain the horrific in a narrative of the natural order of things; more abstractly, the power of the smaller over the larger figure, developed through the latter's responsibility to the powerlessness of the former; and, finally, the death of the innocent if not at, then in the hands of the experienced figure. The novel's central character believes that he alone among adults still hears his youth, still has an innate connection to it and therefore tries to save it. He becomes at times both the father trying to protect children and quiet their fears and the Erl King arising from the mists to offer the most serious threat to children, because his empathy and desire leads to their destruction.

But it is also important to note that Abel begins as a child in Tournier's work and that many of these themes of children and adults, in particular the inversion of positions of weakness and strength, protected and protector, servant and master, are central to the novel's other primary intertext: the story of St Christopher. Christopher was a giant of a man who always sought to serve the strongest master and in due course becomes liege to the devil and, ultimately, to God himself. Asking how he can serve God, he is told to wait by a river and bear across all who come along. He completes this task with ease until a child comes begging to be transported. The strong man is unable to support the weight of this passenger and is saved from drowning only by admitting that he is not up to the task, for the child is, of course, God incarnate. This parable plays a vital role in structuring the novel, for it is the thread running from Abel's childhood experiences in the Catholic French boarding school (St Christopher's), and through his at first inadvertent, then active involvement in the Nazi machinery for maximizing the strength of young Aryan bodies centred at the Castle Kaltenborn. It is also significant in his death in a bog attempting to save a Jewish boy from the flames of the castle in the Germans' hour of final defeat. His attraction to children *and* to figures of power is rooted in his insight into the power of the former and the childlike qualities of the latter.

Abel thus becomes the fulfilment of both the Erl King and St Christopher figures, but with inverted results: the child survives being carried off by the ogre in the bog while the bearer of the child does not. These final reversals are fitting, if mildly ironic, conclusions to a work about a man who believes he has glimpsed the essence of the order of things in the structure of eternally returning oppositions and inversions. Based on these principles of inversion, Tiffauges develops a philosophy of the 'phoric', tapping into the linguistic roots of the joy and power to be gained in his personal dialectic of serving and submitting. 'Euphoria', he philosophizes, is the state of being 'carried away' but also requires the act of carrying something. Metaphors of carrying and being carried abound in the novel, and Abel quickly develops an ability to read the meta-phoric elements in the world around him into a totalizing system of meaning, giving him a sense of mastery even in his most debased moments. Of course, this sense of mastery is aided at every turn by his conviction that fate also has something special in mind for him, that the natural process of inversion comes specifically into play when he is in peril.

Abel positively embraces the notion of fate called upon by so many in reality to resign themselves to non-action and to free themselves of responsibility. This notion accepts the sacrificing of others as a necessity in the order of things and thus becomes an apology for brutality and suffering. The moment of resolution to this structure must be in death, and the moment in the novel at which the consistent inversions of history cease their motions is marked by the resolution of the bifurcation in the narrative voice. The sinister writings of Abel himself, written with a left hand that spontaneously produces his meditations, have alternated with a third person narrator. At first this distinction is absolute, separated by chapters. As the work progresses, the narrator integrates more of Abel's writings, at times quite long passages, yet the reader remains aware of the distinctions maintained between them both orthographically and in perspective. But the sinister voice then ceases as Tiffauges' demise is narrated and the third person speaks from a position that must be subsequent to his death:

He had to make a superhuman effort now to overcome the viscous resistance grinding in his belly and breast, but he persevered, knowing all was as it should be. When he turned to look up for the last time at Ephraim, all he saw was a six-pointed star turning slowly against the black sky.[26]

The novel's final constellation is changed by Schlöndorff. Tiffauges' own voice-over narrates to the film's end, and the image we see to accompany his last, open-ended words about salvation and innocence is shot from behind and above him as he struggles through the moor under the weight of the child.

The change occurs because the director transposes the novel's philosophical ruminations, which Abel Tiffauges provides about his phoric system for understanding the world, into images of carrying and being carried and, most importantly, into the filmic dynamics of screen placement, camera angles and shot composition: i.e. they are translated into cinematic space. The overt presentation of such images is, as we will see, carefully supported by a tension between 'ups and downs' in the fabric of the film. This visually unites the major theme of the St Christopher story, as Abel interprets it, with images of him in the two guises of the traditional ogre: skulking underneath things looking up or towering above looking down. If we follow the movement from one of these positions to the next, tracing out the principle of inversions that captures the spirit of the book, we find that they reflect Tiffauges' sense that the inversions of the world are geared specifically (though not exclusively) to him.

While resigned at one level to the inversions of the world spirit, the novel's main figure also recognizes, and yearns for, the sublimity of their opposite: balance, stasis. It is, of course, a kind of love of death that creeps in here, and this is one of many points at which fascist ideology and Abel's philosophical system converge. But in one passage he considers this in terms that remind us of our opening consideration of the differences between literary and cinematic greys:

In the black–white inversions the grays also undergo a permutation, but a lesser one, and one that grows smaller as they approach a medium gray in which the black and white components exactly balance one another. This medium gray constitutes the pivot, immutable and absolute itself, around which inversion revolves.

Has anyone ever tried to define and produce that *absolute* gray that resists all inversion?[27]

This absolute grey would be a state at which all inversion ceases to matter and, hence, signal the end of history itself.

Now, absolute grey is no more possible in the 'living' world of narrative film than it is in the world Tiffauges envisions. Nevertheless, I would argue that while adjusting it to the narrative mode, *The Ogre* adapts this motif (and perhaps succeeds in raising the question of greyness itself) out of the novel into the cinematic medium by shifting it into a tension between colour and black-and-white footage. Thus, in addition to the analysis of the narrative in light of dynamic screen spaces, we must consider the effects of these shifts in film colour as formal elements within this representation, paying particular attention to images and sequences in which they come together.[28] The colour scheme adds another dimension that aims more at an exploration of the German tradition of self-idealization in general, and the celluloid depictions of that idealization in and around the Nazi period in particular. The French world will be shot in the mild haziness of sepia, and the German landscape often becomes intensely black and white, but there is a third region, that of vivid colour, which plays a vital role here as the promise of fulfilled desires. The promise held out for inclusion in the (national) body of the addressed in cinema will be embedded in repeated compositions that depict each of these hues: Tiffauges in sepia at the left gazes across a black-and-white view toward a stunningly coloured horizon. However, when that area of desire seems to be reached, it turns into lurid Agfa-colour and cannot be sustained. The impossibility of the promised fulfilment returns again and again to haunt Tiffauges, although he continually falls prey to the renewed seduction.

The Ogre begins with three sequences from Tiffauges' days in the provincial boarding school, opening with the sounds and images of pairs of boys one on top of the other attempting to throw each other to the ground. Panning left the camera picks up Abel and his only friend, Nestor, about to successfully join in, owing to Nestor's great girth. This and the following two sequences offer us a wealth of objects and ideas that will be important throughout the rest of the film. For example, the key role that vision will play is indicated by the accent placed on Nestor's glasses. More important than objects, however, are the beginning gestures to vertical hierarchies (ups and downs) embedded in the film, and also the reversal of those hierarchies – the stronger is below and the victim will be punished. We also now see the dominant screen direction of movement and looks left-to-right within the frame that generate a steady rhythm in the film. A further important element here is the hue of the film. Life at St Christopher's seems to be processed in sepia tones of muted brown, although most of Abel's private moments are captured in black and white. At those moments Abel's adult voice addresses us from off-screen.

The second film sequence shows that an element of fate comes into play here as well. Having been sent to be punished for a transgression that was not truly his, Abel stops on the stairs to ask the bronze statue of a man holding a child on his shoulder (recognizable, but not identified as St Christopher bearing Christ) to make a fire and burn the place to the ground. Sure enough, Abel escapes punishment through a catastrophic fire in the cathedral, but Nestor dies trying to quench the flames on his own. Abel will watch as Nestor is carried out, and his voice-over then tells us that he has had a revelation: 'Fate was swift, fate was cruel, and fate was on my side. I would be kept safe while others would suffer terribly.'

The third sequence is marked by an important shift in the screen composition. The secret exchange of the lighter during mass that precedes Abel's punishment and the fire is set up so that Abel appears on the right of the screen and the narrative space for the first time, and his attention is focused to the left.[29] When Abel makes his supplication to Christ sitting astride St Christopher, he is on the right moving to the left up the stairs. Finally, when he understands his special place in fate's designs, he stands at the right of the doorway through which Nestor's body is carried out. Throughout the film, the push from left to right eventually inverts, marking the end of one phase of Abel's journey and leading to another, often by showing him occupying the space of desire, now fulfilled. Here the inversion accompanies the moment when his childhood, such as it was, has ended, to the extent that it will ever end.

Tiffauges is back on the left of the frame when we next view him. He is a grown man, owner of a garage in Paris, and stands inside a window watching children play soccer in the street by his shop. In a wonderfully quirky image, we see Abel 'playing' in the game as well: when the ball (off-screen right) approaches his barred window, he jerks as if to head it back into play. Looking from left to right, Tiffauges now gives a meaning to the directional impulse we sensed in the St Christopher episode: starting on the left, Abel gazes at what he desires, which is or is imagined to be, in that other space. As a child there were no barriers to moving towards it, or at least no walls stood in the way. In adulthood a wall literally stands between him and his imagined desires: to be included, to be with children, to recapture his childhood. Abel's voice begins to show us that he understands himself and his longings to be at one with the movement of the world, a fairy tale of fated desire fulfilled. However, the film will progress to the point of showing the disaster of believing in one's own myths, and the expense of acting out one's fantasies for others. In the first part of the film, the voice seems in concert with the images and action we see, but this will change as Abel becomes more and more convinced of the fable he weaves about himself. Germany under the Nazis will be the land where Tiffauges feels that his union with his fantasies can take place in a manner useful and necessary to both sides.

Three specific images later in the film echo the shot of Abel looking left-to-right at his desires, but in these images outlandish colour takes the place that children have held until now. As a POW Abel is shipped by rail to East Prussia and, while his compatriots plot escapes, he loses himself in the beauty of the autumn landscape by looking out of the barred window across the flat fields toward a brilliantly coloured sky, the first use of bright shades in the film. The screen is divided in three sections: the left comprised of the train car, in sepia tones, from which Abel gazes out with fascination on this land; the central portion is a coldly black-and-white field; and the far right is the fiery sky, unnaturally vibrant in contrast with the other two screen spaces. Exactly as in the scene where he gazes out at what he desires in the children's game, Abel looks here with manifested longing, but remains separated from it as if by the bars of a cage. As he moves deeper into German territory, and into the phantasmagoric world of the Nazis, those bars will disappear.

The moment when the separation between himself and his fantasy initially falls away is marked in the content and form of the imagery as well. It comes a short time later, in the second shot that parallels the image of Abel 'playing soccer' through the barred window. One day, while pursuing a pheasant running along the floor of the trench he is digging, he finds himself suddenly outside the vision of the guards and wanders off to explore. He is playfully scooting on a frozen river when his voice-over begins musing on the words Nestor once spoke to him about the utopia of a hunter's hut becoming real. He starts a turn toward screen right (turning his back to the camera), a turn that is imitated by the camera, which swings right and up to discover a hunter's cabin in the trees. Now no bars separate Abel from the project of his fantasy, materialized certainly enough in this landscape that he loves, removed from him only by a frozen river that he can cross: no cut in the film breaks the continuity of his being in this world. Again, standing left and looking/moving to the right, Abel gazes on what he desires, a world combining both the black and white and the colour of his understanding of being.

When the prisoners' work is nearly completed and they are scheduled to be moved, fate and history seem to work in his favour once again. The forester whom Abel has met at the hut comes looking for replacements for the German apprentices who have all been called up to the war effort on the Eastern Front. He requests that the mechanic be assigned to him to keep the cars in order and generally help out at the estate of 'Rominten', which turns out to be the hunting lodge and grounds of the Third Reich's Master of the Hunt, Hermann Göring. The drive there takes them through a forest brimming with wildlife, such as bucks, boars and birds; but equally important to the Grimm-like quality of this world – Abel will eventually ask if he has fallen into a fairy tale – is the colour. When entering the forest at Rominten we enter a world of hues like those of the sky Abel saw from the train. It is painted like the world of the Nazi period's UFA films,[30] where the connection of fate and history to personality and individual story are the favoured subjects of the great spectacles that helped enlist the audience in the ranks of those who, if not actively involved, were at least not asking questions.

While much of what transpires there is compiled from historical fact, at Rominten we fully enter the world of UFA-style colour and empty promises. Not only the film stock, but the set takes on this colour: the huntsmen's deep greens, the reds of the banners, the perpetual glow of firelight and even the stained-glass swastika intensify the artificial effect. To complete this picture we have all the trappings from myths about Germany: woods teeming with fantastic animals, a medieval order of rank and boundless adventure. As we know, in such tales the lowly can become mighty in a flash, and the most pronounced stylistic element here, after the excessive colour, are the up-and-down dynamics in screen placement. When Göring arrives Abel crouches low behind a planter to peer up at him. Still wearing his prisoner-of-war outfit marked with a 'KG' for *Kriegsgefangener* (POW) on its back, the Frenchman is fascinated by the way in which Göring seems to fill the role of the ogre in 'Puss 'n Boots': the landed lord who delights in excess of all material kinds yet has a child-like sense of mythic wonder as well. The resemblance seems no accident, although here, too, is a reversal: instead of becoming a mouse and being eaten, the ogre 'becomes' a cat that Abel bests by getting lower down than it is and cleaning up its urine. He drives Göring's cat off with a few hand gestures that look oddly like incantations, and remains bobbing in his crouch as he bows before the applauding audience. In another setting, Göring breaks into a childish rage when he is asked not to shoot the forest's prime stag, Candelabra, while Abel is shown in a 'superior' spot above and behind him in the screen composition. The screen positions have been reversed and the most powerful has become the weakest. Nevertheless, both those positions are fully locked into the power dynamic of ritualistic fascism, and what unites the high and the low and allows them to transpose themselves is their unwavering belief in the systems developed to explain the special place in the world of the chosen – their myths.

One repeated gesture in particular pulls together all of these elements of artificial splendour and the dynamics of inversion: for relaxation, Göring dips his hands into a bowl of jewels that can only be described as hyper-colourful. The first time we see him do this it seems to be a strategy to annoy Count Kaltenborn, who detests the nouveau riche aspect of the new power structure. However, the Field Marshall also truly believes that the gems absorb the electricity that gets stored in the body and threatens to explode at some point. The second time he dips his hands in those jewels he not only believes in that power but is dependent on it. He needs it to calm himself after the Count has shot Candelabra, the prize stag Göring had reserved for himself. He learns at the same time that all personnel are being recalled, most moving to the Eastern Front. He orders everyone out except Abel, who crouches at his feet holding the glistening bowl. The spatial hierarchy of high and low (and left and right) balances itself here in a calm moment in the hunting lodge full of props, which represents the gaudy fairy tale of National Socialism in the self-presentation that these two ogres have come to believe. The reality of the slaughter that can be unleashed when the fairy tale becomes real, when the metaphor is actualized, has been demonstrated for the viewers in the massive carnage of the hunt earlier in the day. The final image of the hunt is a shot of the kill displayed on the grounds before the lodge, ordered and photographed as Leni Riefenstahl might have done, in a stark black-and-white image. The world is still comprised of different hues, but Abel has now entered the heart of the radiance that he feels to be both his desire and his destiny.

But then, in the third of the images mentioned above that position Abel at the left looking at his Agfa-coloured desires to the right, he views the majesty of Castle Kaltenborn against an overly colourful sky on the right. During his time at Rominten, Tiffauges comes to be fascinated with the Count even more than with Göring. The aristocrat's lineage, sense of tradition and honour, and his power to defy Göring (unique to this point), all make quite an impression on the prisoner. This fascination increases exponentially when he learns that the castle houses a special school, a *Napola* for the training of boys to join the most elite units of the SS. Of course, children were also missing from the fairy tale at Rominten – or at least children other than Abel and Göring (who is specifically compared visually, and by the voice-over, to Abel's boyhood friend, Nestor). Clearly the rumour of the modern schooling of the boys is an attraction to Tiffauges as well. On the great black roan the forester gives him, Tiffauges emerges out of the sylvan mist hooded and cloaked to arrive at the under-staffed castle and become the 'Ogre of Kaltenborn'.

The fascination of the spectacle which the Third Reich has become in the media is presented in *The Ogre* in a manner that can only be termed over the top. However, as we have seen, the exaggeration of Rominten brings us back not only to the fantasy structures of Nazi ideology, but also to its relation to German film history as well. To complement the Agfa-like colour and the fairy tale stories here we see images reminiscent of the moody greys of the pre-colour age, even back into the silent era. As Abel emerges out of the mists in front of the castle, one cannot help but think of similar shots from Fritz Lang's *Siegfried's Death* (*Siegfried*, 1924), although the image has been reversed to turn the Teutonic hero's light cloak and horse into dark figures. At the same time, the image of Vigo comes to mind, the enlightened traveller of Riefenstahl's *The Blue Light* (*Das blaue Licht*, 1932), who brings disaster to the natural world, for he emerges from the mists in much the same way as Abel does, although on foot. Thus, much as the narrative of the Nazi fairy tale has deeper roots in volkish and feudal structures that pre-date it, Schlöndorff traces the roots of this radiant tale back to the black-and-white sources that first channelled such neo-Romantic desires toward moving images to be coloured in by public consumption.

If Tiffauges believed that he was taken up in the fulfilled fantasy of Göring at Rominten, then he sees the fulfilment of his own inside the walls of Kaltenborn. Here the seduction of inclusion is shown not merely to arise from scared conformism, but from joyful and willing participation. The ceremonies, the games, the night-time torch formations, are, in the words of Count Kaltenborn, quite impressive to the simple minds of children and Tiffauges. He is given a primary task of collecting food from the local farms and villages and sees himself as a protector. But after bringing six new recruits, Abel is made the driving force of conscription of Aryan boys for the school, a further step toward becoming the Erl King, the ogre who out of love takes children from their parents to their deaths. Holding the leash on the four vicious Dobermans of the castle, and shot from low angles, he looks very much the demon that the villagers take him to be, though the voice-over tells us that his mission is a soft one, full of love and care. Sometime later we have a similar tension between the voice and image: checking beds at night, Abel walks the rows of cots with his light passing over the boys. He says they look as if they have been mowed down by a machine gun, which gives the sweeping motion of his light an irony that he himself clearly does not understand. The discrepancies between the voice's self appraisal and these visual images show both how far Abel has gone into believing his own myth and how badly that self-perception misses the mark.

At this point, Abel's trips outside the castle begin to be filmed in black and white, showing stunning images as he moves through the beech trees of the forest. The world of his myth deepens, but the safe world of his Germany begins to be reduced as the Reich implodes and the front approaches. He meets refugees fleeing west in the woods, including some of his old French comrades, who exhort him to join them in an attempt to find a unit and take up the fight against the Germans again. 'I must stay with the children,' Abel replies. He hears of others streaming westward through the woods at night, ghosts driven by the Germans, who are emptying the concentration camps in front of the advancing Red Army. He later witnesses, without commentary, the execution of those who stumble and fall. Among the fallen he hears a sound and finds a small boy, who has escaped by appearing to be dead. As he once hid his pigeons and carried children, Tiffauges secretly tucks the boy under his cloak and takes him to a room in the tower of the castle to nurse him back to health.

But the 'phoric' world is always double-edged. One of the older trainees enters the tower to take up a post with anti-tank equipment, discovers the Jewish child, and begins to sound the alarm, whereupon Abel wraps his arm around the boy's neck and kills him by carrying him up the stairs. Note here the actualization of Tiffauges' world view – and the film's implicit structuring of the St Christopher theme – that now performs the inversion: the euphoria of carrying children, indeed the whole metaphoric system of 'phoric' thinking as a life force, becomes deadly reality. Once again, Abel is on top, shot from low angles as he drags the dead German teenager up the stairs. He is stronger now than the last master he served, which means he must find another. This, of course, requires descending underneath the very weakest: therefore, he picks up the Jewish boy and starts out of the castle, which has come under an attack that will soon level the structure. With the boy cruelly exhorting him on despite the cold and the difficulty, Abel wades off into the night, which at first is lit by the flames engulfing Kaltenborn but then darkens again into an eerie beech bog shot in black and white. His voice begins to relate a story that he once heard a priest tell, about how even the greatest sinner could become cloaked in the mantle of innocence by picking up and bearing a child to safety. He finishes reporting that tale, and concludes elliptically: 'and then …'. The last we see of Abel is his figure in the bog, with the child on his back: the ellipses behind the voice's final words leave his fate indeterminate.

The final image returns us to the three-part screen structure that we remember from the train ride and his discovery of his cabin in the woods. I have interpreted this *mise-en-scène* as a projection of desire from out of the washed out space of sepia tones for the unified but clear dichotomy of colour and black and white that Abel feels reflects his own nature, and that of the world. The significant difference here is that this final image, a long shot from a high angle, shows Tiffauges in the left screen quadrant with his back to the camera and moving to the left. This changes the structure of screen placement and motion we have observed to this point, in which inversions have moved him to the right of the screen. In addition, it also shows for the first time the direction of his look and movement to be away from those starker cinematic shades of light and dark or radiant colour. This alteration changes the character of sepia images from the flattened out shades of the novel's colourless France, which follows Abel through the first half of the film, to a cinematic space of grey that is left for the viewer to ponder.

The collaborator and the victim, both survivors in the abstract sense, advance further into that space together, as the screen blacks out and a dedication to the late Louis Malle appears in white letters. Thus, at the end we have a three-part juxtaposition of the voice's open-ended 'and then …', the *mise-en-scène* that breaks with the patterns that have kept Abel moving into his desires and us into the film, and the written evocation of a French cinematic master shaped by the experiences of the war and the Holocaust.[31] This seems, without doubt, a constellation that asks us to contemplate further the claims about innocence and redemption made in Abel's final voice-over, rather than to close off reflection by accepting them. In this sense the translation of intertextual and metaphoric structures of the novel into the medium of film fosters an interrogation of the relationship between the aesthetic and institutional traditions of German cinema, and the totalitarian fantasies that find expression in the homicidal policies of the Third Reich.

DEUTSCHLAND *PRIVAT*?

Like Schlöndorff's film, Maugg's *The Olympic Summer* concentrates on an individual who is clearly aligned with the perpetrators rather than the victims of German history. It too explores the interconnectedness of private desires with public structures and historical memory. An opening title card points us toward the importance of historical truth in the film to follow. We read that this story is based on 'real occurrences' ('wahre Begebenheiten') that took place in and around the summer of 1936, much in the way that will be depicted here.[32] In addition, this presentation of events has been filmed using an Askania camera 'that is as old as the events themselves'. Hence, we are forewarned that the narrative and, to some extent, the manner in which it has been captured are true. However, the narrator immediately complicates this by introducing the story almost as a fairy tale. To capture the odd sense of a supposedly true story with a fairy tale ambiance used in the film, I break with convention and relate this story in the past tense.

Once upon a time there was a young butcher's apprentice from West Pommerania (*Vorpommern*), who saved for years to buy a bike and, upon getting a used two-wheeler, set out for the nation's capital to watch the Olympic games. Arriving in the confusion of the city, he by chance fell in with a well-to-do widow, who took him to her secluded villa in the south-west part of the city. He lived as a kept man in her boathouse and remained fully unaware of the political events of the day. Completely the innocent when he arrived, the apprentice's only initiation was into the world of sexual desire and personal satisfaction: he remained, as so many have since claimed, totally unconscious of the actions beginning to take shape around him.

To make our suspicions about this tale of political innocence even stronger, it goes on to turn its protagonist into a victim of the regime. He stayed in the boathouse long past the end of the Olympiad, but was eventually moved back into a room in the city as the widow began to tire of him. Her visits and her cash support dwindled away, and the apprentice fell prey to the dangers of the urban environment. A cruising SS officer picked him up, but before his initiation into same-sex pleasure could be consummated, other SS men burst in to shoot their comrade and arrest the butcher's boy. Without knowing why, he was sentenced to two years in prison, which stretched to ten after a failed escape attempt. This attempt took place near the end of his second year, when he could not face the prospect of having the memories of his happiness triggered by the days of late summer. Late in the war he managed to make contact with the woman, who agreed to help him escape and hide him, but at their appointed meeting on a crowded train platform they no longer recognized each other. After the thirty days in darkened isolation that he received for this episode, the apprentice emerged to spend three days with a cloth protecting his eyes, warming himself in the sun. He told his story to an adolescent from the *Volksturm* who had been set to guard the prisoners, and then he died.

There is no denying the transparently apologetic impulse contained in the skeleton of the story presented here. A German man comes of age in the mid- to late-1930s without taking note of even a single aspect of the political situation of the nation. Incarcerated for being socially dangerous if not fully degenerate, he still has no idea about the social hygiene laws of the land. Certainly this seems a quite outrageous manifestation of the 'I-knew-nothing-about-it' chorus that echoed throughout Germany after the war. The Germans here seem succinctly divorced from the Nazis and their war, and their programmes of genocide do not appear at all. Surely, in its barest form, this story exhibits the worst aspects of naïvety and nostalgia, if not of outright revisionism.

But stories are seldom told in their barest form, and narrative films never are. While we cannot ignore the troubling tendencies here, we must also attend to the manner of presentation before drawing our conclusions.[33] To start, *The Olympic Summer* gives viewers a sequence as powerful as any opening in a German film. First, a snapshot of a blue sky with white clouds grows to fill half of the centre of the screen while the initial credits fade in and out. Then, original photos of rural life are edited together in time with a soundtrack that shifts from a light vibraphone score, to a robustly sung folksong, to a swelling accordion melody, a melody that will accompany us throughout much of the film. We first see pictures of a farmyard with figures in the distance, interspersed with 'empty' images of flat fields with distant horizons. These are followed by a series of pictures showing a small girl at play with a pig; through an acceleration of the montage the pig seems to begin a nickelodeon dance. The soundtrack suddenly includes ear-splitting squeals of fear, which both complement and distance the following shots of a splayed out pig. In viewing this sequence, no one who has read them can help but be put in mind of descriptions such as Jean Améry's passage on torture turning 'the other [...] into a shrilly squealing piglet at slaughter'.[34] But the question facing us here regards those who have neither heard that shrieking nor read those words.

This opening segment introduces four formal elements that need to be scrutinized in order to understand fully the implications of this mixture of history, docudrama and fairy tale. The first is the blending of historical, documentary material and the simulated images generated by Maugg himself. The second is the relation of the aural to visual tracks. The third are the manipulations of the film's tempo, from slow motion to fast motion to stop-time and pixilation effects. The final technique is the repetition of images which both evoke and then undermine a kind of empathy with the apprentice. These techniques underscore the thematic of seeing and not seeing that brings us back to questions about complicity in the world of the viewers.

In the opening sequence the division between the historical and the new images is absolute, although the line between them is difficult to discern. After watching the old shots of the farmlands, the yard and the slaughter, the switch takes place at the film's first close ups, those around the bottle pouring out the celebratory libation. An increased proximity to the objects being filmed, and a slight increase in the image quality, mark the move into the new 'old' images. The smooth transition between the historical and the new material, along with this immediacy of objects, seemingly invites a suspension of disbelief and promises the possibility of an illusory recreation of the past; however, that recreation is rendered uncomfortably close as well. The images following the bottle are low-angle, tight shots first of a man's stubbly chin while drinking, then of a woman's mouth, shots that strike this viewer as far too intimate to sustain the safety of the illusion. And though this sequence is laced with a kind of positive bucolic value, the naked brutality underscoring this life also shines through: 'Blood and Soil' indeed. That brutality jars us when the squeals of the pig overpower the music on the soundtrack, even before we see the images of the slaughter. Further displacement of the idyllic comes with the protagonist's introduction, for the first image of the apprentice shows him inadvertently wiping blood on his face while cleaning his cleaver. In the moment that we first see this shot it seems to characterize the lad as a simple, good-natured soul; of course, in the context of a film titled to announce a story from 1936, this besmeared innocence also signals the intention to explore the status of the coincidental (non)participant in momentous historical events.

The notion of 'coincidence' actually becomes the guiding principle of the initial Berlin interlude. Again we begin with historical footage, this time of the Nazi capital prior to the Olympic games: flags, chaotic traffic, and hustle and bustle. The narrator explains that the apprentice is confused by the city, but is also impressed. By chance, he takes his first meal in 'one of those establishments where rolls could be had in any quantity with an order of pea soup at a fixed price', which makes an equally strong impression on him. The end of the Berlin montage is the image of a storefront called 'Aichingers', which is, or stands in for, such an establishment. The film then cuts to the new material, in which we watch the boy eating and taking in his exciting new surroundings. In a point-of-view shot, we then see a host of metropolitan characters, mostly working class but some slightly more elegantly dressed. Down the aisle toward the apprentice's niche comes a poorly-clad man playing an accordion, which is the instrument on the soundtrack even though the visual and aural tracks are not in synch. Shifting to a different angle, but still from the same part of the restaurant, we see a table of Brown Shirts begin to give this man a hard time. The narrator makes no mention of this growing abuse. Tension mounts, but then a cut shows us that the apprentice chances to see something that catches his eye, and another cut uses the implications of an eye-line match to distract our gaze as well. A woman's feet and calves are held in view as she descends some stairs, then her hat tumbles down into the midst of the SA, one of whom clowns by donning it. This act is an affront to the leader of his group, who berates him and throws the hat from his head to the ground at the apprentice's feet before leading the storm troopers off. The musician slips off screen as our sight is directed with the hat travelling off to the side of the action. The film draws no attention to the way this chance saves the man or distracts the apprentice, although in the description of the woman we learn that she 'knows how to make the most of life's coincidences'. This coincidence is a point where personal desire and public memory are forged, and so the disappearance of the musician off screen must be understood literally – as a disappearance made visible.

Immediately afterward, the drive out of town is filmed to the accompaniment of a tango played in part on an accordion. This tango will play repeatedly in the boathouse segment after the widow has seduced her charge by blindfolding *herself* in order to overcome his bashfulness during their first intimate moments together. However, the appearance of the accordion player in the previous scene has made this a very complicated element. In keeping with so many parts of this film, it signifies in two directions at once: the accordion player, like the music, was not completely diegetic, not entirely part of the world of the film. Roughed up by the SA and then forgotten, the player reminds one of the fate of the real victims of fascism. This reminder then haunts the soundtrack as well, with scratchy music that both evokes the historical era and remains decidedly foreign. This almost *diegetic* effect returns each time we hear music, often out of synch but 'coming from' the phonograph that the apprentice carries with them on outings in the boat, to the shore, and even when they dance. Again a doubled reference is at work, for the tango corresponds to the passion and physicality of the lovers on the one hand, and to the weight that they bear with them because of it on the other.

The accordion player himself makes another appearance as a repetition in the apprentice's memory. While serving his jail sentence, the apprentice reconstructs the blissful moments of that fast fading late summer in his fantasy, a daydream which will eventually stop the work of the whole coal-digging detail to which he has been assigned in the prison yard. The events of meeting his lover are replayed in a truncated form, but the musician can still be seen escaping the SA in the background with the entrance of the hat. The apprentice is so transfixed by his memory that he sees neither the brutality of the SA nor the plight of their victim which are embedded there: he only grasps at his desire. We actually see him tossing the hat into the air in the prison yard, still looking up at the late summer sky with a few white clouds. The viewer realizes at this point that the sight of the sky that causes him such unbearably sweet pain is the first picture seen at the opening of the film, which grew larger but never filled the entire screen and thus always remained framed as an image. Now we have seen the nostalgic yearning that finds its trace in that image, but also know that the musician has disappeared from its view, as have the Brown Shirts.

This, again, is a double-edged depiction of individual memory. It tries to acknowledge the importance, perhaps even primacy of individual stories and desires while still showing the occurrence of blindness that accompanies such vision. It is not necessarily just *historically* realistic memory that should carry with it the seeds and burden of coming to terms with complicity, but also the most private memories of innocent pleasure as well. The apprentice does not see what disappears, but the viewer does.

His prison sentence is thematically linked to sight as well, for the narrator tells us he ends up there by becoming involved in 'a murky affair' ('eine undurchsichtige Sache'). Actually the event is not opaque at all; rather, what remains obscured for the apprentice is the murky issue of the interrelation of personal desire and political responsibility. The sequence leading to his arrest begins with another 'Aichingers' shot and takes place there, setting up not only an opposition to the earlier heterosexual encounter, but also a direct parallel and extension of the meeting with the widow. The death of his would-be lover points out in horrible clarity that the personal is political, and yet the apprentice does not get it. But the audience does, in part because this interlude repeats an image of the apprentice's blood-smeared face that we remember from the opening sequence.

Even in the narrative itself our hero is not a victim only of the regime's policies but also of his own memorializing of his sexual 'Olympic summer' and his Pomeranian innocence prior to that. His sentence is relatively light and is almost completed when his memories drive him to an escape attempt. Coincidentally, the escape is another point where a companion, the instigator, dies, while he, the follower, survives. The escape fails because the apprentice cannot bring himself to kill the guard that his companion has immobilized. This action saves him from the gallows but results in his fellow prisoner being hanged. Yet, his innocent nature alone does not keep him from murder for, as the narrator tells us, 'he had only learned to kill animals'. In stereotypically German fashion, he only does what he has been taught to do. Furthermore, the tone of the voice-over combines with the viewer's memory of the anguished squeals of the opening segment to make this distinction between those he will or will not kill less reassuring, particularly given the contemporaneous definition about who does not fall into the same category of 'human' as the Aryan guard. If the fairy tale has made the viewer forget those sounds, the narrator soon brings them back by inserting the effects of history. He says that because of the military situation all hands are needed and so the apprentice is assigned to a work detail in a slaughterhouse, where his training as a killer of animals can be put to use. This historical coincidence keeps him from dying just yet but at the expense of others: simultaneously, it keeps alive our memory of the film's opening as we see him framed against rows of pigs' heads. Despite the privacy and serenity of the piano score, which by now the viewer associates with his moments of memory, the images here keep us from an empathy that might indeed be too fully apologetic.

The tension between the aural and visual, which has accompanied us from the outset, becomes especially acute near the end of the film. At the same time, a referential doubling, or even recurrence, of images and scenes increasingly creates a space of memory within the work that combats the simpleton's single-mindedness. Thus even his death, the point of strongest temptation to see the apprentice as an allegorical figure of victimization, is textured by a troubling ambiguity generated in part by juxtapositions of sound and image. The narrator relates how he emerges to sit blindfolded and pass on his tale before dying, and then: 'speech became more and more difficult for him. He laid himself on the rocks. Thus, he died.'[35] We then see a close up of his interlocutor, the air-force apprentice (*Luftwaffenhilfe*), locked in a silent, Munch-like scream, a silence then broken by the historical radio announcement that 'The Führer is dead'. The coincidence of these two deaths sets up both a parallel, and an opposition, which defy easy pigeonholing. In particular, the transparent spin put on by the radio announcer, who turns Hitler's suicide into a hero's death in defence of the heart of the home front in Berlin, undermines any idea that the apprentice's death occurs solely on the German home front demarcated by private innocence and public victimization. This sequence refuses to equate the average German with Hitler, but also ironically portrays the apprentice as the 'Leader' in the defence of the homeland of silence and forgetting that indeed outlasts the war.

The apprentice's memories have been shown as both powerful and laughable, for he sees what others cannot (his recollected experiences), but in turn cannot see what is around him, or even what should be in his memories. This critique is pushed further by the reappearance of the blindfold as he tells his story to the next apprentice. We should remember that the blindfold, worn by the widow, first appeared as an enabling device at his initiation into sexual activity, and is already bound up with personal desire and the desire not to be seen when it comes into play again in the prison yard. Now the blindfold gives us an image of the apprentice as one who did not – could not – see.

The Olympic Summer is structured by a doubling that is signalled in the formal principles of composition, setting up yet not absolutizing the parallels and oppositions between different spheres: public and private, city and country, straight and gay, political and personal, historical documents and aesthetic recreations. Maugg employs cuts almost exclusively, and uses very few blends, dissolves or fades that urge the viewer to naturalize these images. Instead, the viewer is constantly confronted with the transparency of a privacy that cannot shut out public history by seeing only personal memory. Indeed, the recurrent sequences of Maugg's film invite the audience to understand simultaneously the power and the problems of memory as history, perhaps even for those relative outsiders of us who blindly live in intimate proximity to violence in other contexts as well.

CONCLUSION

In a manner more consequent than any other feature film I have discussed, *The Ogre* and *The Olympic Summer* both seek to put questions of collaboration and fellow-travelling to the test by pursuing their stories along the lines of personal investment, both conscious and unconscious. *The Ogre* reminds us that this period in German history, which has come to be considered by many as the heart of darkness, was one that imagined itself and was experienced as radiant. By exploring the effects of Agfa garishness as self-conjured fairy tale, Schlöndorff's film in a sense reinvests that UFA-colour with 'shades of grey'. At certain moments, the film recreates the visual impression of the entertainment industry that historically took viewers so far away from the great myths circulating outside, and thus reconnects those two worlds of feature fables and grand illusion. Alternating this damaged colour with the black and white of a damaged life does not set up a simple opposition between those public and private worlds, as much as it interweaves them. *The Olympic Summer* explores 'shades of grey' by redeploying the technology of the National Socialist period to achieve a distanced black-and-white depiction. Maugg conjures up the grey areas of personal and sexual happiness in that context in such a way as to make them point beyond that period. Hence, both of these films call upon us to use them as modes of reckoning with the historical role of representation and experience, because they draw attention to these issues at both the levels of content and of form.

If we can speak at all about film's contribution to 'coming to terms' as a process, then we must recognize it to be a process and not a ritually repeated act. Although very few films simultaneously manage to expand our historical knowledge and generate a connection to today, many that work in only one of these areas contribute to 'coming to terms' in small increments. Both documentary and fictional works must play a role here. While recent feature films seem to have shifted to private stories that individualize, and hence weaken, the memory of the collective, the manner of telling those stories can colour in a grey area of aesthetic apprehension of the past and present that no black-and-white account of facts can attain alone. In looking at the privatization of history in contemporary German film, I have been concerned with showing the potential alignment between the 'relative outsider' to the crimes of German history, and the viewer who may unwittingly be in an analogous position to the historical perpetrator. It strikes me that Maugg's aesthetics of recurrence best shows the interrelated nature of personal (sexual) desire and social structures that gestures to this disturbing alignment, and does so in a manner accessible through neither trauma nor transference. This implies that the empathy so often at the centre of Holocaust studies needs to be set aside here and the question of distinguishing 'memory' from 'anti-memory' rethought. This rethinking, as Andreas Huyssen puts it, means recognizing that '[t]he difficulty of the current conjuncture is to think memory and amnesia together, rather than simply to oppose them'.[36] But we should also remember that the most prevalent type of amnesia, medically speaking, is not a disconnection from the distant past, but an ongoing process that prohibits the formation of memories in the present.

Notes

1   Geoffrey Hartman, *Holocaust Remembrance: The Shapes of Memory* (Cambridge, Mass.: Blackwell, 1994), p. 10.

2   Hartman, *Holocaust Remembrance*, p. 20.

3   James E. Young, *The Texture of Memory: Holocaust Memorials and Meaning* (New Haven: Yale University Press, 1993), p. 7.

4   Hartmann, *Holocaust Remembrance*, p. 10.

5   Hartmann, *Holocaust Remembrance*, p. 269. Kupferman was born in Poland in 1923 and spent much of World War II in the Ural and Kazakhstan internment camps. He was the only member of his family to survive. In 1948 he emigrated to Israel to become a world-renowned abstract painter. He was also associated with the Kibbutz movement: he co-founded the 'Ghetto Fighters' Kibbutz', where he lived until his death in 2003.

6   Lawrence Langer also makes extended use of this metaphor in his discussion of Primo Levi's 'Legacy in Grey'. Langer, 'Legacy in Gray' in Robert S. Kremer (ed.), *Memory and Mastery: Primo Levi as Writer and Witness* (Albany: State University of New York Press, 2001), pp. 217–34.

7   The Agfa company, based in Wolfen, produced colour film used in German productions during the Third Reich from 1941 onwards.

8   Anton Kaes, *From Hitler to Heimat: The Return of History as Film* (Cambridge, Mass: Harvard University Press, 1989).

9   For a kinder interpretation of Vilsmaier's *Stalingrad* on account of its anti-war thrust see R. C. Reimer, 'Picture-Perfect War: An Analysis of Joseph Vilsmaier's *Stalingrad* (1993)' in Randall Halle and Margaret McCarthy (eds.), *Light Motives: German Popular Film in Perspective* (Detroit: Wayne State University Press, 2003), pp. 304–25.

10 I would say that the same ultimately holds true for better-intentioned works such as Hans Wilhelm Geißendörfer's *Gudrun* (1992), Bernhard Sinkel's *The Movie Teller* (*Der Kinoerzähler*, 1992), and *Rabbit Hunt* (*Hasenjagd – Vor lauter Feigheit gibt es kein Erbarmen*, 1994), by Austrian filmmaker Andreas Gruber, even though the latter's re-enactment of the slaughter at Mauthausen is of a higher quality and purpose than that of Vilsmaier's work and evokes emotion in a much more specific context.

11 Erica Fischer, *Aimée & Jaguar: eine Frauenliebe Berlin 1943* (Cologne: Kiepenheuer & Witsch, 1994).

12 Saul Friedländer has noted that aesthetic works that have a kind of 'relative "adequacy"' in representing the Shoah are marked by 'an allusive or distanced realism' in which '[r]eality is there, in its starkness, but perceived through a filter' constituted by distance in time and spatial displacement. Friedländer, *Probing the Limits of Representation: Nazism and the 'Final Solution'* (Cambridge, Mass.: Harvard University Press, 1992), p. 17.

13 For a full reading to support this conclusion, see John Davidson, 'A Story of Faces and Intimate Spaces: Form and History in Max Färberböck's *Aimée und Jaguar'*, *Quarterly Review of Film and Video*, 19.4 (2000), 323–41. A similar metaphoric use of the grey of age concentrating on victims is to be found in Jan Schütte's *Goodbye America* (*Auf Wiedersehen, Amerika*, 1993).

14 Günter Graffenberger, 'Janusz Korczak und das geheime Poland', *Die Welt*, 3 April 1990, p. 79.

15 Quoted in Stephen Engelberg, 'Wajda's *Korczak* Sets Loose the Furies', *New York Times*, 14 April 1991, pp. 15–17. Engelberg, along with many voices in the German press, connects the vehemence of Heymann's reaction to French sensitivity due to the desecration of a Jewish cemetery just days before the film's appearance at Cannes. Another of the film's

less shrill but more authoritative critics was Claude Lanzmann, who also felt the film wilfully obscured passive and active participation on the part of Poles in the attempted extermination of the European Jews. One of the film's staunchest defenders was Mareck Edelman, the last surviving leader of the ghetto uprising in 1944.

16   Wajda points directly to Polish anti-Semitism, participation in brutality against Jews and passivity regarding the ongoing situation in at least three instances. The film opens with the cancellation of Dr Korczak's radio broadcast on childrearing and education because of pressure exerted from important places in the local and national government to remove this prominent Jewish voice from the airwaves *long before* the Germans take over. At another point, after the ghetto has been erected, Korczak accosts a Polish guard who is brutalizing children. Finally, the family and employers of a young Polish girl, who has an interest in one of Korczak's orphans, forbid her to see the boy wearing a yellow star again. For some, these instances may not carry enough weight to balance out the self-sacrifice of the young Pole shot for dispersing bread in the ghetto, and the relative absence of other (non-Jewish) Poles. Still, at the very least they indicate an attempt on the director's part not to whitewash what is known about Polish history even as the stress is placed on this figure who comes to represent its 'secret' history.

17   'Dieses Schlußbild ist nicht nur Kitsch, nicht nur Verstoß gegen das Bilderverbot. Es ist eine Spielart christlicher Himmelfahrt.' Peter Körte, 'Der Mann aus Papier', *Frankfurter Rundschau*, 28 March 1991, p. 14.

18   Körte, 'Der Mann aus Papier'.

19   Only one reviewer has, to my knowledge, made this connection (intuitively rather than analytically): 'Yet the milky-white light still points to destruction' ('Doch die milchig weiße Luft verweist noch auf den Untergang'). Hans Günther Pflaum, 'Lehrstück der reinen Humanität', *Süddeutsche Zeitung*, 8 May 1991, p. 10.

20   Here I would agree with Körte that many of the shot compositions are produced as 'proof of a moral superiority. [...] Whenever Korczak speaks, he always expresses himself in polished sentences; the others listen and nod, they don't argue with him and they are ashamed of their simple-mindedness and their immaturity'. ('Anschauungsmaterial einer moralischen Überlegenheit [...]. Wenn Korczak das Wort ergreift, äußert er stets druckreife Sätze; die anderen lauschen und nicken, sie argumentieren nicht und sind beschämt von ihrer Unbedarftheit und Unreife'). Körte, 'Der Mann aus Papier'.

21   Along with *Aimée and Jaguar*, the most famous inclusion of individual desire can be found in Agnieszka Holland's *Europa Europa* (*Hitlerjunge Salomon*, 1991), the story of a Jewish boy whose 'passing' as a German in the Hitler Youth is threatened specifically by what the sexual encounter with the girl he desires might literally reveal. The story of the unwilling perpetrator is told from a different angle there than the one I am pursuing in this section of my essay. A similar take on personal desire and German participation in brutality is Thomas Mitscherlich's *The Denouncer* (*Die Denunziantin*, 1993), the tale of an enigmatic woman who denounces a man critical of the regime, which unfortunately lacks real cinematic power.

22   There are, of course, other works that make choices about (visual) presentation that do not focus on colour. The Brechtian-influenced films of Michael Verhoeven, *The Nasty Girl* (*Das schreckliche Mädchen*, 1989) and *My Mother's Courage* (*Mutters Courage*, 1995), deserve special mention here because of his sovereign management of temporal and spatial distance and his bending of generic boundaries. Far less successful are the elliptically allegorical treatments bordering on farce developed by Armin Mueller-Stahl in *Conversation with the Beast* (1997) and Alexsandr Sokurov's *Moloch* (1999), or on the heroic by Werner Herzog in *Invincible* (2001).

23   For a discussion of this context see John E. Davidson, 'Overcoming Germany's Past(s) in Film since the "Wende"', *Seminar* 33.4 (1997), 307–21.

24   Michel Tournier, *The Ogre*, trans. by Barbara Bray (New York: Doubleday, 1972; originally 1970).

25   English translation in Klaus-Peter Hinze and Leonard M. Trawick, *An Anthology of German Literature of the Romantic Era and Age of Goethe* (San Francisco: EmText, 1993), pp. 40–3

26   Tournier, *The Ogre*, p. 370.

27   Tournier, *The Ogre*, p. 112. Italics in original.

28   According to the head of the sound crew, Schlöndorff claimed to be working without a set plan as to which sequences would be in colour and which in black and white (Karl Laabs, personal conversation with the author). If this anecdote is accurate, then we are not necessarily working at the level of 'intention' here, at least not bound to discern a specific system that is tied directly to a desired understanding of the film.

29   That Schlöndorff seems to make these choices consciously is underscored by the changes instituted in adapting Tournier's work. While this scene combines two distinct episodes, it reverses the position of the characters in the book, where Nestor sits on the left, by the outer wall, Abel in the middle, and a third boy on the right. Tournier, *The Ogre*, p. 57 ff.

30   From 1942 onwards, the entire German film industry was subsumed under one film company, UFA (Universum Film AG).

31   In addition to having been Schlöndorff's mentor in his apprentice years, Louis Malle was himself a child under the Vichy regime, who experienced both the quiet bravery of resisters and the brutality of fascist collaborators. *The Ogre*'s scenes in St Christopher's clearly owe something to the aesthetics of the film account of that experience in Malle's film *Au revoir, les enfants* (1987).

32   The basis of the film is actually a short story by Günther Rücker, entitled 'The Journeyman' ('Der Geselle'). Rücker, *Anton Popper und andere Erzählungen* (Berlin: Aufbau, 1985), pp. 72–75.

33   I myself may have been guilty of reducing this film to its simplest story in my brief comment on it in an earlier article. Davidson, 'Overcoming Germany's Past(s)'.

34   Jean Améry, 'Torture' in Lawrence L. Langer (ed.), *Art from the Ashes: A Holocaust Anthology* (Oxford and New York: OUP, 1995), pp. 121–37 (p. 132).

35   'Das Sprechen wurde ihm immer schwerer. Er legte sich auf die Felsen. So starb er'.

36   Andreas Huyssen, *Twilight Memories: Marking Time in a Culture of Amnesia* (New York: Routledge, 1995), p. 7.

Chapter 3

East German cinema after unification[1]

Daniela Berghahn

THE END OF DEFA

The collapse of state socialism in the German Democratic Republic saw one of the most dramatic and rapid transformations of a country's political and economic system that history has ever witnessed. Against this backdrop, DEFA (Deutsche Film Aktiengesellschaft), just like all other state-owned enterprises, was privatized. For 46 years DEFA had enjoyed monopoly status, being East Germany's only film production and distribution company. At the time of its privatization, DEFA consisted of a feature film studio in Potsdam-Babelsberg, a documentary film studio in Berlin and Potsdam, an animation studio in Dresden and a dubbing studio in Berlin-Johannisthal. There was also copy works, an import and export division, DEFA-Außenhandel, and Progress Film-Verleih, which was in charge of film programming and distribution.[2]

Between 1946, when DEFA was founded in the Soviet occupied zone, and 1992, when the Babelsberg site was sold to Compagnie Immobilière Phénix Deutschland GmbH for 130 million DM,[3] the DEFA feature film studio produced no less than 750 feature films – an average of 15 films per year. Amongst them were critically acclaimed masterpieces, indeed milestones of German film history. When, on the 100th anniversary of cinema in 1995, German film critics and producers were invited to compile a list of the 100 most important German films of all time, no less than 14 DEFA films were nominated.[4] Amongst them were Wolfgang Staudte's *The Murderers Are among Us* (*Die Mörder sind unter uns*, 1946), Kurt Maetzig's *Marriage in the Shadows* (*Ehe im Schatten*, 1947), Konrad

Wolf's *I Was Nineteen* (*Ich war neunzehn*, 1967) and *Divided Heaven* (*Der geteilte Himmel*, 1964), Frank Beyer's *Jacob the Liar* (*Jakob der Lügner*, 1974) and *Trace of Stones* (*Spur der Steine*, 1966/1989), Gerhard Klein's *Berlin – Schönhauser Corner* (*Berlin – Ecke Schönhauser*, 1957) and Heiner Carow's *The Legend of Paul and Paula* (*Die Legende von Paul und Paula*, 1974). What this brief and incomplete list of film titles reveals is that DEFA's reputation was founded on two traditions in particular: the anti-fascist tradition and the socialist realist tradition. This chapter will explore to what extent east German filmmakers stayed true to these two most prominent strands of East German film culture after 1990, notwithstanding the dramatically changed conditions of film production and reception in the wake of German reunification.

Soon after the privatization of the Babelsberg studio site, it became apparent that the new owners had no intention whatsoever of preserving the DEFA heritage. This heritage had been predicated on the assumption that film, alongside the other arts, had a central role to play in the grand project of constructing a socialist society. What the new owners had in mind was to turn the Babelsberg site into a lucrative business with a theme park, prime location real estate, a state-of-the-art media centre and a film studio, which they named Studio Babelsberg Motion Pictures GmbH. The company logo paid tribute to Fritz Lang's film *Metropolis* (1927), which was also made in the film city Babelsberg when UFA was based there.[5] No mention of DEFA was made in the studio's new name, most of DEFA's remaining staff were made redundant and DEFA was officially struck off the register of companies in August 1994.

The west German film director Volker Schlöndorff, who was appointed as the artistic director of the new studio, had visions of creating a Hollywood in Europe. But his dream never came true, for instead of trying to develop a new creative centre of German or European film production, the studio management's strategy was to attract international big-budget productions. However, the number of such productions, including Jean-Jacques Annaud's $80 million epic about Stalingrad, *Duel – Enemy at the Gates* (2000) and Roman Polanski's *The Pianist* (2002), remained small. The attempt to stimulate the development of indigenous film production by setting up Babelsberg Independents – a production and development unit within the studio which aimed to support Berlin-based young directors – resulted in just a few films. One looked hopelessly for the familiar names of ex-DEFA filmmakers who had, it seemed, been ousted from what was once *their* film city in the wake of German reunification. In order to stay economically viable, Babelsberg's loss-making studios had to focus increasingly on television productions, in particular, lucrative soaps and chat shows. The future of film production at Babelsberg remains uncertain: Vivendi, the new owner of Media City Babelsberg, was 35 billion Euros in debt in 2002, and so far Studio Babelsberg has not succeeded in establishing itself in Germany's struggling film industry. In 2004, Vivendi Universal sold Studio Babelsberg to a Munich-based investment group for the notional sum of just one Euro and even took over 18 million Euros of the Studio's existing debt. The prospects for Babelsberg are bleak, or, as Bärbel Dalichow, the director of the Potsdam Film Museum, aptly put it: 'A third life of the film city Babelsberg is unlikely but not impossible.'[6]

'IT'S BETTER TO LIVE IN THE JUNGLE THAN IN A ZOO': FACING ARTISTIC AUTONOMY

While Germany was swept up in a wave of unification euphoria, DEFA's filmmakers could not yet foresee the decline and eventual disappearance of DEFA. Instead, they were exhilarated by the prospect of being able to make films without having to worry about the state's interference and censorship, since in autumn 1989 the newly installed Minister of Culture granted all sectors of culture autonomy from state control. Nominally the Central Film Office (*Hauptverwaltung Film*) – a department in the Ministry of Culture which was in charge of regulating and controlling the GDR's entire film industry – continued to exist until March 1990. However, it effectively ceased to operate when the GDR's last Film Minister, Horst Pehnert, relinquished his post alongside many other cultural functionaries in November 1989. Films could now be produced and distributed without the approval of the Film Office. At last, the time had come to speak the unspeakable and make films that addressed subject matters which had hitherto been taboo. It was now possible to renounce the official aesthetic doctrine of socialist realism, which had, until then, remained mandatory in some form or another, and experiment with an avant-garde aesthetic that was still novel for

east German filmmakers but was long outdated across the rest of
Europe. The time had also come to dig out those 'forbidden films' which
had been banished to the state film archives in the wake of the infamous
Eleventh Plenum of the Central Committee of the SED in December
1965, and prepare their public release.[7] The newly gained freedom was
even accompanied by some modest financial support from the GDR's
last government, which granted DEFA some 18 million DM for the
production of eight final films, the so-called *Überläuferfilme* (run-over
films, i.e. films that had been conceptualized before but were only
realized after the fall of the SED regime). Thus the period of transition
afforded filmmakers the unique opportunity of still receiving funding
from the state without having to conform to its supervisory rigour.

Not surprisingly, this sudden release from strict state control into
complete artistic autonomy proved a double-edged sword for many
filmmakers. The Film Office had not just acted as a censor, but in its
capacity as the patron of the film industry had also assumed the role
fulfilled by a producer in a capitalist system of film production, namely
to weed out badly-crafted scripts or insist on alterations that would
improve a film's quality and audience appeal. In the absence of such
external quality control during the period of transition, some filmmakers celebrated their new creative autonomy in a self-indulgent
manner and lost sight of their audience. Ulrich Weiß's *Miraculi* (1992)
and Herwig Kipping's *The Country Beyond the Rainbow* (*Das Land hinter
dem Regenbogen*, 1992), are illustrative examples of this trend: both are
highly enigmatic parables of life in the former GDR which received
recognition from some critics (Kipping's film even won the Federal
Film Prize at the International Film Festival in Berlin), but failed to
resonate with the public.[8]

Moreover, east German filmmakers were no longer sheltered from
the harsh realities of the market. As a result, even well crafted films
such as Roland Gräf's *The Tango Player* (*Der Tangospieler*, 1991), based
on Christoph Hein's novel of the same name, performed poorly at the
box-office. It was not the film that was to blame, but rather the changed
conditions of film distribution and exhibition in the new federal states.
The film's theatrical release in 1991 coincided with the privatization of
cinemas. Nearly half of the eight hundred cinemas in the new federal
states were gradually being closed, in particular those in provincial areas.

This massive closure severely diminished access to what once used to be a prime leisure activity for young people in the GDR. The majority of the remaining cinemas were taken over by west German cinema chains which modernized them and converted them into multiplexes. The change in cinema ownership had significant repercussions for the type of films that were shown. Whilst in the past DEFA productions had been promoted though centrally devised programming policies which ensured a high visibility of the GDR's national film culture across the country, this artificial protection no longer existed after the privatization of cinemas. Suddenly east German films faced unmitigated competition from Hollywood blockbusters. As Leonie Naughton poignantly states, '[b]y the time *The Tango Player* reached theatres, cinema owners had realized that they could make more money selling popcorn than from screening DEFA films.'[9]

The general transformation of east Germany's cultural economy of shortage, which lacked a developed entertainment industry, into a cultural sphere with a variety of offerings contributed to the rapid decline of cinema audiences. Moreover, prices for cinema tickets, which had been heavily subsidized in the past, more than tripled, making a visit to the cinema an almost unaffordable luxury for many east Germans at a time when they were facing major economic insecurities. In 1988 East German citizens went to the cinema on average four times a year (as frequently as the Americans), by 1992 this figure had dwindled to just one visit per year.[10]

Of equal significance was the fact that the new cultural climate had changed audience expectations and behaviour. Fictionalized accounts of contemporary society in the style of DEFA (*Gegenwartsfilme*), a key 'DEFA genre', had lost favour with east German audiences. Given the choice between socialist enlightenment and sheer escapist entertainment, cinema-goers opted for the latter. Entertainment films and Hollywood imports had been undeniably more popular with audiences even when the Film Office still prescribed what kind of films were deemed suitable viewing. However, domestic productions, and in particular films about contemporary society, had a unique role to play in the GDR's tightly controlled public sphere.[11] Film, albeit to a lesser extent than literature, had provided a platform for oblique criticism and filled an information deficit left in the Party-controlled public sphere.

Readers and audiences had learnt to decipher deviant messages by reading between the lines. Although cultural functionaries, who were not dumb either, understood them too, they often let them pass, depending on the prevailing political climate. Thus, what is usually referred to as the replacement function (*Stellvertreter Funktion*) of art in the GDR constituted a significant aspect of the audience appeal of films which were rumoured to have been only reluctantly approved by the officials. Not all of them became box-office hits on the scale of Heiner Carow's cult film *The Legend of Paul and Paula*, but the lure of the almost forbidden had at least drawn a large share of the educated public. In the post-Wall public sphere, in which freedom of expression was a given, films that spoke the truth had lost their magic spell.

The market for East German films in the old federal states was even smaller. Since the 1980s, Hollywood films have accounted for around 80% of all box-office receipts, leaving only a small share for other foreign imports and domestic productions. Moreover, West German audiences had traditionally shown little interest in the film culture of their brothers and sisters on the other side of the Wall. German unification did not spark a sudden interest in films made in 'the other part of Germany', and to date the only east German film that has appealed to audiences in the old and the new federal states alike has been Leander Haußmann's nostalgic comedy, *Sonnenallee* (1999).

Against this background of a dramatically changing media landscape, DEFA filmmakers were struggling for their artistic survival. DEFA's directors, scriptwriters, cameramen and other artistic staff had been permanently employed by the studio and never had to worry about making a living. For most of them the dismantling of the east German film industry meant a free fall from complete security to total independence, from the status of a once revered artist to a nobody. They lacked vital contacts with producers in the west and independent east German production companies were only gradually being set up. Inexperienced in raising funding for films – they had never had to worry about budgets, which had been centrally allocated by the Film Office and the studio management – DEFA's filmmakers lost their way in Germany's notorious film subsidy jungle.

Only a handful of DEFA's old guard of directors and scriptwriters succeeded in adjusting to these new conditions. Many took early retirement, others went to work for television. Frank Beyer, best known in the west for his banned film *Trace of Stones*, has extensively worked for television since unification. His productions include a 1995 adaptation of Erich Loest's novel *Nicolai Church* (*Nikolaikirche*, 1995), about one of the centres of the GDR's 'velvet revolution' in Leipzig, which was subsequently released in cinemas, and *When All the Germans Are Asleep* (*Wenn alle Deutschen schlafen*, 1994). Like Beyer's Oscar-nominated film, *Jacob the Liar*, this television film is based on a text by Jurek Becker and depicts life in a Polish ghetto. Egon Günther, who had left the GDR in 1978 and worked in Munich for twelve years, returned to Babelsberg to direct two feature films: *Stein* (1991), a dream-like parable about the lost socialist utopia, and *The Mask of Desire* (*Die Braut*, 1998), a film about Goethe's relationship with Christiane Vulpius. Roland Gräf and Rainer Simon both made one more feature film, *The Mystery of the Amber Room* (*Die Spur des Bernsteinzimmers*, 1991) and *Distant Country, Pa-isch* (*Fernes Land Pa-isch*, 1993/2000). Heiner Carow, an exceptionally popular director in the GDR with a dozen feature films to his name, made just one more, *The Misdemeanour* (*Die Verfehlung*, 1991), and thereafter worked for television until his untimely death in 1997. Several of DEFA's scriptwriters, including Christl Gräf, Stefan Kolditz and Wolfgang Kohlhaase, have continued to write screenplays for east and west German feature and television productions. Similarly, many east German actors such as Michael Gwisdek, Sylvester Groth and Corinna Harfouch, to mention but a few, who made a name for themselves in DEFA productions but who were never permanently employed by the studio, have successfully adapted to the changed conditions of film production.

For DEFA's next generation of directors (*Nachwuchsregisseure*), the radical transformation of the cultural sphere was a blessing in disguise. If DEFA had continued to exist, they would have had to embark on a drawn-out studio apprenticeship as assistant directors before being assigned to their own projects, if indeed this ever happened. Instead, the dissolution of the rigid hierarchy in the DEFA studio at the time of the revolution resulted in the establishment of an autonomous artistic working group, DaDaeR, in January 1990. This group is associated with a number of aesthetically innovative or ideologically provocative début films, notably Jörg Foth's *Last from the DaDaeR* (*Letztes aus der DaDaeR*,

1990), Kipping's aforementioned *The Country Beyond the Rainbow*, and Peter Welz's *Banal Days* (*Banale Tage*, 1992). After the revolution, Thomas Wilkening, one of the unit's co-founders, was commercially astute enough to transform it into a limited company, making Thomas Wilkening Filmgesellschaft east Germany's first private production company. Helke Misselwitz's feature film début *Herzsprung* (1992),[12] and her next film, *Little Angel* (*Engelchen*, 1996), as well as Kipping's enigmatic artist bio-pic *Novalis* (1994) were among the first films produced or co-produced by Wilkening.

The most prolific and, in terms of the critical resonance of their films, most successful contemporary east German directors are currently Andreas Dresen and Andreas Kleinert. Both were born shortly after the Berlin Wall was erected, both graduated from the Konrad Wolf Film Academy in Babelsberg when the GDR ceased to exist and both welcomed the abolition of the GDR's centralized system of cultural production, to which Kleinert so poignantly referred in his bon mot: 'It's better to live in the jungle than in a zoo.'[13] Although both filmmakers have made a name for themselves with films which reflect the social and moral dilemmas of reunification, including Dresen's *Silent Country* (*Stilles Land*, 1992) and *The Policewoman* (*Die Polizistin*, 1999), and Kleinert's *Lost Landscape* (*Verlorene Landschaft*, 1992), *Outside Time* (*Neben der Zeit*, 1995) and *Paths in the Night* (*Wege in die Nacht*, 1999), they wish to shake off the label 'East German filmmaker' arguing that they address issues of universal relevance, albeit in a specifically east German social context.[14]

THE LEGACY OF DEFA IN
EAST GERMAN FILMS OF THE 1990s

Even a cursory glance at the films made by east German directors after unification highlights significant continuities and discontinuities with the DEFA tradition. The most startling discontinuity is the almost complete absence of films that would once have been classified as 'anti-fascist' films, the lifeline of DEFA's feature film production.[15] In fact, from its very first film, *The Murderers Are among Us*, until the end of DEFA in 1992, DEFA produced approximately one hundred anti-fascist films. This represents roughly 13% of the entire feature film production. The importance accorded to the theme of anti-fascism in DEFA's feature film production reflects its cultural function as nation-building myth. While the focus of the anti-fascist genre is primarily on the triumphs and tribulations of heroic anti-fascist resistance fighters, it also comprises numerous remarkable films about anti-Semitism and the Holocaust, notably Kurt Maetzig's *Marriage in the Shadows*, and Konrad Wolf's *Stars* (*Sterne*, 1959) and *Professor Mamlock* (1961).

In the wake of German unification, this great DEFA tradition has been largely abandoned. This is all the more astounding given that the search for a new and shared German identity after reunification resulted in a renewed interest in the Third Reich and the Holocaust, not least because after four decades of division these traumatic events provided the only common memory of German nationhood. Given the different interpretations of National Socialism in the GDR and the FRG, the democratization of memory in the wake of reunification resulted in a contestation and a rapid succession of public debates about whose memory would be represented in the new German national identity. West German filmmakers were quick to respond by making numerous films about the Third Reich and the Holocaust. The theme of anti-Semitism, in particular, received unprecedented attention in films such as Max Färberböck's *Aimée and Jaguar* (*Aimée und Jaguar*, 1999), Rolf Schübel's *Gloomy Sunday – A Song of Love and Death* (*Gloomy Sunday – Ein Lied von Liebe und Tod*, 1999), Michael Verhoeven's *My Mother's Courage* (*Mutters Courage*, 1995), Joseph Vilsmaier's *Comedian Harmonists* (1998) and Dani Levy's *The Giraffe* (*Meschugge*, 1998).[16]

What the small number of films about the Nazi past that were made by east German filmmakers in the 1990s all have in common is that they break with the conventions of the anti-fascist tradition and instead continue the trend that first manifested itself in a number DEFA films of the 1980s. Namely, they question the myth of heroic anti-fascist resistance,[17] and acknowledge that the east Germans, too, are not free from guilt.[18] They also redefine the relationship between Germans and Russians,[19] asserting for the first time that the Russians were not (as official memory in the GDR had it) perceived as the eagerly awaited liberators, but instead as the 'Bolshevik menace' or simply the enemy. Notwithstanding a few remarkable films about Germany's Nazi past,

east German filmmakers made relatively few contributions to the east–
west German memory contest during the 1990s. This was presumably
because they were too preoccupied with coming to terms with a more
recent past and its ramifications for the present. They were anxious not
to repeat the sins of their fathers, who made peace with the perpetrators,
but wanted instead to critically examine the GDR's Stalinist dictatorship
through their films.

This preoccupation with the GDR's immediate past and its repercussions for the present is reflected in the numerous films that address
concerns close to the heart of east Germans at the time. Thus many of
the social issue-based films made by east German filmmakers after the
collapse of the SED regime can be considered as a continuation of
DEFA's films about contemporary society (*Gegenwartsfilme*), the second
most important lifeline of the feature film studio. Films about contemporary society began to play a prominent role in DEFA productions
from the 1950s onwards, when filmmakers were encouraged to support
the state's socio-economic agenda, the 'construction of socialism'
(*Aufbau des Sozialismus*) and the 'consolidation of socialism' (*Ankunft im
Sozialismus*) by making films that depicted the lives of ordinary people
in socialist society. These films are not exactly the kind of stuff that
celluloid dreams are made of. They dwell on problems at the workplace,
examine the relationship between the individual and the socialist
collective, and in many respects look like an illustrated social history of
the GDR. Some are didactic and aim to help people master the problems
they face in contemporary society; others (notably the more popular
ones) provide counter-narratives to the official master-narrative of
socialism.[20] What many of the east German films of the 1990s have in
common with DEFA's films about contemporary society is that they are
socially committed films that are firmly grounded in the experience of
ordinary life in east Germany, shortly before or after the end of state
socialism. They are indebted to the aesthetic principles of a strong
realist tradition, but one that has at last been liberated from the
restrictions imposed by the hitherto mandatory qualification 'socialist'.
Consequently, heroes no longer have to be positive, problems do not
necessarily have to come with solutions and an optimistic and
progressive outlook on life is no longer obligatory. Eighteen years after
Erich Honecker's frequently invoked remark that there would be no

more taboos in the realm of art and literature, the promise has at last come true.

Many of the films made shortly after the demise of the East German regime look back in anger at the GDR and accuse the paternalistic state of having abused its authority and suppressed its children. In particular, the all-pervasive surveillance by the *Stasi* (short for *Staatssicherheit*, the State Security Service) is a prominent theme in several post-unification films of the early 1990s. The *Stasi*'s hydra-like surveillance network infiltrated every sphere and niche of GDR society. Everybody could be potentially spying, being spied on or both. In the feature film studio alone, some 60 to 70 unofficial informers (*inoffizielle Mitarbeiter*) had been working during the 1970s and 1980s, and files on both victims of the *Stasi* (*Opferakten*) and *Stasi* employees and unofficial informers (*Täterakten*) who had worked for DEFA were lodged with the Ministry for State Security.[21]

In the initial years after the opening up of the *Stasi* archives, 'the public developed a lurid fascination with the stories of victims and perpetrators of the East German secret police'.[22] It became an extremely popular theme on talk shows that were trying to boost audience ratings with sensational revelations of victims and perpetrators. The *Stasi* became the voraciously consumed subject of infotainment, but also the concern of more serious attempts to come to terms with the past. The numerous feature films made by ex-DEFA directors during the early 1990s, which centre on the victims and perpetrators of *Stasi* surveillance can be seen as an important contribution to working through the past.

Frank Beyer's film *The Suspicion* (*Der Verdacht*, 1991), based on the east German writer Volker Braun's *Unfinished Story* (*Unvollendete Geschichte*, 1975/1988),[23] provides an evocative account of the mistrust and fear sown amongst people by the omnipresence of the *Stasi*. It is shown to destroy the humanity and dignity of peoples' lives, to break up families and relationships. In *The Tango Player*, the protagonist and victim of *Stasi* allegations and manipulations suffers from an acute loss of identity as a result of his imprisonment. Michael Gwisdek's *Farewell to Agnes* (*Abschied von Agnes*, 1994) is a dark comedy which revisits the *Stasi* experience from the vantage point of the early 1990s. Heiner, an unemployed academic and writer, spends his days mourning the loss of his beloved wife, Agnes, recording his memories of her on a tape recorder. The *tristesse* of his isolated and eccentric existence is suddenly interrupted when a young man named Stefan forces his way into Heiner's flat, seeking refuge from a pack of journalists in pursuit of him. As the two men end up living together, a somewhat sado-masochistic dependency with homoerotic undertones develops between them, which again and again prevents Heiner from getting rid of his unwelcome guest. When it transpires that Stefan, a former *Stasi* major (hence the media witch-hunt directed towards him) knows the most intimate details of Heiner's dreams and fears, details which only Heiner's wife Agnes can have conveyed, Heiner kills the former spy by throwing him out of the fourth-floor window. The sinister suggestion that Heiner's farewell to Agnes took a similar form adds to the ambiguity of the film, which is essentially a psychograph of the complex relationship between victim and perpetrator.[24]

Another theme that preoccupied east German filmmakers after unification was Germany's erstwhile division. The theme itself was not new, but the ideological slant with which it was approached changed after the fall of the communist regime in the GDR. During the days of DEFA several productions had made reference to Germany's division, most notably the four so-called 'Wall films' (*Mauerfilme*) of the 1960s which present the erection of the Berlin Wall in the most positive and partisan terms.[25] Even films which provide a much more balanced and discursive comment on Germany's division, such as Konrad Wolf's *Divided Heaven* and Roland Gräf's *The Escape* (*Die Flucht*, 1977), ultimately confirm the superiority of socialism and the GDR, albeit without condoning the enforced imprisonment of East German citizens in their own country.

Although Wolf's and Gräf's films were daring for their times in that they addressed the taboo topic of illegal emigration from the Republic (*Republikflucht*), predictably, those films which were made or completed after the fall of the Wall are much more outspoken about the inhumanity of the enforced division between the German people and the sense of isolation and imprisonment that was part of the East German experience. In Heiner Carow's melodrama *The Misdemeanour*, the 'forbidden' love between Elisabeth, a middle-aged cleaning woman in a desolate East German border town, and Jacob, a dockworker from Hamburg, is tragically destroyed through the German–German border and a system of surveillance and betrayal. More poignantly, even when the Wall comes down and the lovers could be reunited at last, they have just missed each other:[26] Elisabeth, the victim of a political system that has deprived her of personal fulfilment, has avenged herself by shooting her oppressor and has been sentenced to prison. She thus becomes ineluctably entangled in the power structures of the GDR's totalitarian system from which she cannot escape even after its demise.[27]

Andreas Kleinert's film *Lost Landscape* gives a retrospective account of the childhood of its protagonist, Elias, in the GDR. His parents have done precisely what the GDR's paternalistic state also did: they have built a high fence around their home to protect their child from the harmful and deceitful influences of the outside world. The son eventually escapes and becomes a successful politician in the West. Kleinert's film is a parable, not just about the 'fenced-in' German Democratic Republic, but also about fences and barriers in a more symbolic sense. The barrier of estrangement that Elias finds almost impossible to overcome when he visits his parents in the former GDR after decades of separation corresponds to the estrangement east and west Germans experienced when the Wall came down. For Elias's parents, just as for Elisabeth in *The Misdemeanour*, freedom has come too late: they commit suicide.

Violent death and suicide are prominent motifs in several films that depict the social and personal problems of east Germans in the wake of reunification. Herein lies another violation of an erstwhile taboo: death was a theme which DEFA filmmakers were to avoid, with the exception, that is, of sacrificial or heroic death for a good cause, such as the fight against the fascists or the class enemy. The depiction of ordinary death, be it by accident or illness, was considered to be pessimistic and thus incompatible with the optimistic and progressive pathos of socialist art. Hence films which touched upon the theme of death, let alone suicide, such as Egon Günther's *The Keys* (*Die Schlüssel*, 1974), *The Legend of Paul and Paula*, and Konrad Wolf's *Solo Sunny* (1979) invariably gave rise to controversy and debate. But the prominence of the death motif in several east German films of the 1990s cannot simply be explained by filmmakers' fascination with what used to be taboo.

While the murders committed by the protagonists in *Farewell to Agnes* and *The Misdemeanour* are symbolic acts of liberation from the GDR's totalitarian rule and its representatives, the violent deaths that occur in several other post-unification films are less readily explained in terms of their symbolic significance.[28] In particular in Andreas Kleinert's second feature film, *Outside Time*, the murder of a Russian deserter is embedded in an ambiguous web of references. The film is set in a small town somewhere in Brandenburg, a place which, as the title suggests, is rapidly falling 'outside time' since it cannot keep pace with the changes brought about by unification and the transformation of the former GDR. The Russian troops stationed there have withdrawn and their barracks have turned into rat-infested ruins; the intercity trains do not stop there any more and even the regional railway link to Berlin is going to be suspended. Most young people are leaving. Against this backdrop, the film tells the fateful love story of a young east German woman, Sophie, and Sergej, a Russian deserter. When Sophie introduces her lover to her mother and her brother, Sergej becomes embroiled in the incestuous tensions underlying the relationship between Sophie, her brother Georg and her mother. The mother is drawn towards Sergej because he reminds her of her own adulterous affair with a Ukrainian soldier shortly after the war. At the same time Sophie's mother and brother are jealous of Sergej and fear that he will take her away from the family. The arrival of the Russian implodes the claustrophobic sham existence that held this dysfunctional family together. As so often in Kleinert's films, the family functions as a microcosm in which such universal themes as self-deception, guilt and destiny are acted out in a clearly defined socio-historical context. This combination of the universal with the specific lends the film a parabolic dimension: both Sophie and her mother choose Russian men as lovers; both do so at historically significant moments which mark the beginning and the end of the GDR; in both cases the involvement with a Russian results in tragedy, namely the suicide of the mother's jealous husband and the murder of Sophie's Russian boyfriend at the hands of her brother. Within the microcosm of the family, Russian men become the pivot of complex family dynamics, evoking passionate and conflicting feelings and triggering a twofold tragedy. Within the macrocosm of East Germany's geopolitical context, the character constellation parabolically mirrors the ambivalence which characterized the relationship between East Germans and Russians, the GDR and the Soviet Union.[29] It embodies the changing power structures between the

Russians and the east Germans after the collapse of communism: once the victors and imposers of communism, the Russians have become the losers who have to withdraw now that the ideological battle has been won by capitalism.[30]

Kleinert's next film, *Paths in the Night*, culminates in the suicide of its protagonist Walter, a man in his late 50s who used to be the powerful and well-respected director of an electricity combine. However, in the wake of unification and the ensuing privatization of industry, he has lost his job. At first it may seem that Walter's social decline is the cause of his tragic end. However, Walter is not depicted solely as a victim who deserves our pity. Admittedly, he is a victim of the west German take-over of the east as well as a victim of 'decades of tutelage and crippling authoritarian structures [that have made him master] in the art of self-deception, disavowal and denial'.[31] But he is also a perpetrator who has been complicit with the totalitarian system, and who has internalized the authoritarian principle to such an extent that it ultimately leads to his self-destruction.[32] To give his life meaning and in order to regain self-respect, Walter becomes the self-appointed boss of a vigilante team, consisting of himself, Gina and René, who patrol Berlin's commuter and underground trains at night. At Walter's command, the two adolescents beat up hooligans who are molesting passengers, seemingly to enforce law and order in a world that has gone out of kilter, but in reality to find an outlet for their pent-up aggression. Walter sees himself and his violent helpmates as precursors of a better time to come in which he is to occupy a central place as a new leader. Driven by his frustrated desire for power, Walter becomes more and more entangled in a series of acts of violence, randomly directed at hooligans but also at his accomplice, Gina, when she renounces her obedience and respect. A moral abyss opens up as Walter's self-deception begins to crumble and he realizes that at the bottom of his declared mission to reinstate justice and order is a fascistic desire for power that he is unable to satisfy in the new social order of post-Wall Germany, in which he has been degraded to a powerless underdog. Unable to adjust to the new social order, Walter commits suicide.

Kleinert's film provides a complex psychograph of a man who is portrayed as a fossil of the *ancien regime* and whose mental disposition reflects the totalitarian power structures of the former GDR. Implicit in his fate is a symbolic dimension and the message that has concerned Kleinert in all three of his post-unification films, each of which advocates the need to change. Invariably those characters, namely Elias, Sophie and Walter's wife Sylvia, who embrace change survive, or better still, are granted a new lease of life, whereas those who resist change perish.

The same holds true for Hanna in Oskar Roehler's *No Place to Go* (*Die Unberührbare*, 1999), which some critics consider to be the west German counterpart of Kleinert's *Paths in the Night*.[33] The protagonist Hanna, who is based on Gisela Elsner, a west German author and the mother of the film director, also refuses to accept the need for change, as her out-dated 1960s make-up and hairstyle suggest. As she witnesses the fall of the Berlin Wall and the collapse of communism, she stubbornly clings to an ideal of communism that has little in common with the realities of real existing socialism in the GDR. Hence the end of the GDR instils her with fear, since it deprives her of her spiritual home. Like Walter she is deluded about her own identity: she considers herself to be a radical left-winger, a communist at heart whose spiritual home is the GDR, while indulging in the most decadent consumerism capitalist society has to offer. Like Walter she pays with her life for her self-deception and inertia.

With a few notable exceptions such as the road movie comedies *Burning Life* (Peter Welz, 1994), and Peter Kahane's *To the Horizon and Beyond* (*Bis zum Horizont und weiter*, 1999), the majority of post-Wall films made by east German filmmakers paint a gloomy picture. They consequently stand in stark contrast to the countless comedies made by west German filmmakers during the 1990s. These are predominantly relationship comedies, which totally ignore the historic event of German unification, arguably because for the majority of west Germans unifi-cation was of little consequence other than leading to a small increase in their tax burden, the so-called solidarity surcharge (*Solidaritätszuschlag*).[34] However, a number of road movie comedies, notably such box-office hits as Peter Timm's *Go, Trabi, Go!* (1991) and Detlev Buck's *No More Mr Nice Guy* (*Wir können auch anders*, 1993), depict the comical side of east Germany's take-over by the west. These films help to take the sting out of the problems and hostilities *Ossis* and *Wessis* (easterners and westerners) experienced as they were trying to overcome decades of division which had led to a serious state of estrangement between them. In the eyes of east German filmmakers, however, the process of a rapid acculturation to social, political and economic structures imposed by westerners was no laughing matter.

Another reason for the scarce number of comedies made by east German filmmakers in the wake of unification is the under-representation of this genre in the DEFA tradition. Not just comedies, but genre cinema as a whole, was held in low regard by the GDR's cultural officials, mainly because the role assigned to film art was not diversion and entertainment but rather education and enlightenment. As a result, DEFA's foremost filmmakers never dirtied their hands with genre cinema. DEFA did employ a number of directors and scriptwriters who specialized in genre cinema, but generally audience demand for most popular genres had to be satisfied by Western imports.[35]

However, ten years after the fall of the Wall, things were beginning to change. Old traditions fell into abeyance and a new generation of filmmakers acutely aware of audience demand came to the fore. More importantly, the east Germans' attitude towards their past underwent a dramatic change. After their initial embrace of all things western, they had become wary of 'their experience of living in the GDR [...] being elided from the German historical record' and of losing their Eastern identity.[36] Moreover, they were keen to move on from a tainted memory of their past and the stigma of the 'Stasi state' that has dominated the public debate about the former GDR. As memories of the old GDR were becoming somewhat blurred, 'magnifying its achievements while forgetting its repression',[37] a wave of Ostalgie (nostalgia for East Germany – literally, 'eastalgia') swept across the new federal states. East German brands enjoyed revived popularity; websites devoted to GDR memorabilia, Honecker, Trabis and the GDR's national anthem mushroomed on the internet; east Berlin nightclubs capitalized on 'a "GDR revival" with "old-time" sing-alongs, employing staff dressed up as party officials and border guards, and even Erich Honecker look-alikes.'[38] Unmistakably, the time had come to look back at everyday life in the GDR through a rose-tinted camera lens.

On 7 October 1999, the day that would have marked the 50th anniversary of the GDR, Leander Haußmann's Ostalgie-comedy Sonnenallee was released. A month later, on 9 November 1999, the 10th anniversary of the fall of the Berlin Wall, Sebastian Peterson's comedy

Heroes Like Us (*Helden wie wir*) premiered, based on Thomas Brussig's best-selling 1995 reunification novel of the same name. What both films have in common, apart from being based on screenplays written or co-written by Brussig, is that they are feel-good movies about the GDR. Audience demand for such reconciliatory retro-comedies continues, as the box-office success and critical acclaim of *Goodbye, Lenin!* (2003), made by the west German director Wolfgang Becker, proves. All three films are grotesque satires about everyday life in the GDR conveyed from the vantage point of adolescents.

This narrative perspective is of particular significance in explaining the reconciliatory stance of *Sonnenallee*. As Micha, the film's protagonist and narrator, explains in a voice-over comment at the end of the film: 'Once upon a time there was a country and I lived there. If you ask me how it was? It was the best time of my life, for I was young and in love.'[39] The conflation of memories of the GDR with memories of the experience of first love and youth legitimizes a nostalgic idealization of the GDR, which ultimately paves the way for a normalization of the GDR's totalitarian legacy. In other respects too, *Sonnenallee* promotes the project of normalization.[40]

The film tells the story of a group of adolescents who live at the shorter end of the Sonnenallee, a five-kilometre-long street that stretches from the West Berlin suburb of Kreuzberg to Treptow in the East and that was, until 1989, divided by the Wall. In spite of living right next to the border fortifications, the film argues, they are normal teenagers and do what teenagers do the world over: they fall in love, experiment with drugs, and try to impress their peers by wearing the hippest clothes and listening to the coolest pop music. What sets the lives of these East Berlin teenagers apart from their peers in the West is the economy of shortage and the all-pervasive authority of the state. Both aspects are at the centre of the film's satire: much-coveted Western consumer goods such as a Rolling Stones album are only available on the black market; recreational drugs are entirely unavailable, and home-made substitutes concocted from herbal asthma remedies and the GDR variety of Coca-Cola have to suffice.

Sonnenallee is a far cry from DEFA's critical films about contemporary life. Haußmann's film does not purport to give an authentic picture of life in the GDR during the 1970s. Instead it projects a nostalgic fantasy that is in equal measure a tribute to the romanticized notion of youth as the best time of our lives, and a reconciliatory offer to east Germans to make peace with the problematic past and thus regain a positive identification with their part of German history. It is thus only right that this self-conscious fictionalization of the GDR's erstwhile everyday culture abounds in inter-textual references to its fictional status. For example, the film pays homage to DEFA's cinematic tradition by recreating the artificial Orwo-Color look. This was a distinctive feature of DEFA colour films, many of which were made with Orwo-Color film stock, the GDR brand that was a bestseller across the Eastern Bloc.[41] Colour, as the film's final sequence in which colour fades to black and white suggests, stands for an embellished fictional reality that has little in common with the greyness typically associated with real life under socialism. The notion that only the prettification through the colourful medium of film can transfigure the drabness of real life is further underscored by Nina Hagen's song 'You Forgot the Colour Film', which accompanies the fade from colour to hues of grey at the end.[42]

More importantly, *Sonnenallee* alludes to DEFA's cult film *per se*, *The Legend of Paul and Paula*. When Mischa runs across the street to put his life (in the shape of his forged diaries) at Miriam's feet, we hear the most memorable song from this 1970s *Gegenwartsfilm*, 'Go to Her and Let Your Kite Fly High'[43] by the popular East German band Die Puhdies. Rushing up the stairs, he encounters Paul, played by the same actor (Winfried Glatzleder) as in Carow's film, who asks him whether he needs an axe. This is a reference to a famous scene from *The Legend of Paul and Paula* in which Paul smashes Paula's front door after she has refused ever to see him again.

The oblique social critique that made Carow's film, as well as many other DEFA films about contemporary society, so controversial is here reduced to a series of more or less empty signifiers that produce nothing more than nostalgic recognition and laughter. Thus *Sonnenallee* neutralizes DEFA's tradition of social realism to a postmodern pastiche that is witty, entertaining and reconciliatory, rather than critical or subversive. Although to date *Sonnenallee* is the most popular east German film in the west, it is in many respects untypical of the eastern cinematic discourse on unification, which has remained more or less faithful to DEFA's tradition of socially committed films about contemporary issues.

That social critique does not necessarily have to exclude humour has been proven by Andreas Dresen's recent feature films. *Silent Country, Night Shapes* (*Nachtgestalten*, 1999) and *Grill Point* (*Halbe Treppe*, 2002) transfigure what is essentially the depiction of a drab or even miserable existence through humour. *Silent Country* is a subtle comedy that captures the historic moment when the Wall came down from the periphery of a small provincial theatre, where a young director and his cast are rehearsing Samuel Beckett's absurd play *Waiting for Godot* (1952). The film is a light-hearted parable of the sense of stagnation and inertia that pervaded every aspect of life in the GDR. *Grill Point* is an immensely funny film about adultery and marital conflict that is set in a bleak prefabricated housing estate (*Plattenbausiedlung*) in Frankfurt an der Oder, near the Polish border. The protagonists' desire to break out of their stale marriages poignantly mirrors the desire of many east Germans to leave their past behind and start a new life in the new Germany. Yet, as the film suggests, the habit of a lifetime may prove more enduring than the thrill of the new. *Night Shapes* traces the meandering paths through Berlin at night of a number of people living on the margins of society: a homeless couple expecting a baby, a heroin-addicted child prostitute, a young boy from Africa who is seeking asylum in Germany and a middle-aged underdog, who has lost touch with his emotions. Although these characters' lives are ostensibly miserable, the film argues that they are not beyond hope and redemption. Each and every one of them is touched by divine mercy, which momentarily lights up the all-encompassing darkness around them. As Dresen commented, through seemingly profane yet ultimately spiritual experiences, these marginalized and desperate individuals discover a core of human dignity and moral integrity in themselves that is ultimately indestructible.[44]

Dresen's feature films are unmistakably indebted to DEFA's cinematic tradition, in terms of their thematic concerns, the humanist approach taken to the characters and their aesthetics. Notably, DEFA's documentary realist tradition has been a strong formative influence on Dresen's filmmaking.[45] His training at the Babelsberg Film Academy and with DEFA's masters of documentary realism has taught the director to use images rather than words, to carefully research and observe his characters and their social environment rather than invent them, and to apply this documentary approach to feature films. However, Dresen has taken these stylistic principles merely as a starting point and developed a distinctive style of his own: the shaky hand-held camera, the grainy film stock, jump cuts and tracking shots, the near absence of floodlights, often combined with improvised acting, are the hallmarks of Dresen's true-to-life aesthetics. What distinguishes Dresen's films from other probing explorations of post-Wall German misery in the east is the light-heartedness of his approach. This trademark of his style may also explain why some of his East Side stories proved much more popular with audiences in the west than the majority of other films originating in the new federal states.

What then is the legacy of DEFA in the works of contemporary east German filmmakers? Though none of the post-Wall films surveyed here could have been made in the days of DEFA, because they fly in the face of the doctrine of socialist realism and broach taboos that would have provoked the censors, they are indebted to DEFA's tradition of social realism. Like DEFA's films about contemporary society, east German films of the 1990s are socially committed films that are driven by a strong humanist and utopian impulse. Unlike the 'cinema of consensus' that has been identified as the dominant strand of west German film culture during the 1990s,[46] the films discussed here are based on the premise that film has to play a social function; precisely the premise that was at the core of socialist film art in the German Democratic Republic. The idea of film performing a social function was also at the root of the socially committed author's film (*Autorenfilm*) in the Federal Republic during the 1960s and 1970s. New German Cinema was in many respects a counter-cinema that critically examined the social ills of contemporary west German society. When a new generation of west German filmmakers abandoned this tradition in favour of socially conformist comedies during the 1990s, east German filmmakers entered into an all-German film culture which they enriched through a specifically eastern variety of a cinema of social concern.

Notes

1   For an in-depth discussion of many of the issues and films referred to in this chapter, see my book *Hollywood behind the Wall: The Cinema of East Germany* (Manchester: Manchester University Press, 2005).

2   In view of the limited scope of this chapter, I shall only be able to examine the impact of unification on DEFA's feature film studio and the legacy of DEFA's feature films in post-Wall Germany.

3   CIP was a subsidiary of the French utilities and communications conglomerate, Compagnie Générale des Eaux (subsequently Vivendi and since 2000 Vivendi Universal). After the takeover, the DEFA feature film studio was renamed DEFA Studio Babelsberg GmbH. On 9 August 1994, the name DEFA was eliminated from the register of companies.

4   Barton Byg, 'Introduction: Reassessing DEFA Today' in Barton Byg and Betheny Moore (eds.), *Moving Images of East Germany: Past and Future of DEFA Film* (Washington, D.C.: American Institute for Contemporary German Studies, 2002), pp. 1–23 (p. 6).

5   The German film company UFA (Universum Film AG), which was founded in 1917, produced such internationally acclaimed masterpieces as Friedrich Wilhem Murnau's *Nosferatu* (1922), Fritz Lang's *Metropolis* (1927), and Joseph von Sternberg's *The Blue Angel* (*Der blaue Engel*, 1930). In 1937 the Nazi Party took over UFA's shares, and in 1942 UFA, alongside other film companies, was subsumed under the UFA holding company into which the entire Nazi film industry was organized. After World War II UFA ceased to exist as a legal entity when the Reich's film industry was dismantled, but was soon revived in a different business configuration. Cf. Klaus Kreimeier, *Die UFA-Story: Geschichte eines Filmkonzerns* (Frankfurt/Main: Fischer Taschenbuchverlag, 2002).

6   'Ein drittes Leben der Filmstadt Babelsberg ist unwahrscheinlich, aber nicht ausgeschlossen.' Bärbel Dalichow, 'Das letzte Kapitel 1989 bis 1993' in Ralf Schenk (ed.), *Das zweite Leben der Filmstadt Babelsberg: DEFA Spielfilme 1946–1992* (Berlin: Henschel Verlag, 1994), pp. 328–53 (p. 353).

7   Frank Beyer's *Trace of Stones* and Kurt Maetzig's *The Rabbit Is Me* (*Das Kaninchen bin ich*, 1965/1989) are the most famous forbidden films. For a detailed discussion of the twelve films that were banned in 1965/66 see Christiane Mückenberger, *Prädikat: Besonders schädlich* (Berlin: Henschel Verlag, 1990); Stefan Soldovieri, 'Negotiating Censorship: GDR Film at the Juncture of 1965/66' (unpublished doctoral thesis, University of Wisconsin-Madison, 1998); Daniela Berghahn, 'The Forbidden Films: Film Censorship in the Wake of the Eleventh Plenum' in Diana Holmes and Alison Smith (eds.), *100 Years of European Cinema: Entertainment or Ideology?* (Manchester: Manchester University Press, 2000), pp. 40–51.

8   *The Country Beyond the Rainbow* was seen by just a thousand viewers. It took two years for *Miraculi* to find a distributor and then it was taken off cinema programmes after just five days. See Leonie Naughton, *That Was the Wild East: Film Culture, Unification and the 'New' Germany* (Ann Arbor: University of Michigan Press, 2002), p. 66.

9   Naughton, *That Was the Wild East*, p. 67.

10 Johannes Klingsporn, 'Zur Lage der deutschen Kinowirtschaft', *Media Perspektiven*, 12 (1991), 793–805 (p. 794); Naughton, *That Was the Wild East*, p. 74.

11 For a discussion of the 'public sphere' in the GDR's social context see David Bathrick, *The Powers of Speech: The Politics of Culture in the GDR* (Lincoln, Nebraska and London: University of Nebraska Press, 1995); Marc Silberman, 'Problematizing the "Socialist Public Sphere": Concepts and Consequences' in Marc Silberman (ed.), *What Remains?: East German Culture and the Postwar Public* (Washington, D.C.: American Institute of Contemporary German Studies, 1997), pp. 1–37.

12   Herzsprung is the name of a village, but literally means 'crack in the heart'.

13   'Besser im Dschungel, als im Zoo.' Cited by Andreas Dresen in an interview with the author in Potsdam, 19 July 2002.

14   This claim appears to be more justified in the case of Dresen's films. In particular *Night Shapes* (*Nachtgestalten*, 1999), which renders life in Germany's new capital from the perspective of those on the margins of society, could be set in any metropolis. For a detailed account of Dresen's and Kleinert's oeuvre to date and the numerous prizes their films have been awarded, see Kerstin Decker, 'Neben der Zeit: Die Filme von Andreas Dresen and Andreas Kleinert' in Ralf Schenk and Erika Richter (eds.), *Apropos: Film 2001. Das Jahrbuch der DEFA Stiftung* (Berlin: Verlag Das Neue Berlin, 2001), pp. 328–43.

15   On DEFA's anti-fascist films cf. Christiane Mückenberger, '*Sie sehen selbst, Sie hören selbst …*': *Die DEFA von ihren Anfängen bis 1949* (Marburg: Hitzeroth, 1994); Barton Byg, 'The Anti-Fascist Tradition and GDR Film' in 'Proceedings, Purdue University Fifth Annual Conference on Film', West Lafayette, 1980, pp. 81–87; Daniela Berghahn, 'Liars and Traitors: Unheroic Resistance and Anti-Fascist DEFA Films' in Daniela Berghahn and Alan Bance (eds.), *Millennial Essays on Film and Other German Studies* (Oxford and Bern: Lang, 2002), pp. 23–39.

16   For a discussion of representations of the Third Reich in film since unification, including an analysis of *Aimée and Jaguar*, see John Davidson's chapter in this volume.

17   For example, Ulrich Weiß's *Your Unknown Brother* (*Dein unbekannter Bruder*, 1982).

18   For example, Frank Beyer's *The Turning Point* (*Der Aufenthalt*, 1983), Heiner Carow's *The Russians Are Coming* (*Die Russen kommen*, 1968/1987), and Rainer Simon's *The Case of Ö* (*Der Fall Ö*, 1991).

19   For example, *The Russians Are Coming* and Maxim Dessau's film *First Loss* (*Erster Verlust*, 1990).

20   Joshua Feinstein distinguishes between 'films of contemporary life' (*Gegenwartsfilme*) and 'films of everyday life' (*Alltagsfilme*). The latter, he argues deny the progressive vision of history inscribed in socialism. Feinstein, *The Triumph of the Ordinary: Depictions of Daily Life in the East German Cinema 1949–1989* (Chapel Hill and London: University of North Carolina Press, 2002), pp. 6–7.

21   Axel Geiss, *Repression und Freiheit: DEFA-Regisseure zwischen Fremd- und Selbstbestimmung* (Potsdam: Brandenburgische Zentrale für politische Bildung, 1997).

22   Alison Lewis, 'En-Gendering Remembrance: Memory, Gender and Informers for the Stasi', *New German Critique*, 86 (2002), 103–34 (p. 105).

23   Braun's story appeared in the journal *Sinn und Form* in 1975, but when the text's provocative nature was discovered half of the journal's print run was quickly destroyed. The text was not published in the GDR until 1988 and was subsequently adapted by Ulrich Plenzdorf, who wrote the screenplay for Beyer's film.

24   Other films in which surveillance through the *Stasi* is a prominent theme are Lienhard Wawrzyn's *The Informer* (*Der Blaue*, 1994), *Nicolai Church*, and Sybille Schönemann's autobiographical documentary *Locked-Up Time* (*Verriegelte Zeit*, 1991).

25   The 'Wall films' are Frank Vogel's *… And Your Love Too* (*… Und deine Liebe auch*, 1962), Heinz Thiel's *The Knock-out Punch* (*Der Kinnhaken*, 1962), Gerhard Klein's *Sunday Driver* (*Sonntagsfahrer*, 1963) and the episodic film *Stories of That Night* (*Geschichten jener Nacht*, 1967), directed by Karlheinz Carpentier, Ulrich Thein, Frank Vogel and Gerhard Klein.

26   The film's original German title, *Die Verfehlung*, can also mean 'just missed'.

27   Margarethe von Trotta's German–German love story, *The Promise* (*Das Versprechen*, 1995), can be considered as the West German counterpart of Carow's film.

28   The protagonist Johanna of Helke Misselwitz's *Herzsprung* falls victim to a racially-motivated arson attack committed by neo-Nazi skinheads. However, she does not die in the flames but apparently of heart failure shortly after the attack. The numerous incidents of suicide in films, including *Herzsprung*, Peter Welz's *Burning Life* (1994) and Peter Kahane's *To the Horizon and Beyond* (*Bis zum Horizont und weiter*, 1999) are motivated by the disenfranchisement of east Germans in the wake of unification.

29   See Hans-Jörg Rother, 'Georg, wo ist dein Bruder Sergej?', *Frankfurter Allgemeine Zeitung*, 1 October 1996.

30   Andreas Kleinert and Erika Richter, 'Anarchie der Menschlichkeit', *Film und Fernsehen*, 5/6 (1996), 52–55 (p. 53).

31   Lewis, 'En-Gendering Remembrance', p. 106, referring to Hans-Jürgen Maaz's influential study *Gefühlsstau: Ein Psychogramm der DDR* (1992), in which the psychologist argues that all east Germans have been psychologically crippled and deformed by the experience of totalitarian control and manipulation.

32   In the original script, Walter was conceived as a high-ranking *Stasi* official. However, the actor Hilmar Thate who plays Walter insisted that the protagonist's former profession be changed in order to make Walter a more likeable character. Hans-Jörg Rother, 'Das Spiel ist aus: *Wege in die Nacht* von Andreas Kleinert', *Film und Fernsehen*, 3/4 (1999), 8–9 (p. 8).

33   See for example Merten Worthmann, 'Wege in die Nacht: Oskar Roehlers Film "Die Unberührbare"', *Die Zeit*, 19 April 2000. For a further discussion of Roehler's film, see Paul Cooke, 'Whatever Happened to Veronika Voss?: Rehabilitating the "68ers" and the Problem of Westalgie in Oskar Roehler's *Die Unberührbare* (2000)', *German Studies Review*, 27 (2004), 33–44.

34   For a discussion of these comedies, see Dickon Copsey's chapter in this volume.

35   The only genre which DEFA successfully adapted to the requirements of socialist society was the Western. Between 1966 and 1979 the Babelsberg studio made twelve so-called 'Indian films' (*Indianerfilme*). See Gerd Gemünden, 'Between Karl May and Karl Marx: the DEFA "Indianerfilme" (1965–85)', *Film History*, 10 (1998), 399–407.

36   Paul Cooke, 'Performing "Ostalgie": Leander Haußmann's *Sonnenallee*', *German Life and Letters*, 56.2 (2003), 156–67 (p. 160).

37   Konrad H. Jarausch, 'Reshaping German Identities: Reflections on the Post-Unification Debate' in Jarausch, *After Unity: Reconfiguring German Identities* (Providence and Oxford: Berghahn Books, 1997), pp. 1–23 (p. 19).

38   Naughton, *That Was the Wild East*, p. 20.

39   'Es war einmal ein Land und ich habe dort gelebt. Wenn man mich fragt, wie es war? Es war die schönste Zeit meines Lebens, denn ich war jung und verliebt'.

40   For a different perspective on Haußmann's film, see Seán Allan's chapter in this volume.

41   Orwo, short for Original Wolfen, is an East German brand of film stock that was created in the 1960s. Originally, the German company Agfa had manufactured film at Wolfen, but in the early 1960s reserved the brand name for films produced in West Germany. From 1964 onwards most DEFA films were made with Orwo, while a few were made with Eastmancolor. *Sonnenallee* is made on Kodak.

42   'Du hast den Farbfilm vergessen'.

43   'Geh zu ihr und laß deinen Drachen steigen'.

44   Personal interview with the author, Potsdam 19 July 2002. Dresen himself has attributed the spiritual or even religious concern of *Night Shapes* to the strong influence which East European cinema had on him. However this existentialist concern can also be found in the films of Lothar Warnecke, who studied theology before joining DEFA and who was nicknamed the 'moralist'.

45   Documentary realism is usually associated with the third generation of DEFA directors, notably Lothar Warnecke, Rainer Simon and Roland Gräf.

46   Eric Rentschler, 'From New German Cinema to the Post-Wall Cinema of Consensus' in Mette Hjort and Scott MacKenzie (eds.), *Cinema and Nation* (London and New York: Routledge, 2000), pp. 260–77.

Chapter 4

Ostalgie, fantasy and the normalization of east–west relations in post-unification comedy

Seán Allan

For those brought up on a diet of Rainer Werner Fassbinder, Wim Wenders and Volker Schlöndorff, the years immediately following German unification represent something of a lacuna in German film history. There were, of course, still directors who sought to assess the impact of the events of the unification process within the explicitly socio-political idiom characteristic of the New German Cinema. With *The Promise* (*Das Versprechen*, 1995), Margarethe von Trotta produced a film about a love affair spanning the two Germanys which, for all the novelty of its theme, had a familiar look and feel. In the east, films such as Egon Günther's *Stein* (1991) offered a tantalizing glimpse of what might have been in the GDR, had cultural policy been willing to tolerate a greater degree of formal experimentation, whilst Peter Kahane's *The Architects* (*Die Architekten*, 1990) exemplified the talents of the youngest generation of DEFA filmmakers, a group whose time seemed to have passed even before it had arrived. But despite their merits, all of the above films found themselves swimming against the tide. For the rapidly changing cinematic landscape in the post-unification period was characterized not by a renaissance of the kind of political filmmaking that had charac-terized the 1970s and 1980s, but rather by a revival of popular cinema. This took two forms: on the one hand, the market was dominated by such well-known Hollywood blockbusters as *Pretty Woman* (1990), *Basic Instinct* (1992) and *Jurassic Park* (1993); and on the other, the late 1980s and early 1990s saw the emergence of a plethora of (often low-budget) comedies targeted specifically at German audiences. Such films included the romantic comedies of Sherry Hormann, *Women Are Something Wonderful* (*Frauen sind was Wunderbares*, 1994) and *Doubting Thomas* (*Irren ist männlich*, 1996), and 'proletarian comedies' *German Spoken Here* (*Man spricht deutsh*, 1998) and *Ballerman 6* (1997) directed by Hanns Christian Müller and Tom Gerhardt respectively. In addition, there was a series of comedies directed by Wolfgang Büld – *Manta-Manta* (1991) – and Peter Timm – *Go, Trabi, Go!* (1991) and *Manta – Der Film* (1991) – which exploited the social and cultural clichés associated with two brands of car and their drivers: the (East German) Trabant and the (West German) Opel Manta. Many of the comedies referred to above are formulaic and banal; but to some extent at least, the (commercial) success of these films was to shape the way in which issues relating to German unification and the legacy of the GDR would be handled in the popular cinema. For within this wave of 'new German comedy', the emergence of a new sub-genre – the 'unification comedy' – is clearly discernible, of which Wolfgang Becker's *Goodbye, Lenin!* (2003) is the most recent, and perhaps most successful, example. While some of these unification comedies have been decried for promoting an uncritical attitude to the GDR past (often referred to as *Ostalgie* or 'ostalgia'), and for ignoring the implications of political developments in the post-unification era, it is important not to underestimate the contribution these films have made to the 'normalization' of German–German relations in the popular imagination. As we shall see, the strength of *Goodbye, Lenin!* is precisely the manner in which it both validates a sense of GDR cultural identity, and at the same time presents a critique of sentimental *Ostalgie*.

THE WILD EAST: THE 'TRABI-FILMS' AND *NO MORE MR NICE GUY*

The first of the 'Trabi-films', *Go, Trabi, Go!* was released in 1991 and follows the adventures of the Struutz family, who drive from Bitterfeld to Rome in their Trabant. Directed by Peter Timm (who had been expelled from the GDR in 1973), this blatantly commercial film is little more than an early tryout of the formula that was to be applied so successfully in the 'Manta-films' later that year. As such the film deals almost exclusively in crude clichés, and for the most part, takes care to bypass any politically sensitive issues. Even so, when the Struutz family call on their city-dwelling relatives in Regensburg, the west Germans are shown in a wholly negative light as vulgar, shallow, mean and quite unwilling to put themselves out to help their relatives from the east. By contrast, the east Germans are depicted as warm, helpful, kind-hearted, always willing to make the best of a bad job and with a respect for education and the arts that their western counterparts lack. But despite such moments where the film appears to be gesturing towards an agenda of national and cultural identity, the warm light in which the Struutz family is depicted is essentially a reflection of their naïve provincialism. And while this provincialism has much to do with their GDR origins, that particular German–German issue is never explicitly foregrounded. Indeed the bulk of the film is set not in Germany but in Italy, and its comic potential stems from the valiant efforts of the father to defend himself, his car and his attractive young daughter from the unwelcome attentions of a variety of cunning, roguish Italians.

Throughout the film Udo, the father, is portrayed as an exotic figure, a point that is underlined by his adherence to unmistakably east German fashions and his total loyalty to his faithful Trabant, 'Schorsch'. Indeed this element of GDR exoticism is explicitly foregrounded in the film during the 'Trabi Peepshow' sequence. But the corollary to Udo's reluctance to embrace the new capitalist consumerism is his firm conviction that the past can be a reliable guide to the future. This is reflected in the film, above all, in the way that his voyage of discovery is mediated by his reading of Goethe's *Italian Journey* (*Italienische Reise*, 1816–1829). Despite his obstinacy in everyday matters, Udo's imagi-nation and ability to endorse the values of Goethe's humanist narrative underline his status as an individual who refuses to allow his sense of beauty and adventure to be dimmed by the obstacles that are placed in his way by an increasingly commercialized and hostile world. And it is striking that while the other members of his family laugh at him initially for bringing along his copy of the *Italian Journey*, by the end of the film even his daughter Jacqueline is quoting Goethe, reading out the diary entry for 9 March 1787: 'One agreeable aspect of travel is that even ordinary incidents, because they are novel and unexpected, have a touch of adventure about them.'[1] For the Struutz family, the euphoria of the *Wende*,[2] symbolized here by the newly discovered possibilities for travel, still outweighs the harsh economic realities that were to become increasingly emphasized in the sequel.

If the first 'Trabi-film', *Go, Trabi, Go!* was a comic road movie underscored by Goethe's *Italian Journey*, the follow-up, *Go, Trabi, Go! 2 – That was the Wild East* (*Go, Trabi, Go 2 – Das war der wilde Osten*) was, as its title suggests,[3] a parody of a Western, though one permeated by references to another work of German classical literature, this time Goethe's *Faust II* (1833). Released one year later in 1992 and directed by Reinhard Klooss and Wolfgang Büld, the second 'Trabi-film' picks up from where *Go, Trabi, Go!* left off. The Struutz family return home from Italy only to find that their house in Bitterfeld has been bulldozed to make way for a new golf complex. However, the shock of losing their home is offset by the news that they have inherited what turns out to be a garden gnome factory. In contrast to *Go, Trabi, Go!*, the action of the sequel is far more closely tied in to contemporary political developments following German unification and, in particular, to the issue of property speculation in the east. Indeed, the extent to which the sequel seeks to embrace not only a west German but also an east German audience is reflected in the casting of Jaecki Schwarz (a highly popular GDR star from numerous DEFA productions) in the role of a provincial lawyer.

The harsh realities of life in the east after the fall of socialism are immediately apparent. The Bitterfeld to which the Struutz family return has the air of a run-down outpost in the Wild West, an impression underlined by the rotting 'carcasses' of abandoned Trabants scattered by the roadside. Like its predecessor, this 'Trabi-film' also operates in terms of well-worn stereotypes. Whilst the naïve *Ossis*[4] remain technically backward, their places are being taken by those who have embraced the ideology of capitalism. But although the GDR citizens are gently mocked for their provincialism, the real target of the film's satire is the patent absurdity of the slogans that have accompanied the arrival of the new ideology of corporate capitalism. The mayor is now to be seen taking the local civil servants on a training run so that they are 'fit for the market'.[5] Charlie, the self-styled businessman whom Udo befriends, has not only adopted an English name, but has no shame in marketing anything that will sell (here banana-flavoured condoms decorated with the colours of the German flag). And in the cigar-smoking figure of William Buck, the aptly named millionaire in New

York whom Udo tracks down in his search for a financial backer, we are presented with a grotesque parody of an American capitalist.

To a considerable extent, the comedy of *Go, Trabi, Go! 2* stems from the efforts of the Struutz family to adapt to the new circumstances. As in the first 'Trabi-film', mother and daughter are shown to be more flexible than their obstinate father. Udo's wife celebrates her new role as the wife of an entrepreneur by buying an outfit to match, whilst Jacqueline embraces the 'freedom' the new economy offers by teaming up with her friend, Diana, and taking a job in a newly opened strip club. Nonetheless, although both women adapt quickly, it is clear that the construction of these new identities is essentially a matter of performance, and these identities are shed as effortlessly as they are assumed. In Udo's case, however, the transformation is more extreme. When he finally decides to embrace the new ideology, he throws himself into his role so completely that even Charlie is taken aback. His development – an obvious satire of the rags-to-riches myth of American capitalism – takes him from the local casino (where he makes a fortune gambling the solitary mark his factory is said to be worth), to Wall Street where he strikes a deal with William Buck to supply a million dollars' worth of garden gnomes, thereby saving his factory, and with it, the jobs of his workers. This comic fantasy highlights the absurdity of the newspaper headline we see in the local newspaper – 'Success comes to those who want it'[6] – as well as the promise held out by the advertisement: 'You came as an *Ossi* – you left as a manager.'[7] At one level, it is tempting to see *Go, Trabi, Go! 2*, like so many genre comedies, as an example of 'cultural thinking', that is to say as a film offering an imaginary solution to the very real contradictions with which its audience is confronted (notably the need to reconcile the GDR's out-dated manufacturing processes with the desire to preserve a sense of community and non-alienated labour). But at another level, it would appear that what Udo has done, albeit unwittingly, is to transform 'socialism' into a commodity that can be purchased by the individual with sufficient financial backing. Thus whilst the film criticizes the ideology of corporate capitalism at one level, it reinstates it at another.

For all the humour in the film, it is hard to avoid the inescapable conclusion that the way of life represented by Udo's gnome factory is doomed, and that its – and its owner's – good fortune, is, quite literally, too good to be true. This is further emphasized by the intertextual references in the film to Goethe's *Faust II* (significantly the only book to have survived the destruction of the Struutz family home). Like the Emperor's kingdom in the second part of *Faust*, the east Germany to which Udo and his family return is 'like a weary dream, | Where one deformity another mouldeth, | Where lawlessness itself by law upholdeth, | And 't is an age of error that unfoldeth'.[8] And in this post-GDR setting, the place of Baucis and Philemon's hut that is such a 'vexing blot'[9] in the Emperor's grandiose schemes is taken by Udo's gnome factory, which stands in the way of the mayor's scheme for a ghastly urban complex in the midst of the beautiful countryside of Landwitz. But while the gnome factory, together with the natural idyll of Landwitz survive in this updated version of the Faustian legend, it is hard to ignore the fact that in Goethe's *Faust II*, Baucis and Philemon's hut is razed to the ground by Mephistopheles and his assistants. The 'happy ending' that we are presented with in *Go, Trabi, Go! 2* is, however, one that is required by the conventions of comedy. The ethos of an uncritical and sentimental *Ostalgie* that reverberates throughout the film is reflected in the idyllic, low-tech way of life that has been given a stay of execution. The reappearance of the family Trabant, 'Schorsch' (now fully restored to mint condition after being unceremoniously dumped onto a barge-load of scrap iron) acts as a catalyst for the restoration of harmony within the Struutz family itself. And in the final sequence of the film, their mission accomplished, the sharply contrasting figures of Udo and Charlie go their separate ways like Old Shatterhand and Winnetou in a Karl May Western. Each has learned from the other, and they part not as enemies, but as 'blood brothers', a rare (but genuine) example of a rapprochement between east and west. Charlie's decision to abandon the former GDR for destinations further east still suggests that, for the time being at least, east Germany has ceased to be a lawless frontier country with easy pickings for opportunists like him. But despite the reassurance of his parting words ('This used to be the wild East. Used to be, Udo. But now there's nothing more for me here')[10] they cannot disguise the fragility of the film's fantasy denouement in which the logic of comedy takes precedence over the logic of capitalism.

The notion of the GDR as a new 'Wild West' also lies at the heart of Detlev Buck's deliciously ironic portrayal of post-unification Germany, *No More Mr Nice Guy* (*Wir können auch anders*), a hugely popular film released in 1993. The film begins with a thinly-disguised reference to the opening up of the border between the two German states as Rudi Kipp emerges from the institution that has looked after him up until then and vigorously asserts that he is free to go 'wherever he pleases'. Here too the east is presented as a frontier region awaiting colonization, an impression that is further enhanced by the image of a surveyor in the background taking measurements of the surrounding terrain. It is a land in which the old order is crumbling, but one in which, as yet, nothing new has emerged to take its place. Indeed the further Rudi and his brother, Moritz, venture into the hinterlands of Mecklenburg-West Pomerania in their adventures, the more we see how little the pace and style of living has changed.

The most original aspect of *No More Mr Nice Guy*, however, is not so much its portrayal of the GDR, but rather its characterization of the two brothers, Rudi and Moritz, and the fact that, in this world in which reality appears to have been turned on its head, naïvety triumphs over sophistication. Whilst in any other unification comedy the naïvety of the protagonists would point to their origins in the east, in *No More Mr Nice Guy* we discover that they are in fact provincials from the west. Rudi's willingness to view every situation as an occasion for a celebration, together with a seemingly limitless capacity to come up with a platitude to suit every occasion, marks him out as the *'kleiner Mann'* par excellence. He is a figure who is, if anything, more at home in the low-key provincial setting of the east than in the west. For all his conventionality, however, he (and his brother, Moritz) are consistently portrayed as well-meaning and open-minded, and it is this that Viktor (the deserting Russian soldier who hijacks their truck) comes to recognize and which convinces him that it is almost his duty to take care of these accident-prone bumpkins. By the same token, Nadine (the waitress they encounter in their final desperate action) also recognizes that far from being 'dangerous killers', these comical figures are not only quite harmless, but possess a far greater sense of warmth and humanity than the foul-mouthed customers she serves in her bar.

In this way, Buck's comedy upholds the appealing fantasy that those whose heart is in the right place can succeed against all the odds. An integral part of this fantasy, of course, involves the dispensation of a kind of 'comic justice' visited (for the most part unwittingly) on those who consider themselves to be far superior to the two brothers. Nowhere is this clearer than in the case of the macho detective hunting down the fugitives; he may declare scornfully, 'It's like the Wild West here!',[11] but the defeat of the police, assisted as they are by every high-tech device imaginable, is a moment to be savoured. Moreover, although Rudi and Moritz are content to remain within the constraints of their very limited existences, as a result of so doing they discover (quite literally) a whole new world in Viktor's village in Russia. Just as in *Go, Trabi, Go! 2*, the final sequence of Buck's film presents the provincialism of the east, with its emphasis on human community (albeit in a spirit of *Ostalgie*) as a utopian 'pre-unification' way of life.[12] The simple values of Rudi and Moritz (values not shared by the high-handed westerners they encounter on their travels) are reflected in the idyllic setting of the final sequence, an idyll in which both east and west, young and old are united in harmony. It is a world that is on the retreat, but one which, as the film suggests, can still be found in the east for those willing to go far enough in search of it.

A LIFE LESS ORDINARY: *SONNENALLEE*

By the end of the 1990s, the concept of *Ostalgie* was itself being subjected to increasingly intense scrutiny. Perhaps the first signs of such a shift in thinking are to be seen in Leander Haußmann's hit comedy *Sonnenallee* (based on a script written by himself and Thomas Brussig). Premiered on 7 October 1999 – a significant date in that it marked the 50th anniversary of the founding of the GDR – *Sonnenallee* broke new ground by being, in the words of its director, the first comedy to be made about the Berlin Wall. In opting for a comic treatment of such a sensitive subject, Haußmann (born in 1959) and Brussig (born in 1965) display the irreverence of a new generation of filmmakers, coupled with the self-confidence that comes from having an insider's perspective on events. Indeed, as Thomas Brussig noted, 'only an *Ossi* could have made this film'.[13] Yet this did not prevent the film being sharply criticized for trivializing the sufferings of those who had fallen foul of the SED regime.[14] Only more recently – largely as a result of two important essays by Helen Cafferty[15] and Paul Cooke[16] – has a rather more differentiated view of the film started to emerge.

In *Sonnenallee*, Haußmann and Brussig make little or no attempt to address conventional political issues on the wider stage; what interests them instead is what might be termed as the 'heroism of the ordinary'. Indeed one of the factors that persuaded Brussig to collaborate with Haußmann was the latter's reluctance to just tell a conventional story about a totalitarian system. In setting *Sonnenallee* in the GDR of the 1970s, Haußmann and Brussig were able to tap into the vogue for retro-culture that was so widespread during the late 1990s, and this was no doubt a factor in the film's appeal to a wide audience. But there was much more at stake in choosing this particular milieu, for as Haußmann goes on to suggest, somewhat tongue in cheek: 'The GDR was always stuck in the 1970s.'[17] Focusing on the 1970s allows the filmmakers to explore the collective memories of a generation of GDR citizens whilst avoiding the need to address the vicissitudes of German–German political develop-ments during the late 1980s. Nonetheless, Haußmann emphatically rejects the suggestion that the film is in any sense apolitical: 'the whole film is political; in almost every scene the characters are confronted with political issues'.[18]

The song accompanying the opening titles, where the repeated refrain warns us 'You don't know what it's like here', points to the film's 'corrective' agenda. No one knows less what life is like in the GDR than Micha's Uncle Heinz from the West. His distorted impressions are little more than a collage of clichés derived from the Western boulevard press. On his numerous visits to the family, he 'smuggles' what he, in his naïvety, mistakenly believes to be contraband goods (nylon stockings and coffee). Moreover, as the film makes clear, the sense of danger that Uncle Heinz experiences is not real but imagined, and stems from the dull routine life he lives in the West. His distorted view of the GDR is mirrored at various points in the film, but perhaps most comically when Micha and his friend Mario run behind a bus full of western tourists, screaming, 'Hunger! Hunger!' However, by playing up to the absurd prejudices of those who would look down on them as objects of pity – and thereby reversing the roles of observer and observed – Micha and Mario re-affirm their refusal to assume the passive role of the victim. Thus whilst Heinz and the tourists on the viewing platforms remain trapped within their clichéd vision of life in East Berlin, *Sonnenallee* offers the viewer a glimpse of an altogether different reality, a reality that is also referred to in the opening song with its reference to 'Different people with different lives | And many ways they can live them'. It is this desire to portray such diversity, and in so doing challenge the perceived wisdom of life in the GDR as a monotonous grey existence, that is reflected in the film's subtitle 'In Colour' ('Farbfilm').

By adopting the structure of a 'rites of passage' film and focusing on the drama of teenage youth, the creators of *Sonnenallee* lay claim to a certain universality of experience. Whilst certain references in the film – notably jokes revolving around particular consumer products – can only be understood by those with first hand knowledge of the GDR, the experiences that Micha, Mario, Wuschel and his friends undergo are the kind with which audiences from both east and west can easily identify. As Haußmann notes: 'When a boy meets a girl for the first time – that's something everybody understands.'[19] However, the film's contribution to a normalization of German–German relations is due to its capacity to mobilize two contrasting modes of spectatorship: on the one hand, the boys' escapades are shown to be not GDR-specific, but part of the universal experience of teenage youth; on the other, the GDR setting of this universal rites of passage story endorses a concept of East German cultural identity by legitimizing their memories of the past.[20] This aspect of the film's agenda is, in part, reflected in Thomas Brussig's remark that: 'I grew up in the GDR. That doesn't make the GDR any better. But I still have fond memories of that childhood.'[21] Moreover, for all the irony running through the film, it is impossible to ignore the positive aspects of the milieu in which their lives are played out: the strong sense of a community in which – despite life's daily tiffs – everyone knows everybody; the loyalty of the mother to her family as shown when she cannot go through with her decision to travel to the West on a stolen passport; and the optimistic outlook of Micha together with his determination to make the best out of what he has. This latter point is illustrated at the end of the film, when his crazy performance as an air-guitarist convinces the inconsolable Wuschel that although his LP is not in fact the Stones album he so covets, it is not without its merits.

Micha's performance in the final carnivalesque sequence of the film, in which the protagonist's fantasy enables him, quite literally, to transcend the physical barrier of the Berlin Wall, bears witness to the power of the imagination generally in overcoming the obstacles of everyday reality. Indeed for all the GDR teenagers in the film, fantasy and the imagination play a crucial role in how they explore and define their sense of self-identity. The clearest example of this occurs during the sequence in the family bathroom in Micha's home where he adjusts his FDJ shirt[22] as he rehearses his speech of 'self-criticism', whilst at the same time his sister, Sabine, receives instruction on how to perform her audition piece for the drama school. Here, the explicit theatricality of Sabine's rehearsal is contrasted with the implicit theatricality of Micha's attempt to address the party's youth brigade (in the hope of winning favour with his beloved Miriam). When his plan works – to the extent that he succeeds in forging a bond with Miriam – his ecstatic hymn to the Marxist–Leninist doctrines underpinning the GDR underscores the extent to which the ideological trappings of everyday life are merely a façade against which the real dramas of youth, and above all the infatuation with the opposite sex, are played out.

Micha's success in attracting the admiration of Miriam, however, marks a turning point in his development. Following the scenes of drug-induced anarchy during the party at Mario's flat, Micha has the task of restoring his standing in the eyes of Miriam (whose antipathy towards the East is thinly concealed). To this end he has to create the (non-existent) diaries that he has promised to show her, and – in a manner not unlike Alexander's attempt to recreate a fictional version of the GDR for his mother in *Goodbye, Lenin!* – he embarks on a process of 'remembering' in which he, quite literally, rewrites his own identity and with it, his attitude to the GDR. Yet rather than portray this as a dubious act of revisionism, the film reminds us (humorously) of the way in which memory and the construction of personal and political histories are conditioned by the needs and desires of the present. The irony of these sequences is twofold: on the one hand, it arises from the obvious discrepancy between the rebellious attitude of Micha's adolescent reflections and the (alleged) age of the 'diarist' recording them: 'Today we learnt the last letters. At last I can write an important word that I'm always thinking – shit!';[23] but on the other, it derives from the discrepancy between Micha's actual childhood experiences and his *post hoc* construction of an childhood dogged by state oppression that he has not in fact experienced. Nonetheless, for all the comic potential of these episodes, they have a serious function, triggering as they do an important process in Micha's personal development, for as he observes: 'I thought about this country and what it means to live here, and about why Miriam always appeared so unhappy.'[24] That is to say, in rewriting his personal memories Micha embarks on a process of exploring a range of contrasting attitudes towards the GDR.

The filmmakers' decision to focus on the personal and emotional development of the protagonists has prompted many to condemn *Sonnenallee* for its alleged failure to address the more uncomfortable aspects of life in the GDR. This question is perhaps most urgently raised in the sequence towards the end of the film where the policeman in charge of the district (the ABV or *Abschnittsbevollmächtigte*) shoots at Wuschel in the (mistaken) belief that he is attempting to escape. Although Haußmann had originally planned to include the boy's death in the film, in the finished version Wuschel survives, his heart protected by the coveted Rolling Stones LP that has borne the brunt of the bullet's impact. Yet the avoidance of tragedy here is not quite as complete as it might appear, for in the eyes of the Stones-obsessed Wuschel, the loss of his precious LP outweighs any consideration that he is lucky to be alive. As Brussig notes: 'It can't be Wuschel who gets shot, but his record – that's far worse.'[25] Here Brussig's remarks underline the alternative agenda that lies at the heart of *Sonnenallee*: namely, what is at stake in the film is not conventional politics, but rather the subjective realities of the youthful protagonists, and the role of fantasy in their quest for self-identity. Indeed it is in this sense that Haußmann's claim that every scene in the film is political is to be understood. *Sonnenallee* deals with its subject matter not in terms of a political agenda set by conventional Western liberal democracies, but seeks rather to redefine the political in terms of the characters' subjective experience of everyday life in the GDR of their adolescence. In so doing, it challenges the grey, stereotypical image of the state by offering a glimpse of an alternative (and more colourful) GDR, an agenda that is reinforced by the lyrics of the Nina Hagen song 'You Forgot the Colour Film' ('Du hast den Farbfilm vergessen') that accompanies the final credits.

ADIEU GDR: *GOODBYE, LENIN!*

There can be little doubt that the cinematic event of 2003 in Germany was the release of Wolfgang Becker's *Goodbye, Lenin!* Becker's film so completely caught the public's imagination in both the old and new federal states that by June of that year some 5.5 million tickets had been sold; a phenomenal achievement by any yardstick. Indeed the film was regarded as such a landmark event that a special screening was even arranged for the members of the German parliament. Set in the year leading up to German unification, *Goodbye Lenin!* continues the trend set by *Sonnnenallee* some four years earlier, insofar as it strives for a more differentiated understanding of the concept of *Ostalgie*, whilst at the same time highlighting the importance of memory (both individual and collective) for the citizens of the former GDR. Far from presenting a conventional critique of life under the SED regime, the film explores the bond that exists between Alex, the film's youthful protagonist, and his mother, Christiane, a dedicated socialist. As Bernd Lichtenberg, the Cologne-born author of the screenplay comments: 'I didn't want to produce a film about the problems of the GDR but one about a close-knit family where history bursts in like an unexpected guest.'[26] For Alex, the implications of the fall of the Wall have less to do with history and the socio-economics of life in a united Germany than with his belief that his mother, who has just emerged from a coma and thus knows nothing of the unification process, should be spared the trauma of discovering that the GDR no longer exists. By focusing on the love between mother and son, and showing how each constructs a web of lies to protect the other, the film presents the viewer with a theme which, on the surface at least, would appear to transcend the ideological boundary between the two German states. Indeed, as Lichtenberg continues: 'I'm sure that such families where people deceive each other and lies obscure the truth – that's something you find in both East and West.'[27] Nonetheless, by setting this 'universal' story within a specifically GDR context, the film simultaneously offers two distinct modes of spectatorship. On the one hand, for non-GDR viewers it 'corrects' the received picture of the GDR by reminding them that family relationships in the East were not fundamentally different to those in the West; on the other hand, for viewers from the former GDR, the fact that this 'universal' story is set in East Berlin offers them the opportunity to draw on the insider knowledge necessary to decode the numerous references to a specifically East German way of life, and thereby affirm a sense of their unique cultural identity.

Although the film focuses primarily on the drama played out within Alex's family, it does not shy away from offering a critique of some of the more absurd aspects of political culture in the GDR. We are reminded of the hollowness of the SED regime's rhetoric when images of a hung over Alex sitting in front of a propaganda poster bearing the message 'Socialism revolves around the individual'[28] are juxtaposed with larger-than-life images of Honecker and Gorbachev sitting on the tribune watching the military parade to mark the 40th anniversary of the founding of the GDR. Nonetheless, Alex's cynical voice-over ('There was a wind of change in the air, whilst right in front of our house a shooting club with an overinflated sense of its own importance was performing for the last time')[29] contributes, once again, to the film's 'normalizing' agenda. This reminds the viewer that people in the GDR were just as capable of seeing through the pomp of the state's extravagant displays of military power as their counterparts in the West. But it is, above all, through the characterization of Alex's mother, Christiane, that the film succeeds in providing a corrective to stereotypical notions of the GDR generally, and of socialist activism in particular. When Christiane's husband fails to return from a congress in West Berlin (for reasons which only later become clear) she is traumatized at first, but then decides to commit herself to the GDR so wholeheartedly that Alex describes her as married to the state. Nonetheless, she is quite the opposite of the doctrinaire party member typified by the likes of Frau Nizold, the headmistress in *Sonnenallee*. Alex's mother is adored by all who come into contact with her, and the photographs of her posing dressed up as a mermaid for the 'Neptune Festival' with the children from her class underline her warmth and humanity. So committed is she to her beliefs that some, including the headmaster of the school where she works, are inclined to see her as being even too idealistic. Yet this niggardly view of her is firmly contradicted by the humorous pragmatism she displays when helping the neighbours to compose letters of complaint (*Eingaben*) to the manufacturers of various defective products in the GDR. And when she believes (mistakenly, of course) that people from the Federal

Republic are fleeing to the GDR, her insistence that the family should extend a welcoming hand to the new 'refugees' mirrors the spirit of 'German–German' comradeship displayed when the first GDR citizens crossed into West Berlin on 9 November 1989. By portraying her not as a fanatical ideologue, but as a compassionate, devoted mother with serious beliefs tempered by a mischievous sense of humour, the film marks her out as a figure whose qualities transcend the boundaries of East and West. Once again, however, the fact that it is an *Ossi* who embodies these universal qualities creates the potential for a different (and supplementary) act of identification for the viewer from the former East. The characterization of Christiane addresses both a need and a desire to cherish positive memories of a GDR past, and it is hardly coincidental that this potential for empathy is further facilitated through the casting of the well-known GDR actress, Katrin Saß, in the role.

A similar strategy is discernible in the way the film presents the Federal Republic. Just as it does not shy away from showing some of the shortcomings of life in the GDR, so too the film draws attention to some of the less palatable aspects of the unification process (and, in particular, the currency union). Every time Alex visits the local hospital to check on his mother's progress, he discovers that yet another GDR-trained doctor has been lured to the west by the prospects of better pay. Likewise, the east Germans' willingness to unite behind the new 'all-German' (i.e. West German) soccer team during the World Cup is cynically exploited by the manager of the west German satellite TV business, X-TV, as an opportunity to expand his company's market share. Nonetheless, for all the rampant commercialism of the firm's operations, we should not forget that they provide the backdrop to a genuine rapprochement between east and west as symbolized by the friendship that develops between Alex and Denis (the young TV technician from west Berlin his firm pairs him up with). Thus just as the film's characterization of Alex's mother calls into question clichéd notions of the *Ossi*, so the depiction of Denis contradicts the stereotypical notion of the *Wessi* as essentially arrogant and exploitative. When Alex's mother wants to watch the news, it is Denis who comes to his friend's aid, suggesting he show her old news bulletins recorded on video, and even supplying a set of recordings of the news programme 'Aktuelle Kamera'. Furthermore, when Denis assures Alex that his mother will never notice that the programmes are from last year, remarking that 'it was always just the same old rubbish!'[30] his words are not intended as an aggressive put-down of his GDR colleague, but are symptomatic of a healthy scepticism that corresponds to Alex's own views on the relationship between truth and politics: 'the truth was something that was pretty questionable and could easily be adapted to fit the way my mother saw things'.[31]

Throughout the course of *Goodbye, Lenin!* the viewer is presented with a variety of different attitudes to the phenomenon of *Ostalgie*. At one end of the scale, there is the complete rejection of everything associated with the East – essentially the stance taken by Alex's sister, Ariane. After the fall of the socialist regime in the GDR she abandons her studies, takes a menial job with Burger King and plunges into a new relationship with Rainer, her west German boss. It is she who is the driving force behind what Alex terms the 'Westernization' of the family home; and the belly-dance she performs for Rainer, which panders to 'Rainer's enthusiasm for the customs of the Orient',[32] underlines that, paradoxically, she has no qualms in exploiting her status as an exotic Eastern 'Other' in order to 'Westernize' her private life. Indeed her reluctance to go along with Alex's elaborate scheme (a reluctance which prompts him to accuse her of wishing their mother were dead), together with her rage when she discovers that their mother has concealed the letters sent by their father from West Berlin, hint at a deep-seated desire on her part to distance herself from everything that reminds her of her GDR past, whilst at the same time embracing a new (non-GDR) identity.

Ariane is, of course, young, and her willingness to turn her back on the past is in part due to the fact that she still has the opportunity to carve out a new identity for herself in the future. But if her attitude represents a rejection of *Ostalgie* in any form, the attitude of the elderly residents in the block of flats where Alex lives represents the very opposite, namely a desire to cling to an idealized image of the GDR and to reject everything associated with the Federal Republic. For Herr Mehlert, Frau Schäfer and Herr Ganske, there is no realistic prospect of them establishing a new identity within a unified Germany; for them unification means the obliteration of their past identity as GDR citizens. Accordingly when Alex tells them that his mother has never even heard of the end of the GDR, Herr Mehlert remarks that she is someone to be envied. For him and his co-residents, the opportunity to play a part in Alex's fictional world is, quite literally, an opportunity to be transported back into a past they wish they had never left behind. This is a past in which their identity as GDR citizens had a legitimate basis; and it is this feeling that is underlined by Frau Schäfer's 'ostalgic' remark: 'It's so nice to chat with your mother. It makes you feel that things are still the way they used to be.'[33]

Whilst for Ariane, change cannot take place fast enough, Herr Mehlert and his co-residents are assailed by a feeling that they, like so many GDR citizens, have simply been left behind by the pace of change. Moreover, as the time-delayed images of the frantically revolving clock – the famous *Weltzeituhr* at the Alexanderplatz – remind us, the more rapidly change occurs, the stronger the desire becomes to cling to the memories of the past. Even Alex is not immune to this, for once he has established his fantasy GDR world within the flat, he finds himself increasingly at home there: 'There, far away from the hectic pace of life of the new era, was a place for calm quiet reflection.'[34] These reflections offer the viewer an intriguing insight into the psychology of *Ostalgie* as well as into the reason behind Alex's construction of a fictional GDR. Although he embarks on his project believing that – like Herr Mehlert, Frau Schäfer and Herr Ganske – his mother will be unable to come to terms with the sudden collapse of the GDR, it becomes increasingly clear that it is he who cannot come to terms with the abrupt loss of his idyllic childhood (a loss symbolized by the collapse of the GDR). Just as Christiane's temporary awakening from her coma provides the young protagonist with an extended opportunity to prepare himself for the eventual trauma of losing his mother, so the 'extra time' the 'GDR' enjoys, also gives him an opportunity to make the transition from the old to the new world order. In this way, the film maps out a middle way between the two extremes represented on the one hand, by Ariane (who rejects the past), and on the other, by the elderly residents (who reject the future). Indeed *Goodbye, Lenin!* is a rites of passage movie in a double sense, since the successful conclusion to Alex's development takes place at both a personal and a political level. What we witness is a process of mourning for both his mother *and* for the GDR: at a personal level he succeeds in transferring his emotional attachment from his mother to Lara; at a political level, he is able to come to terms with the end of the GDR and thereby embrace the new future. This is symbolized by the firework display on the eve of unification that he watches with Lara from the rooftop of the hospital. This moment of transition, a moment in which the personal and the political merge, is underscored in the penultimate sequence in the film in which he scatters his mother's ashes across both east and west using one of the model space rockets of his childhood. At the same time, the elision of this sequence with the concluding section of what is supposedly super-8 footage (an idyllic collage of childhood memories) reminds the viewer that for any individual to make a genuine transition to a new future, he or she must be allowed to cherish the memories of the past.

One of the great strengths of *Goodbye, Lenin!* is the way in which it prompts the viewer to reflect on the complex relationship between history, memory and fiction. In particular, the film reminds us that the past is never simply there as a given, and that, as in *Sonnenallee*, engaging with the past is a process that is almost always highly conditioned by the needs of the present. This can be seen in the fictional 'GDR' that Alex constructs for his mother. Following the news bulletin he and Denis have put together to account for the presence of imported cars in the East following an influx of 'refugees' from the West, Alex reflects that: 'The GDR that I created for my mother came increasingly to resemble the GDR that I might have wished for myself.'[35] That is to say, Alex assembles in the realm of the imaginary a version of the GDR that is free from the contradictions he has experienced at first hand. At one level, it is tempting to see a parallel between the workings of Alex's fantasy and the activities of the SED regime's propagandists; for in both cases an attempt is being made to 'make good' some of the more obvious shortcomings of the GDR. Indeed it is hardly coincidental that (apart from Ariane) the one character who urges him to tell his mother the truth is Lara, who, as a young woman brought up in the Soviet Union, has direct experience of the consequences that can ensue from a systematic distortion of the truth. Nonetheless, there is a clear difference between the motives behind Alex's attempt to draw attention to the positive aspects of the GDR, and the SED propagandists' more cynical manipulation of the truth. Lara's affection for Alex enables her to recognize that the relationship between truth and falsehood is not always as straightforward as it might seem, and that there are circumstances when the integrity of people's memories (however inaccurate) should be preserved and legitimized so that the individual can come to terms with what they have lost. Even though she may not agree that Alex's mother should be kept in the dark, she recognizes that Alex's fictional GDR represents both a gift of love to his mother and an expression of his own need to preserve a memory he can look back on and treasure. And, as the ending of the film underlines, this gift is reciprocated by his mother. For ultimately, it is Alex and not Christiane who is shielded from the truth. When he brings his estranged father to visit his mother in hospital, we see Lara telling Christiane about the political changes that have taken place; and the bemused look Alex receives from his mother makes it clear to the viewer (though not to him) that she has indeed grasped what is going on. Nonetheless, as her 'endorsement' of the speech delivered by the 'new premier' (alias the taxi-driver-cum-Sigmund-Jähn-lookalike)[36] underlines, now it she who seeks to preserve the fiction of her 'ignorance' (and with it her son's happiness). Although Alex may tell himself 'I think it was good that she never discovered the truth. She died happy',[37] the fact is (as Lara knows) that she died happy despite knowing the truth.

CONCLUSION

In both *Sonnenallee* and *Goodbye, Lenin!* there is a marked change in the way in which the GDR and, above all, memories of the GDR are presented. For the most part, the early unification comedies offer a crude and distorted picture of the GDR in which the *Ossi* appears as an exotic 'Other', as an individual incapable of being assimilated within a new political structure. This element of exoticism (which is reflected in the crude stereotyping of a film like *Go, Trabi, Go!*) is further exacerbated by an equally clichéd notion of the GDR as a new Wild West, a *terra incognita* at the mercy of the new speculators. Running parallel to the new spirit of entrepreneurship, represented by the likes of Charlie in *Go, Trabi, Go! 2*, is a sentimental idealization of outmoded and ineffective working practices (such as Udo Struutz's gnome factory). By contrast, *Sonnenallee* and *Goodbye, Lenin!* offer a much more differentiated picture of the East. Their success is due, in no small measure, to the way in which they highlight many of the positive aspects of life in the GDR whilst avoiding the trap of lapsing into an uncritical attitude of *Ostalgie*. In particular, both films explore what lies at the heart of such 'ostalgic' tendencies, namely the need for former GDR citizens to preserve the sense of a cultural identity that is both distinct from that of their west German counterparts, and which reflects the experiences that are unique to their historical and political past. By setting their 'universal' stories within specifically East German settings, *Sonnenallee* and *Goodbye, Lenin!* open up a new perspective on the East for audiences with little or no firsthand experience of the GDR. In so doing, these films make an important contribution to the normalization of German–German relations. At the same time, both films recognize the crucial role of the past and memory in the construction of both an individual and national sense of identity. In this way, the viewer is led to understand that, if the process of German unification is to take place at a cultural level, it will be necessary to find a middle way between the two extremes represented by, on the one hand, a total rejection of the GDR past, and on the other, a sentimental idealization of a past that never existed. It is in this sense that *Goodbye, Lenin!* offers the viewer a corrective to the way in which all memories of the GDR seemed to be swept aside in the drive to unification following November 1989. For as Alex comments: 'We were to celebrate the anniversary of the founding of our Socialist Fatherland one last time. But in contrast to reality this time it would be a dignified farewell.'[38] For whilst the 'new premier', 'Sigmund Jähn', announces the removal of the border between the Federal Republic and the GDR (and with it the end of a divided Germany), his speech also reminds the viewer (from both East and West) that, for all its shortcomings, the GDR was founded on a vision that will continue to exist long after the state has perished. For as 'Jähn' remarks: 'We know that our country is not perfect. But what we believe in has again and again inspired people all over the world.'[39]

Notes

1 Johann Wolfgang Goethe, *Italian Journey*, tr. by W. H. Auden and Elizabeth Mayer (Harmondsworth: Penguin, 1962), p. 197.

2 *Wende* (turning point) is the term used by Germans to describe the fall of the communist regime in the GDR.

3 The title clearly alludes to the classic Western *How the West Was Won* (Henry Hathaway, John Ford and George Marshall, 1963) which in German is known as *Das war der wilde Westen*.

4 The terms *Ossi* and *Wessi* were used (almost always pejoratively) as a shorthand for citizens from the GDR and the Federal Republic respectively.

5 'Fit für den Markt'.

6 'Erfolg muß man nur wollen'.

7 'Sie kommen als Ossi ... Sie gehen als Boss!'

8 Johann Wolfgang Goethe, *Faust: Parts 1 & 2*, tr. by Bayard Taylor (London: Sphere, 1969), p. 202.

9 Goethe, *Faust*, p. 418.

10 'Das war der wilde Osten. *War*, Udo. Hier habe ich nichts mehr zu suchen'.

11 'Hier ist es wie im Wilden Westen'.

12 For a discussion of the film's relation to the *Heimat* tradition in German cinema, see Leonie Naughton, *That Was the Wild East: Film Culture, Unification and the 'New' Germany* (Ann Arbor: University of Michigan Press, 2002), pp. 155–64.

13 'Diesen Film durfte nur ein Ossi machen.' Peter Zander, '"Im Theater sitzen die Spielverderber": Interview mit Leander Haußmann', http://archiv.berliner.archiv 1999/991006/feulliton/story01.html

14 Help e.V. – an organization supporting victims of political violence – launched a lawsuit against the filmmakers on the grounds that the film insulted those who had suffered persecution under the SED regime.

15 Helen Cafferty, '*Sonnenallee*: Taking German Comedy Seriously in Unified Germany' in Carol Anne Costabile-Henning, Rachel J. Halverson and Kristie A. Foell (eds.), *Textual Responses to German Unification: Processing Historical and Social Change in Literature and Film* (Berlin and New York: DeGruyter, 2001), pp. 253–71.

16 Paul Cooke, 'Performing "Ostalgie": Leander Haußmann's *Sonnenallee*', *German Life and Letters*, 56 (2003), 156–67.

17 'Die DDR war eigentlich immer in den Siebzigern.' Sandra Maischberger, '*Sonnenallee* – Eine Mauerkomödie: Interview mit Leander Haußmann und Thomas Brussig' in Leander Haußmann (ed.), *Sonnenallee: Das Buch zum Farbfilm* (Berlin: Quadriga, 1999), pp. 8–24 (p.11).

18 'Der ganze Film ist politisch, fast in jeder Szene werden die Figuren mit der Politik konfrontiert.' Maischberger, '*Sonnenallee*', p. 12.

19 'Wenn ein Junge zum ersten Mal ein Mädchen sieht – das ist etwas, was jeder versteht.' Maischberger, '*Sonnenallee*', p. 21.

20 See Cooke, 'Performing "Ostalgie"', p. 163.

21 'Meine Kindheit hat in der DDR stattgefunden. Das macht die DDR nicht besser. Aber ich erinnere mich trotzdem gerne an die Kindheit.' Maischberger, '*Sonnenallee*', p. 24.

22 The FDJ, or *Freie Deutsche Jugend* (Free German Youth), was the communist youth organization in the GDR.

23 'Heute haben wir die letzten [Buchstaben] gelernt. Endlich kann ich ein wichtiges Wort schreiben, daß ich ganz oft denke: Scheiße!'

24 'Ich machte mir über dieses Land Gedanken, was es bedeutet hier zu leben, und warum Miriam so unglücklich wirkte'.

25 'Nicht Wuschel muß erschossen werden, sondern seine Platte – das ist viel schlimmer.' Maischberger, '*Sonnenallee*', p. 12.

26 'Es ging mir [...] nicht darum, einen Film mit DDR-Problematik zu entwerfen, sondern um eine kleine Familie, bei der die Historie wie ein unangemeldeter Gast hereinplatzt.' Alfred Holighaus, 'Eine Familiengeschichte: Gespräch mit dem Drehbuchautor Bernd Lichtenberg' in Michael Töteberg (ed.), *Goodbye, Lenin!: Ein Film von Wolfgang Becker* (Berlin: Schwarzkopf & Schwarzkopf, 2003), pp. 148–51 (pp.148–9).

27 'Ich denke, solche Familiengeschichten, in denen man sich belügt, wo es Lügen gibt, die der Wahrheit im Wege stehen, die kennt man im Westen wie im Osten.' Holighaus, 'Eine Familiengeschichte', p. 149.

28 'Der Mensch steht im Mittelpunkt der sozialistischen Gesellschaft'.

29 'Die Zeit roch nach Veränderung, während vor unserem Haus ein überdimensionierter Schützenverein seine letzte Vorstellung gab'.

30 'War doch immer derselbe Quatsch'.

31 'dass die Wahrheit nur eine zweifelhafte Angelegenheit war, die ich leicht Mutters gewohnter Wahrnehmung angleichen konnte'.

32 'Rainers Begeisterung für die Sitten und Gebräuche des Morgenlandes'.

33 'Es ist so schön, sich mit deiner Mutter zu unterhalten. Man hat das Gefühl, es ist so wie früher'.

34 'Doch weit ab von der Hektik der neuen Zeit lag ein Ort der Stille, der Ruhe und der Beschaulichkeit'.

35 'Die DDR, die ich für meine Mutter schuf, wurde immer mehr die DDR, die ich mir vielleicht gewünscht hätte'.

36 As is made clear in the early part of the film, Alex's boyhood hero – Sigmund Jähn from the GDR – was the first German in space.

37 'Ich glaube, es war schon richtig, dass sie die Wahrheit nie erfahren hat. Sie ist glücklich gestorben'.

38 'Ein letztes Mal noch sollten wir den Geburtstag unseres sozialistischen Vaterlandes feiern. Aber im Gegensatz zur Wirklichkeit als einen würdigen Abschied'.

39 'Wir wissen, dass unser Land nicht perfekt ist. Aber das, woran wir glauben, begeisterte immer wieder viele Menschen aus aller Welt'.

Chapter 5

Turkish–German cinema: from cultural resistance to transnational cinema?

Rob Burns

The last thirty years have seen the development of a considerable body of films made in Germany which draw on the multifarious experiences of Turkish migrants in the Federal Republic. This Turkish–German cinema has its roots in two areas of cultural practice. Firstly, what gradually took on the character of a 'sub-state cinema'[1] emerged initially as part of a 'politically critical national cinema', subsumed under a broader thematic category within the New German Cinema of the 1970s, namely films which addressed themselves to the plight of so-called 'guest-workers' (*Gastarbeiter*). This initial focus on the inhuman living and working conditions of foreign labourers is typified by *Lowest of the Low* (*Ganz unten*), the fly-on-the-wall documentary that was released in 1986 as a companion to Günter Wallraff's record-breaking literary reportage of the same title. Disguising himself as a Turkish worker, Wallraff spent some two years recording his experiences in a variety of dangerous, insanitary and badly paid jobs. Despite the everyday manifestations of fascistic behaviour he unmasked, Wallraff was not spared criticism himself from those who felt that *Lowest of the Low* presented a patronizing and stereotyped portrait of the Turk as uneducated, unskilled, naïve and pitiful. Arlene Akiko Teraoka goes even further and argues that *Lowest of the Low* 'is not really about Turks at all'; rather, Wallraff 'is taking their experience as paradigmatic for the experience of oppression in general'.[2] The same point has been made about another film from this earlier period, *Shirin's Wedding* (*Shirins Hochzeit*, 1975), written and directed by the German filmmaker Helma Sanders-Brahms. Made in the mid-1970s, at a time when the voice of feminism was beginning to make itself heard in the cultural sphere in Germany, the film has been criticized for collapsing the specifically Turkish dimension of the pro-tagonist's story into a generalized narrative about women's oppression under patriarchy.[3]

Secondly, and more generally, the development of Turkish–German cinema must also be seen against the background of various initiatives to promote migrant culture in Germany. In the early 1980s organizations were founded to co-ordinate the creative efforts of Germany's migrant population, and to facilitate what was expressly and affirmatively desig-nated as 'guest-worker literature'. Such writing laid claim to counter-cultural status, hence the insistence on using the official term for migrant labour, 'guest-worker' (just as 'many Asian, African and Caribbean people in Britain chose to adopt the term "Black" as an umbrella political category').[4] Conceived as an instrument of 'cultural resistance', this was to be above all a 'literature of the affected'[5] which consequently gave priority to the authenticity of personal experience. In view of the lack of authenticity betrayed by the New German Cinema's representations of alterity, such an aesthetic provided a creative stimulus to migrant filmmakers in Germany, as well as helping to shape a climate in which films addressing problems of ethnic difference could be expected to attract production subsidies from the public service broadcasting corporations and the federal and regional funding authorities.

A 'CINEMA OF THE AFFECTED'
AND A 'CINEMA OF *MÉTISSAGE*'

Both in its thematic emphases and its recurrent imagery centred on the trope of incarceration, the work of Tevfik Başer is wholly representative of this first phase of migrant cinema. The Turkish-born director, who moved to Germany in the early 1980s,[6] released his first feature film, *40 m² of Germany* (*40 m² Deutschland*), in 1986, the same year as *Lowest of the Low*, but although one of the two principal figures in Başer's film is a Turkish guest-worker, we are shown nothing of his life outside the domestic sphere. To have done so, Başer has stated, would only have yielded clichés.[7] Similarly, although the film, like *Shirin's Wedding*, portrays a Turkish woman in circumstances of extreme oppression, the specifically *cultural* dimension of that oppression is precisely what is foregrounded in Başer's movie. The '40 square metres' in question define the film's sole location, a three-room flat in a Hamburg tenement building that must seem almost palatial to its new occupant, Turna, who has been brought over from rural Anatolia to live with her husband, Dursun. It is Turna's task to transform this space into a little pocket of Turkish culture which will offer Dursun refuge after his work at the factory, and safeguard his wife from the moral depravity he sees pervading German society. In reality, however, as endless days pass filled only with cleaning, washing and cooking, it proves to be a domain of domestic drudgery in which, since Dursun keeps the flat door permanently locked, Turna is quite literally imprisoned.

Not the least disturbing aspect of Turna's plight is her lack of resistance. So conditioned is she to her husband's patriarchal authoritarianism that she cannot, or dare not, utter more than the mildest of protestations. In her growing frustration Turna cuts off her long black plaits, an act of transformation she repeats on her doll after she becomes pregnant. If this is to be seen as a gesture of cultural protest by embracing a Western hairstyle, then it quickly gives way to feelings of shame that she tries to conceal under a headscarf. Similarly, the effect of cutting the doll's hair is to make it appear male, an act not so much of self-assertion as compliance with her husband's demands for a son and heir. Ironically, the only real opportunity Turna is offered of experiencing the outside world she herself forfeits not by denying but by proudly affirming her cultural identity. Dursun finally gives in to Turna's entreaties and agrees to take her to the fair, though only in order that she might see for herself how immorally the Germans entertain themselves. On the morning of the promised outing she wakes up early and prepares herself for the big occasion, fastidiously applying her most brilliant make-up and donning a traditional outfit resplendent in billowing shawls and multi-coloured scarves. However, such a dazzling assertion of her Turkish femininity merely strengthens Dursun's resolve to keep Turna under lock and key. Sensing that his wife's overt 'Otherness' will attract attention, and afraid that she in turn will be contaminated by any contact with German customs and mores, Dursun reneges on his promise and goes out alone.

Apart from as a household drudge and sexual slave, Turna's only other value to Dursun lies in her capacity to bear him a male offspring. Significantly, the only occasions on which Dursun appears to demonstrate concern for his wife relate to his increasing frustration at her failure to conceive. When she falls ill, principally as a consequence of her living conditions, Dursun fetches not a doctor but the *hodja*, a Muslim holy man, who proceeds to carry out a fertility rite on Turna unperturbed by her blank incomprehension at his ministrations. The meaning of the Koran text the *hodja* inscribes on Turna's belly is inaccessible to her because she cannot read or write. Her powers of articulation decline progressively, in tandem with her physical and mental deterioration, to the point where eventually language breaks down totally and she is reduced to anguished screams or neurotic whimpering. Deprived of social intercourse and treated like a caged animal, a woman denied a voice has become a woman without a language. Incapable of resisting her captor but lacking any external liberator, Turna can finally only secure her release when Dursun suffers a fatal epileptic attack. Yet, even in death, he maintains the role of his wife's jailor by blocking the doorway. Moreover, the fact that the camera declines to follow Turna as she finally escapes from the Stygian gloom of her internment and staggers into the radiant sunlight of the street would seem to suggest that a whole set of new problems awaits her in the foreign environment to which she has only now gained access. For, as Başer has argued, Turna has been incarcerated twice over: first, in her role as a Turkish woman, and secondly, as an immigrant in an alien world.[8]

The trope of imprisonment is pursued in Başer's second movie, *Farewell to a False Paradise* (*Abschied vom falschen Paradies*, 1989). In the so-called 'guest-worker literature' of the 1970s and early 1980s, the notion of paradise was invariably used ironically to signify the flagrant discrepancy between the immigrants' initial projections of a promised land of opportunity and affluence and their actual hellish reality of discrimination and exploitation. *Farewell to a False Paradise* reverses this trajectory: moving from Turkey to Germany in her teens and sentenced in 1984 to six years in a German jail for the killing of her violent husband, Elif, the film's protagonist, enters what she at first perceives as a netherworld of punishment and humiliation, only to discover an elysian sanctuary offering liberation and a new self-awareness. Mostly shot from Elif's point of view, the film repeatedly underscores through its imagery the ethereal connotations contained in its title. When she falls ill during her period of remand, Elif's sense of isolation is diminished by her joyous discovery of a package dangling on a rope outside her window. Containing an orange and a message wishing her a speedy recovery, this simple gift marks Elif's entry into the clandestine service network the inmates have developed to counter the rigours of prison life. If here the serpentine rope, the forbidden fruit (the orange) and the voice from on high (of the woman in the cell above) evoke the earthly paradise of the Garden of Eden, then this prefigures Elif's subsequent loss of innocence when she is moved to the penitentiary proper. Similarly, her ascent of the prison stairs bathed in a celestial neon light, following directly on from a disembodied male voice pronouncing judgment on her, all suggests the stairway to heaven.

Accordingly, Elif comes to experience this institution as an essentially harmonious environment conducive to female bonding. While still on remand, she is invited by Christine, one of the long-term inmates, to come up and join them in the prison. That Elif's new friend has also killed her husband (albeit, in this instance, to end his suffering not hers) establishes a bond between the two women to which Christine gives an ideological seal with her comment that in similar circumstances men are typically convicted of manslaughter and not, as in their case, murder. In contrast to the other two Turkish women in the prison, who remain steadfastly aloof, Elif quickly realizes that the gestures of female solidarity she receives demand reciprocity on her part. Hence she readily goes along with her caseworker's offer to learn Turkish if Elif will learn German. Indeed, in the case of Gabriella, with whom Elif later shares a cell, the reciprocity borders on the erotic as is evident from a series of short scenes showing the two women talking intimately, eating, smoking and showering together. Correlatively, the strength of this female bonding is underscored by the wholly negative role played in the film by men. Thus prison offers Elif a hitherto unknown freedom to explore new possibilities of female identity and, by integrating herself into this sisterly community, she gradually frees herself from what she now perceives as the patriarchal constrictions of Muslim culture. The most dramatic index of Elif's transformation is her new attitude to clothes, which, initiated by her decision to discard the traditional headscarf, is ultimately symptomatic of her changing sexual identity. The striking image of Elif on the day of her release, dressed in jeans, trainers and a man's jacket, is but the final manifestation of her new self-awareness. Just as telling is her complete lack of self-consciousness as she takes a communal shower and sensuously washes her cellmate's back, since this contrasts markedly with the shame and humiliation she felt on arrival at having to expose her body in the course of a routine strip search.

Seen from Elif's point of view, life in this institution is more than a little idyllic. Judged by empirical standards, too, this jail – where cells are havens of domesticity, where the warders are not particularly authoritarian and where, amongst the inmates, there is no hierarchy, no brutality and, crucially in this context, virtually no racism – does, it is true, represent something of a utopia. The visionary dimension is, however, undercut by the film's conclusion: with her sentence reduced for good behaviour and her emotional ties to her family and her homeland now severed, Elif is to be sent back to Turkey. There she faces either another trial for the same crime, or certain death at the hands of an avenging brother-in-law, a fate she unsuccessfully seeks to avoid by attempting suicide. Furthermore, that Elif's temporary sanctuary itself represents only a 'false paradise' is indicated in the opening credits sequence which, by showing the demolition of the prison, long since officially closed down, symbolizes the necessity for Elif's emancipation to extend beyond the (for her) protective walls of this jail.[9]

The title of Başer's film, however, is susceptible to a different reading, for this prison idyll undoubtedly represents a fake paradise for those who, like Deniz Göktürk, see its matriarchal community not as a microcosm of multicultural integration, but merely as the site of Elif's acculturation. Accordingly, *Farewell to a False Paradise* is informed by a 'social-worker approach' to ethnic relations in so far as it 'illustrates the cinematic imprisonment of immigrants within the parameters of well-meaning multiculturalism feeding on binary oppositions and integrationist desires'.[10] As such it epitomizes a type of cinema that Cameron Bailey has defined in the following terms:

Social issue in content, documentary-realist in style, firmly *responsible* in intention – it positions its subjects in direct relations to social crisis, and attempts to articulate "problems" and "solutions to problems" within a framework of centre and margin.[11]

The 'cinema of the affected', as represented by Başer's work, can thus be seen as continuing the tradition of the 'guest-worker cinema' (*Gastarbeiterkino*) of the New German Cinema, the perspective it brought to bear on the alien culture was one in which the focus was unremittingly on alterity as a seemingly insoluble problem, on conflict of either an intercultural or intracultural variety. Georg Seeßlen has assigned the generic label of 'Kino der Métissage' to films foregrounding such intracultural tensions, in which the family frequently appears as the site where battle is waged between the old and the new culture, between the generations and the sexes.[12] The 1990s, however, saw the emergence of a younger generation of Turkish directors in Germany seemingly motivated by a common desire to break with the dominant image sustained by the 'cinema of the affected', that of the Turk as victim.

A CINEMA OF 'YOUNG TURKS' AND THE SHIFT FROM CULTURAL STEREOTYPES

The difference in approach between the two schools of filmmaking is exemplified in their treatment of one of the 'hot' topics in post-unification Germany, that of political asylum. While Başer's third feature, *Farewell, Stranger* (*Lebewohl, Fremde*, 1991), is a typically earnest and tragic tale, it centres this time, however, not on a female migrant worker but on a male asylum seeker. He is the oppositional writer Deniz Varlin, who has escaped from imprisonment in Turkey and arrives, along with three other political refugees (from India, Pakistan and Africa), on the North Sea island of Langeness to await the outcome of his application for asylum in Germany. Another difference from Başer's previous two films is that the narrative point of view is located not exclusively with the Turkish victim, but also with a German who becomes embroiled in his fate. Hence the film opens with the arrival on the island of Karin, a photographic artist living in Hamburg. She may be an outsider to this community, but since she was born on Langeness her periodic presence on the island is accepted. No such tolerance is shown to the four refugees, who from the outset meet with open hostility. Forced to live in an abandoned builder's wagon, they are deprived of even this primitive abode when it is destroyed in an arson attack; while the mysterious death by drowning of the Pakistani occurs after he embarks on an affair with the daughter of one of the farmers. Finally, when the refugees stay put, the authorities are called in to have them removed from the island. Deniz evades detection only because he is given refuge by Karin, who has befriended him in the meantime. Gradually, despite the absence of verbal communication (since neither of the couple can speak the other's language) the friendship blossoms into a love affair, and this in turn helps sustain Deniz's linguistic creativity. For in a short epilogue the film concludes with Karin, now back in Hamburg, receiving in the post a volume of poems Deniz had written while on the island. The book bears the dedication 'for Karin, whose love gave me a new life'.[13]

Like the film itself, the volume of poetry carries the ambiguous German title *Lebewohl, Fremde*, and in accordance with the more obvious meaning, 'farewell, stranger', the main narrative strand of the movie ends with the couple's brief moment of parting before Deniz is taken away by the police. (As a farewell gesture Deniz wraps his lover's body in his overcoat, in which, as Karin subsequently discovers, he has put the manuscript of his poems.) As well as 'stranger' the word 'Fremde' also has connotations of 'strange land' (as in the meaning 'foreign parts') and, indeed, *Farewell, Stranger* is the only one of Başer's three films to be set in a visually recognizable geographical space. The prison in *Farewell to a False Paradise* is not given a specific location, nor, apart from the flashbacks conveying Elif's memories of her homeland, is the viewer permitted access to any reality external to this institution. *40 m² of Germany* is nominally located in the Hamburg district of St Georg, but the public space shown is restricted to what Turna can see of the street below as she peers through her apartment window. By contrast, *Farewell, Stranger* is set on a tiny Hallig island off Germany's northern coast in Schleswig-Holstein. Yet, for all Başer's exploitation of the topography of this location, the film still exudes the same sense of entrapment and isolation that pervaded his previous work.

For although, unlike those two films, *Farewell, Stranger* is dotted with visually stunning images, the prevalent atmosphere thus evoked is one of an all-pervasive bleakness: boundless icy seas, gloomy grey skies and arid, forbidding landscapes epitomized by the recurring shot of a dilapidated, windswept cemetery, and underscored by the use of long shot that frequently captures those inhabiting these desolate spaces as vulnerable, isolated figures against an omnipresent horizon. All these features coalesce into a strikingly pictorial *mise-en-scène* redolent of a Caspar David Friedrich painting. Nor, despite those scenes portraying the growing rapport between Karin and Deniz, do domestic spaces offer any real refuge from this intrinsically hostile environment. In a manner that recalls Fassbinder's use of domestic interiors to construct images of incarceration (but without that director's recourse to modes of anti-transparency realism) Başer often frames his characters within the horizontal and vertical lines of doorways and windows, so that they appear trapped within the depth of the frame or overpowered by the surrounding space. Moreover, given the relative sparseness of the dialogue, the resulting silences on the soundtrack are conspicuously filled by the aural representation of an inhospitable Nature: crashing waves, howling winds, lashing rain. Two particular moments encapsulate the threat posed to Deniz by an environment to which he is actually appealing for sanctuary. Perturbed by a photograph she has found in his shirt pocket, Karin bursts into Deniz's study and unwittingly unleashes a gust of wind that scatters his manuscript through the open window where he is working. The ensuing, largely futile, paper chase eventually leads him to the burnt-out shell of the builder's wagon, which, as he only now discovers, has been the target of xenophobic violence. If Deniz is thereby confronted with the destructive capacity of wind and fire, that of a third element, water, is demonstrated soon after when a torrential storm floods the island. In an awesome aerial shot – comparable with the spectacular natural vistas that punctuate the films of Werner Herzog – made all the more arresting for its contrast with the predominantly low camera angles used to capture the landscape elsewhere in the film, Başer shows the whole island virtually submerged. He then focuses on Karin's farmhouse, which is now reduced to a tiny plot of land encircled by an irresistibly encroaching sea. Although Deniz and Karin are airlifted to the mainland by a navy helicopter, this apparent act of rescue ultimately proves to be the opposite as he is then immediately handed over to the authorities. When his application for asylum is finally rejected, Deniz is deported back to Turkey where shortly after, as a voice-over and the film's final shot reveal, he dies in prison.

Farewell, Stranger ends with the uncredited intertitle, 'Not to be able to speak in one's own country is worse than death'.[14] Although this might be taken to imply that Deniz had committed suicide,[15] the film as a whole, far from asserting the indispensability of speech, illustrates Zafer Şenocak's contention that intercultural dialogue is not precluded by the absence of a voice:

> When those without speech stand across from each other, they must rely on their senses and their bodies. Their bodies develop a new, immediate relationship to space and thus also to each other. They move and interpret the movements of the Other. They coordinate their movements with one another. They cannot shed the fear of being determined by the Other, but at the same time they are guided by a drive to observe the Other, to recognize him and to know him. There is a process of cognition, at the end of which something like a coexistence of the One with the Other could stand. Recognition, getting to know each other, and acknowledgment are interdependent. They are the physical, pedagogical, and psychological steps in a process that moves inexorably toward the elimination of speechlessness and the development of a new shared language.[16]

This process is also depicted in Sinan Çetin's *Berlin in Berlin* (1993), which likewise centres on the relationship between a German and a Turk who lack the verbal means to communicate. Furthermore, like Başer's three films, *Berlin in Berlin* portrays a figure subjected to extreme confinement, but in a reverse scenario whereby the German finds himself living in a state of quasi-exile within a Turkish family in Berlin. Thomas, an engineer on a building site, becomes infatuated with Dilber, the wife of a Turkish colleague whom he then accidentally kills. Some time later, after trying to re-establish contact with the woman in order to explain his innocence, he is pursued by her brothers-in-law and in his frantic efforts to escape them he breaks into an apartment, only to realize that his place of refuge is none other than the dead man's family home. When his presence is eventually discovered, he is saved from the vengeance-seeking brothers by the insistence of their father and grand-mother that this German is there at God's behest and that so long as he remains under their roof no harm shall befall him. In broader political terms, the German has been granted the equivalent of asylum, but since the safe territory in question only extends as far as the door of the apartment he is in effect trapped there. Thus Thomas's experience of liminality is the mirror-image of that undergone by asylum seekers in Germany: his status as refugee may be decreed by those in authority (in this case, the family elders), but in the rest of the community, the extended family of four generations, he encounters attitudes ranging from mocking curiosity through to bitter resentment and murderous hostility. Gradually, however, there develops a form of uneasy co-existence predicated on a grudging mutual respect, with Thomas being drawn into an increasingly willing participation in the household's customs and rituals.

Like *40 m² of Germany*, Çetin's movie ends with the release of its incarcerated protagonist as, following one final climactic confrontation, Thomas is allowed to leave the apartment accompanied by Dilber. That the viewer is unlikely to respond in the same way to these seemingly similar moments of liberation, however, can be attributed in part to a fundamental formal difference between the two films. Defending his movie against the charge of stoking anti-Islamic sentiment, Başer has rejected the criticism that *40 m² of Germany* merely perpetuates the stereotypes of aggressive (male) villain and passive (female) victim.[17] In Başer's view Dursun is just as much a prisoner as his wife in that he is helpless, unable to adapt and fearful of a society which is foreign to him.[18] Yet, it is less easy for the viewer to empathize with Dursun's situation since the film focuses almost exclusively on Turna's suffering and shows nothing of her husband's life outside the apartment. Moreover, Başer seeks to maximize the degree of identification between the audience and Turna, either by privileging her point of view directly (as, for example, in the scenes of sexual intercourse, which focus on her facial expressions of displeasure and humiliation, and in the use of subjectivized flashbacks and nightmares), or by evoking the hermeticism of her experiential world. The latter is achieved through the prevalence of tightly framed medium shots, close-ups and tracking shots in which the camera itself roams round the flat like a caged animal. Brief, or apparent, shifts in the point of view only serve to emphasize the degree of suture between Turna and the spectatorial position. On one occasion it appears she has plucked up the courage to challenge Dursun over his tyrannical behaviour: in an extended close-up she pleads direct to camera to be allowed more freedom, only for the camera to track back and reveal that, in a speech she can only rehearse but never deliver, she is not addressing her husband but her own reflection in a mirror. On the other occasion when she rebels against her internment, the viewer is similarly locked into Turna's perspective. On the day of the promised outing to the fair, in growing frustration at Dursun's failure to return from supposedly fetching the paper, she angrily pulls on the front door handle and discovers to her astonishment that it is not in fact locked. Venturing apprehensively out of the flat on to the darkened hallway she starts to descend the unlit stairway but abruptly abandons her foray into this uncharted territory when she hears someone coming in down below and the hallway light suddenly comes on. Terror-stricken she rushes back to the safety of the flat, but in her panic tries to open the wrong door and is confronted by an elderly lady, who clearly does not understand a word of Turna's garbled apology. By now a number of other residents have gathered in the hallway. Staring in amazement at this exotic apparition, decked out in all her finery, they react to Turna much in the same way as Dursun had no doubt envisaged. For Turna this brief excursion outside her forty square metres of Germany has become a traumatic ordeal. At this juncture Başer momentarily alters the point of view: whereas for most of the scene he has used *chiaroscuro* and a distorting wide-angled lens, together with an eerily echoing soundtrack to evoke the sense of a nightmare world as Turna perceives it, the dominant visual effect is now the brilliant colour of Turna's garments. Additionally, for once Başer eschews the use of German subtitles, thus placing the viewer in the bedazzled and uncomprehending position of Turna's neighbours, while nevertheless continuing to foreground Turna's emotional state of 'liminal panic',[19] which only ceases when she reaches the safety of her apartment.

Berlin in Berlin contains a sequence very similar to this one, in which Thomas makes his bid for freedom. It begins with a shot of him sitting in his usual position on the floor. All the men in the household have gone out and the mother, who has never approved of Thomas's presence, exploits this opportunity by pointedly leaving the door to the flat open and telling him, in Turkish, that he can go. Moving to the window to check out the street below, Thomas exchanges looks with the grandmother before assuring her, also in Turkish, that he is not a murderer and bidding her farewell, 'In Allah's name'. Çetin then cuts to two of the brothers, Mürtüz and Yüksel, sitting at a table outside the family café. A close-up of a revolver, partly hidden under a newspaper, reveals that Thomas, whose feet are then shown in close-up descending the stairs, has been set up. Reaching the exit to the building, Thomas sees Yüksel crossing the street and realizing that it is a trap he runs back into the tenement courtyard where, reflecting his state of dislocation, the camera executes a 360-degree tracking shot around him, followed by a point-of-view shot of the sky. Any metaphorical connotations of freedom this image may carry are immediately nullified by a graphic match subsequently revealed as the gaze up at the sky by the gun-toting Yüksel standing outside on the street. A repeat close-up of Thomas's feet, now hurriedly ascending the stairs, is followed by a pronounced point-of-view shot down the stairwell of Yüksel hot in pursuit of his prey. Paralleling the identical moment of panic in Turna's retreat in *40 m² of Germany*, Thomas frantically hammers on the door of a woman neighbour, who leaves it on the chain and refuses to answer his anguished cry for help. Çetin then cuts back to the family flat where Dilber surveys the now empty space usually occupied by Thomas. With an inscrutable expression that might signify either relief or disappointment, she moves to the door to the apartment and opens it slightly at precisely the moment that Thomas reaches the threshold. As he steps towards her, the couple exchange looks, and although Dilber then pushes the door to, she leaves it ajar so that Thomas is able to follow her back into the flat and resume his usual seated position on the floor by the window.

This sequence differs from its equivalent in *40 m² of Germany* in one crucial respect: in Çetin's film the point of view is not wedded to the imprisoned protagonist but is dispersed amongst a number of the characters. This formal distinction serves to reinforce the shift from an isolated, oppressed victim with only false hopes of liberation, to an active individual whose efforts at self-emancipation attract alliances (principally from the women of the household). In the case of Dilber, two particular moments in the sequence underscore the sense of a bond burgeoning between her and Thomas. Her act of looking at Thomas through a slight opening in the door, then pushing it to, reprises an earlier scene when she watches him trying to entertain her son, Mustafa. On that occasion, however, her facial expression manifests clear disapproval, which she then signals further by calling the little boy over to her and pointedly shutting the door on Thomas. Secondly, at that point in the escape sequence when Dilber realizes Thomas has gone, there is an abrupt change on the soundtrack from a tense, agitated musical score to a slow, rather schmaltzy theme played on an acoustic guitar. This is in effect a form of aural flashforward since it anticipates the very melody that, in a later scene, Thomas plays on the guitar, ostensibly for the entertainment of the family but clearly meant as a love song to Dilber. Although the film's closing image of the couple walking away from the flat hand-in-hand would suggest that Thomas's feelings for Dilber are reciprocated, for Çetin this is less the tacked-on happy ending typical of melodrama, than an encapsulation of the film's underlying social statement: 'At the end of the film you see that nationality is unimportant. Whenever people live together they are forced to get on.'[20]

Those sentiments would doubtless be endorsed by the Turkish-born director Hussi Kutlucan who chose to make (and star in) a comedy, *Me Boss, You Sneaker* (*Ich Chef, Du Turnschuh*, 1998), out of the unlikely subject matter of political asylum. In a comic odyssey that takes him from the Hamburg docks to a Berlin building site, Dudie, the film's asylum-seeking hero, always manages to rise above adversity. Not even the accidental killing of the young woman Dudie falls for, who has agreed to marry him and thereby provide him quite legitimately with German citizenship, can dent his optimism. Crucially, the audience laughs with, not at, Dudie, not least because refusing to inhabit the role of pitiable victim, he is an empowered (and empowering) figure, who deploys his anarchic humour to resist the attempts of various nefarious Germans to exploit him. In one scene, for example, Dudie hides in a wardrobe from a landlord vociferously demanding his rent. On leaving his refuge and being asked what he was doing there, Dudie replies: 'I was praying. In my religion we pray in the dark',[21] an explanation the landlord accepts without demur. Nor is the film's positive trajectory altered by an ending which sees the hero finally deported, for by this point the bond between Dudie and his dead lover's young son has grown so strong that he leaves Germany as an adoptive father, and thus immeasurably richer than when he arrived.

For all its comic intent, Kutlucan's film still addresses an aspect of Germany's immigration policy that continues to attract controversy. Other young Turkish directors advocate films in which all explicit problematization of alterity is avoided and the issues explored are not principally connected to the question of ethnicity. Thus, describing Deniz, the young woman of migrant background at the centre of his film *A Fine Day* (*Der schöne Tag*, 2000), Thomas Arslan has stated that 'she is a person with her own secrets, contradictions and distinctive features that cannot be reduced to her ethnic origin'.[22] Similarly, *Dealer* (1998) – the second in his trilogy of Berlin films – represents (as the director would have it, at any rate) a psychological portrait of a drug-pusher who just happens to be a Turk, rather than a Turk who is coincidentally a dealer. The same understated approach is applied to the location, for with its coldly detached, observant camera style reminiscent of Fassbinder's early chamber pieces, *Dealer* projects a decidedly anonymous Berlin whose empty streets and somnolent housing estates could be almost anywhere. By contrast, in *Lola + Bilidikid* (1998) Kutlug Ataman foregrounds Berlin's familiar topography as a narrative space populated by Turks drawn from the capital's gay and transvestite scene. Here Germans feature only in passing, as they also do in the Hamburg underworld of Fatih Akin's gangster movie *Short Sharp Shock* (*Kurz und schmerzlos*, 1998). The film centres on three friends: Gabriel the Turk, Bobby the Serb and Costa the Greek, who are caught in a trap of their own making arising from Bobby's hopes of becoming a big name in the Albanian mafia in Hamburg. Throughout, the mixing of ethnicities, far from being problematized, is pointedly underplayed or indeed naturalized. When Gabriel and Costa gently rib their friend about the unlikely constellation of a Serbian working for an Albanian, Bobby responds with an ironic remark about the current vogue for 'multicultural' relations rather than pointing out that a blood-brother friendship between a Turk and a Greek might seem equally improbable. Similarly, when his sister Ceyda breaks up with Costa, Gabriel chides her not because her new lover is German but simply out of loyalty to his friend. His comment that hitherto he had always stood by her might hint at generational tensions in the past, but the film nevertheless carefully eschews the image of the family in exile as the source of cultural conflict.

Akin began his career not as a director but as an actor, and the main reason he started to make his own films was because he was no longer willing to play the 'stereotype Turk' in film productions where 'migrants could only appear in one guise: as a problem'.[23] Admittedly, in their determination to extricate themselves from the discourse of victimization, these filmmakers may run the risk of merely exchanging one set of clichés for another. For movies in which Turks appear variously as pimps, prostitutes, drug-pushers, thieves, petty hoodlums and gangsters might serve to reinforce populist stereotypes of the foreigner as anti-social malingerer or inveterate criminal. Significantly, in *Me Boss, You Sneaker* Kutlucan, although in fact Turkish, chose to make himself Armenian since he did not want to alienate Turks in Germany by playing Dudie as a Turk to be laughed at. While alert to this danger of perpetuating stereotypes, Thomas Arslan nevertheless clings to the hope that 'in using such images as the point of departure it might be possible gradually to dismantle them in such a way that something else becomes visible'.[24] Similarly, whereas the 'cinema of the affected' tended to foreground women, albeit those seemingly 'trapped in subaltern positions',[25] the new transnational cinema appears decidedly male-oriented, either marginalizing women or restricting them to the role of escape route for oppressed or endangered male characters.

A RENAISSANCE IN POLITICAL CINEMA?

Reservations notwithstanding, the recent 'boom in Turkish–German cinema' has been greeted with acclaim, not least by critics detecting a welcome resurgence of political filmmaking.[26] This claim seems somewhat exaggerated and, in truth, more a comment on the state of German cinema since unification, 'a cockily mainstream, brazenly commercial cinema that wants to have no truck with the former quality label "art-cinema"'[27] boasted by its New German Cinema predecessor. This is a 'post-ethnic' cinema only in the sense that it has turned its back on the latter's persistent concern with questions of national identity and big historical themes, whereas for Akin, the term denotes a cinema in which problems of ethnic difference, if not erased from the cultural imaginary altogether, recede ever further into the background.[28] That this can be at the cost of any real engagement with the social and political reality of contemporary Germany, however, becomes apparent if *Short Sharp Shock* is compared even briefly with Mathieu Kassovitz's *La Haine*, the French movie of 1995 that clearly provided Akin with his basic constellation of three ethnically diverse 'angry young men'.

For a film set in Altona, the most prominently multicultural district of Hamburg, *Short Sharp Shock* amazingly avoids even the merest hint of the existence of racial conflict. Indeed, the one German character in the film simply serves to extend the image of ethnic harmony embodied by the mixed-race central trio. Alice, Bobby's German girlfriend, not only runs a jewellery shop with Gabriel's sister but also immediately embarks on a love affair with Gabriel when she ends the relationship with Bobby on account of his links with the mafia. *La Haine*, set in a multi-ethnic working-class suburb of Paris, depicts a milieu evincing both a high degree of racial integration and an increasingly hybridized culture, but in significant contrast to Akin's film, it does so without sweeping racism under the carpet. Inspired in the first instance by the real-life murder of a young Zairean in a Parisian police station, Kassovitz's movie picks up on the well-documented racism of the French police. This is shown in both the racist humiliation to which two of the protagonists are subjected, and in the film's focus on the role of the police in the suburban riots. The prominence of the latter underpins *La Haine*'s portrayal of alienated underclass youth in an environment where chronic male unemployment can only be countered by dealing in drugs or stolen goods, and where the family provides no refuge from social desolation. Significantly, none of the three young men has a visible father, and in their aggressively masculinist stance, manifested both physically through random violence, and rhetorically in their use of backslang as a form of gang-speak, they express their alienation from a society in which, as Ginette Vincendeau has suggested, the only patriarchal figures are the 'bad fathers' of the police.[29]

By contrast, in the opening sequence of *Short Sharp Shock* Gabriel is released from prison to be met by his family including his father, a devout Muslim, who momentarily shocks his son by slapping him in the face. Signalling both his disapproval of his son's misdemeanours and the assertion of paternal authority, this gesture is immediately followed by a loving, conciliatory embrace signifying Gabriel's acceptance back into the family. Three times in the course of the film Gabriel is invited by his father to pray with him. Twice he declines but on the third occasion, following the killing of Bobby and Costa by the Albanian godfather whom Gabriel then executes, the invitation is gratefully accepted: clearly, at a moment of great personal crisis familial and cultural bonds prove to be a source of enduring support.

Correlatively, Akin's film conveys little sense of the city as a constraining environment. Despite the current mass unemployment in Germany – in which the rate amongst the migrant population is double that of the national average – this is not an issue in *Short Sharp Shock*. Newly released from prison, Gabriel not only immediately finds work as a taxi driver, but also by some unexplained process secures a job at the post office for the eminently unemployable Costa. Similarly, the locations of social interaction are many and various, including numerous scenes in comfortable apartments, bars, exotic clubs and discos, while the trio are frequently shown purposefully walking the streets in a manner that suggests a sense of freedom, not boredom. In contrast with the protagonists of the 'cinema of the affected', who typically are constrained by, or even hermetically sealed off from, their German environment, these three characters confidently own these urban spaces. In short, they do not encounter any obvious social exclusion,[30] and their entry into a world of violence appears to be one of their own making. By contrast, the *banlieue* of Kassovitz's making is a desolate, whitewashed estate, comprising multi-storeyed blocks of cramped flats in which the three youths spend as little time as possible. Instead they walk around empty streets, squares and car parks; they meet in a burned-down gym, a vandalized petrol station and an empty train station, with the result that 'the dominant image is of a dead space which visualises the boys' boredom'.[31] That it is, nevertheless, still their terrain becomes apparent when they embark on their disastrous trip to Paris, for at this point Kassovitz executes a change in style. Whereas the estate was shot during the day, in stereo and favouring travelling shots and 'short focal distances to integrate characters in their surroundings', the city was filmed predominantly at night, in mono and with a hand-held camera, using 'long focal distances in order to detach the figures from the background'.[32] This serves to underscore what their subsequent experiences demonstrate, namely that the hapless trio are more at home on the barren estate than in this alien city.

It is symptomatic of the difference in emphasis between the two movies that whereas Kassovitz seeks to differentiate between two environments, Akin also employs separate camera styles but for the purpose of characterizing and individualizing his three protagonists. In short, *La Haine* covers much contested terrain, interweaving as it does 'root causes of social and political unrest in France today: immigration, racism, exclusion, poverty, crime and violence'.[33] Moreover, if the film's continued resonance was dramatically attested to by the startling success of the neo-fascist Jean-Marie Le Pen in the 2002 Presidential elections, then this can be attributed not least to Kassovitz's ability to understand the politics of cinematic language. For although the sociological anchorage of *La Haine* is abundantly clear, it remains at the same time a highly stylized film that is anything but an exercise in bleak naturalism.[34] Akin's aesthetic allegiance, however, is wholly to popular narrative cinema. While the mixing of ethnicities was clearly inspired by *La Haine*, the angry young men of *Short Sharp Shock* are introduced in the manner of *The Good, the Bad and the Ugly* (1966) or *Trainspotting* (1996), with each character given a sequence establishing their persona and culminating in a fusion of freeze-frame and subtitle. Thereafter the three figures are characterized by three different camera styles: Costa is filmed statically and quickly cut; Bobby, in accordance with his restless, nervous character, is shot with a handheld camera; while Gabriel, as the classical hero, is filmed with steady shots and fluid motion. Similarly, Quentin Tarantino's influence is apparent both in some of the slightly surreal, *Pulp Fiction*-type dialogue and in the way Akin attempts to counteract both the melodramatic and the horrifically violent with comic moments. This is illustrated by the scene of the *pietà* in which Gabriel cradles the expiring Costa who uses his dying breath to burst into song. Undoubtedly, however, the real mentor behind Akin's film is Martin Scorsese, both in its reinventing of 'Hamburg as a generic gangster movie location',[35] and in its representation of the three 'Goodfellas' and their life of crime, with no assignment of blame or sociological explanation offered for their actions. Akin's commitment to the models of popular cinema was confirmed by his second feature film, *In July* (*Im Juli*, 2000), a romantic road movie in which a chance encounter with a beautiful young Turkish woman inspires a somewhat hapless German teacher to embark on a journey across south-eastern Europe in pursuit of the girl of his dreams. In fact, the latter turns out to be the equally beautiful young German woman who accompanies him on this quest. Here both the choice of genre and the casting (featuring two of Germany's most bankable stars, Moritz Bleibtreu and Christiane Paul) clearly evidence aspirations to be a commercial filmmaker on the part of a director who proclaims he has 'no message to impart' and 'simply wants to tell a cool story'.[36]

Post-unification Germany, notable less for cool stories than for outbursts of xenophobia, racial violence and the periodic recrudescence of right-wing extremism, has shown itself to be anything but a post-ethnic society. Just as the 'cinema of the affected' arose in part as a response to certain socio-political conditions, so the present climate in the Federal Republic, in which migrants do all too often find themselves in the position of victim, hardly renders anachronistic renewed efforts at 'cultural resistance'. That this need not be incompatible with the shift towards a transnational cinema is evident from *Lola + Bilidikid*. Among the few Germans featuring in Ataman's film are a small band of neo-Nazi youths, who repeatedly menace the Turkish transvestite Lola, and her gay little brother, Murat. Although the viewer is invited (mistakenly) to assume it is these racists who have murdered Lola, their role in the narrative transcends that of supplying a twist in the plot, and extends to a tragic denouement in which (quite possibly to the viewer's pleasure) Lola's Turkish lover exacts a bloody retribution. This political subtext is underscored by the use of Berlin's landmarks: for example, Murat, persecuted as much for his sexuality as on racial grounds, is first beaten up by the modern fascist thugs in the historically resonant environment of the Olympia Stadium; while Lola's corpse is discovered floating in the Landwehr Canal where, in another era, the most famous victim of the ultra-nationalist right, Rosa Luxemburg, was dumped. That such historical specificities are seamlessly integrated into a film which successfully contests essentialist notions of identity marks it out as the work of a director who clearly can think both within and beyond Turkish–German parameters, and exploit productively the tension generated by the push-and-pull between national and transnational cinemas. It is undoubtedly one measure of its political versatility that *Lola + Bilidikid* was shown in London at three different festivals in 1999: the Festival of Turkish Cinema, the Festival of German Cinema and the Festival of Gay Cinema.[37] Moreover, as demonstrated by such (otherwise quite different) films as Kadir Sözen's *Winter Flower* (*Winterblume*, 1996), Yilmaz Arslan's *Yara* (1998) and Ayşe Polat's *The Foreign Tour* (*Die Auslandstournee*, 1999), popular forms like the road movie can be deployed in the service of socially engaged narratives without compromising their makers' serious intent. Just when international cinema is exploring the issues of immigration and asylum with a new urgency, as evidenced by a recent wave of movies such as Pawel Pawlikowski's *Last Resort* (2001), Stephen Frears' *Dirty Pretty Things* (2002), Michael Winterbottom's *In This World* (2003) and Lukas Moodysson's *Lilya 4-Ever* (2003), it would seem a strange moment for the German cinema to abandon what, over the last twenty years, has been one of its principal social and political concerns.[38]

Notes

1 'Sub-state cinemas […] may be defined ethnically in terms of suppressed, indigenous, diasporic, or other populations asserting their civil rights and giving expression to a distinctive religion, language, or regional culture. Catalan, Québecois, Aboriginal, Chicano and Welsh cinemas are examples.' Stephen Crofts, 'Concepts of National Cinema' in John Hill and Pamela Church Gibson (eds.), *Oxford Guide to Film Studies* (Oxford and New York: Oxford University Press, 1998), pp. 385–94 (p. 390).

2 Arlene Akiko Teroaka, 'Talking "Turk": On Narrative Strategies and Cultural Stereotypes', *New German Critique*, 46 (1989), pp.104–26 (pp. 117 and 119).

3 Compare Stefan Reinecke, 'Projektive Übermalungen: Zum Bild des Ausländers im deutschen Film' in Ernst Karpf, Doron Kiesel and Karsten Visarius (eds.), *"Getürkte Bilder": Zur Inszenierung von Fremden im Film* (Marburg: Schüren, 1995), pp. 9–19 (p. 15); Annette Brauerhoch, 'Die Heimat des Geschlechts – oder mit der fremden Geschichte die eigene erzählen: Zu *Shirins Hochzeit* von Helma Sanders-Brahms' in *"Getürkte Bilder"*, pp. 109–15.

4 Sarita Malik, 'Beyond "the Cinema of Duty"? The Pleasures of Hybridity: Black British Film of the 1980s and 1990s' in Andrew Higson (ed.), *Dissolving Views: Key Writings on British Cinema* (London: Cassell, 1996), pp. 202–15 (p. 204).

5   'Literatur der Betroffenen' ('Literature of the Affected') is the title of a programmatic essay by Franco Biondi and Rafik Schami, in *Zu Hause in der Fremde: Ein bundesdeutsches Ausländer-Lesebuch*, ed. by Christian Schaffernicht (Fischerhude: Atelier im Bauernhaus, 1981; Reinbek bei Hamburg: Rowohlt, 1984), pp. 136–50. In 1980 Biondi and Schami had been instrumental in setting up the so-called PoLi-Kunstverein (Association for Polynational Literature and Art) and the publishing collective Südwind, who organized a series of anthologies of literary texts in German by immigrant writers called 'Südwind gastarbeiterdeutscher', a title specifically designed to draw attention to the authors' outsider status in relation to both their social experience and the dominant culture.

6   Born in 1951, Başer studied at the College of Visual Arts (Hochschule für bildende Künste) in Hamburg and acquired German citizenship in 1989. His work, which includes both fiction and non-fiction films, is much garlanded in Germany: his first two feature films were nominated for the Federal Film Prize and his third (all discussed above) served as Germany's official entry to the Cannes Film Festival in 1991.

7   See Franz Ulrich, 'Parabel über eine Gettosituation – Interview mit Tevfik Başer', *Zoom*, 38.17 (1986), pp. 13–16 (p. 14).

8   Ulrich, 'Parabel über eine Gettosituation', p. 14

9   Alternatively, this sequence might serve to underscore the intended 'parable' nature of Başer's film (Ulrich, 'Parabel über eine Gettosituation', p. 16), for as the viewer watches Elif's story unfold, s/he is already aware that, even at the fictional level, this institution does not exist.

10   Deniz Göktürk, 'Turkish Women on German Streets: Closure and Exposure in Transnational Cinema' in Myrto Konstantarakos (ed.), *Spaces in European Cinema* (Exeter and Portland: intellect, 2000), pp. 64–76 (p. 68).

11   Quoted in Malik, 'Beyond "the Cinema of Duty"?', pp. 203–4.

12   Georg Seeßlen, 'Vertraute Fremde', *Freitag*, 17 May 2002, pp.11–13 (p. 11). In Başer's work this 'position between two cultures' is exemplified by the changes and attendant tensions experienced by Elif in *Farewell to a False Paradise*; at its most problematical, if not to say most simplistic, it is epitomized by the fate of the eponymous heroine in Hark Bohm's *Yasemin* (1988), a Turkish 'Juliet' imperilled by her romance with a German 'Romeo'. In the 1990s, films centring on the family, such as Thomas Arslan's *Brothers and Sisters* (*Geschwister Kardesler*, 1996) and Yüksel Yavuz's *April Children* (*Aprilkinder*, 1998), typically no longer depict life between two cultures as inevitably posing an existential threat to their protagonists; rather, the intention is to show how reaction to, and identity in, an 'in-between culture' can take myriad forms.

13   'Für Karin, deren Liebe mir ein neues Leben gab'.

14   'In seinem eigenen Land nicht sprechen zu können, ist schlimmer als der Tod'.

15   The film's final shot of Deniz's body slumped on the floor in the prison corridor would suggest otherwise, however, particularly as it reprises the moment in one of his nightmare sequences where he is taken out of his cell and brutally beaten up. Moreover, the fact that the voice-over narrating the circumstances of Deniz's death is accompanied by the sound of a howling wind would seem to evoke the part played in his tragic end by the country that had refused him asylum.

16   Zafer Şenocak, *Atlas of a Tropical Germany: Essays on Politics and Culture, 1990–1998*, tr. and ed. by Leslie A. Adelson (Lincoln and London: University of Nebraska Press, 2000), pp. 47–8.

17   See Sigrid Weigel, 'Literatur der Fremde – Literatur in der Fremde' in Klaus Briegleb and Sigrid Weigel (eds.), *Gegenwartsliteratur* (Munich: Deutscher Taschenbuch Verlag, 1992), pp. 182–229 (p. 223); Heidrun Suhr, '*Ausländerliteratur*: Minority Literature in the Federal Republic of Germany', *New German Critique*, 46 (1989), 71–103 (p. 95).

18   Ulrich, 'Parabel über eine Gettosituation', pp. 14–15.

19   Hamid Naficy, 'Phobic Spaces and Liminal Panics: Independent Transnational Film Genre' in Rob Wilson and Wimal Dissanayake (eds.), *Global/Local: Cultural Productions and the Transnational Imaginary* (Durham and London: Duke University Press, 1996), pp. 119–44.

20   Quoted in Christoph Wingender, 'Berlin als Paradigma einer kulturellen Werkstatt' in Michael Kessler and Jürgen Wertheimer (eds.), *Multikulturalität: Tendenzen, Probleme, Perspektiven im europaischen und internationalen Horizont* (Tübingen: Stauffenburg, 1995), pp.165–75 (pp. 174–5).

21   'Ich habe gebetet. In meiner Religion betet man im Dunkeln'.

22   Quoted in Tobias Hering, 'Irgendwo muss das Leben ja stattfinden', *Freitag*, 23 November 2001, p. 48.

23   Quoted in Moritz Dehn, 'Die Türken vom Dienst', *Freitag*, 26 March 1999, p. 13.

24   Quoted in Dehn, 'Die Türken vom Dienst', p. 13.

25   Göktürk, 'Turkish Women on German Streets', p. 74.

26   See Dehn, 'Die Türken vom Dienst', p. 13; Georg Seeßlen, 'Leben in zwei Kulturen', *Kulturchronik*, 18.5 (2000), pp. 38–42; Seeßlen, 'Vertraute Fremde', pp. 11–13.

27   Thomas Elsaesser, 'Introduction: German Cinema in the 1990s' in Thomas Elsaesser and Michael Wedel (eds.), *The BFI Companion to German Cinema* (London: BFI, 1999), pp. 3–16 (p. 3).

28   See Ania Faas, 'Papa Courage', *KulturSpiegel*, 8 (2000), pp. 13–15 (p. 14).

29   Ginette Vincendeau, 'Designs on the *Banlieue*: Mathieu Kassovitz's *La Haine*' in Susan Hayward and Ginette Vincendeau (eds.), *French Film: Texts and Contexts* (London: Routledge, 2000), pp. 310–27 (p. 316).

30   On the other hand, through its focus on crime, the underworld and dealing in drugs and illegal arms the film does encapsulate one striking feature of Hamburg in the late 1990s. With an estimated 10,000 drug addicts, over 2,000 dealers and a robbery every three minutes Hamburg had the highest per capita crime rate in Germany and one which in 2001 leapt by 12%. See *The Guardian*, 18 May 2002, p. 17.

31   Vincendeau, 'Designs on the *Banlieue*', p. 313.

32   Myrto Konstantarakos, 'Which Mapping of the City? *La Haine* (Kassovitz, 1995) and the *cinéma de banlieue*' in Phil Powrie (ed.), *French Cinema in the 1990s: Continuity and Difference* (Oxford and New York: Oxford University Press, 1999), pp. 160–71 (p. 163).

33   Kevin Elstob, 'Hate (*La Haine*)', *Film Quarterly*, 51.2 (1997), 44–9 (p. 45).

34   For a discussion of the ways in which *mise-en-scène* in *La Haine* supports its social project, see Vincendeau, 'Designs on the *Banlieue*', pp. 316–23.

35   Göktürk, 'Turkish Women on German Streets', p. 72.

36   Quoted in Faas, 'Papa Courage', p. 14.

37   For drawing this to my attention I am indebted to Deniz Göktürk, who has, however, long argued against some of the assumptions about political cinema informing this chapter. The most recent statement of her position is to be found in Deniz Göktürk, 'Beyond Paternalism: Turkish German Traffic in Cinema' in Tim Bergfelder, Erica Carter and Deniz Göktürk (eds.), *The German Cinema Book* (London: BFI, 2002), pp. 248–56.

38   Significantly, Fatih Akin's most recent film marks a distinct move in the direction of the 'cinema of *métissage*'. For in *Head On* (*Gegen die Wand*, 2004) Akin has addressed directly the question of intracultural conflict, albeit while remaining true to his credo that the representation of intergenerational tensions should not merely reproduce or reinforce cultural stereotypes. One measure of the film's success in achieving that aim was the award of the Golden Bear at the 2004 Berlin International Film Festival, the first time in eighteen years that a German entry has won the prize for best film.

Chapter 6

In search of home:
filming post-unification Berlin

David Clarke

It goes without saying that capital cities and representations of them have a significant function in defining national self-perceptions. This is especially the case for Berlin, in that it achieved its status as 'a full-blown metropolis, totally unlike any other city in Germany'[1] only in the latter decades of the nineteenth century, in the same period as the Germans came to terms with their situation as part of a newly united Empire under the Hohenzollerns. The buildings of the Wilhelmine period, including the Victory Column (*Siegessäule*), the Cathedral and the Reichstag, all testify to a desire for national self-assertion, as channelled through the dynastic ambitions of the Prussian emperors. Under Adolf Hitler and his architect Albert Speer, the link between city building and empire building took on even greater proportions in Speer's plans for the transformation of the city into 'Germania', a capital of ten million dominated by an architecture which was to serve as a monument to Germany's (and Hitler's) new greatness.

In the wake of World War II, the city, at least in cinematic terms, became a metaphor for the senseless destruction of the conflict unleashed by National Socialism and for the disorientation of the immediate postwar situation.[2] As it became clear that the Western allies would not be able to co-operate with the Soviets after the defeat of Nazi Germany, Berlin came to represent the faultline between the capitalist West and the communist East, a division which found its most potent symbol in the Berlin Wall which was erected by the communist leaders of the German Democratic Republic in August 1961. Until the euphoria of the opening of that same Wall in November

1989, the city represented national division and the burden of the past, rather than national unity and self-confidence.[3]

Since unification, the place of the capital in debates surrounding Germany's past and the shape of its future as a nation has, unsurprisingly, been central. Indeed, as Frank Trommler puts it, the last decade has seen an 'explosion of symbolism' in the city.[4] The decision of the Federal Parliament on 20 June 1991 to relocate the legislature and the government to Berlin raised spectres of an uncomfortable past, and some commentators warned that the city's associations with an aggressive nationalism were too strong.[5] The urban fabric of the city has proved to be equally controversial, with various heated debates focusing on what should be removed, what should be added, and what should be altered in order to create a capital which looks forward without forgetting the horrors of the past. Berlin is, in this sense, a 'palimpseste'[6] and a 'haunted' city,[7] in which even street names become a site of ideological struggle. More visible architectural changes, such as the removal in 1992 of the gigantic Lenin memorial on what is now called United Nations Square (Platz der Vereinigten Nationen) in east Berlin, the slow demolition of Erich Honecker's Palace of the Republic (Palast der Republik) or the building of a Holocaust memorial adjacent to the redeveloped Postdamer Platz have all been the source of sometimes bitter disputes in Berlin and beyond.[8]

Turning towards the future, however, Berlin has also been celebrated as the habitat of a new, resourceful, go-getting generation,[9] and as one of the hot spots of a pan-European youth culture epitomized by the annual 'Love Parade' open-air rave.[10] The city has been perceived as a work in progress, the ballet of the cranes above the city's skyline over the last ten years providing a powerful image for the new start promised by the coining of the term 'the Berlin Republic'. Berlin is, as Bodo Mohrshäuser suggests, 'the capital of unification'[11] and thus plays an important symbolic role in any possible redefinition of what it means to be German in the twenty-first century.

This sense of German-ness as an identity still under construction, which finds its metaphorical counterpart in the material transformation of the city, is suggested, as Sabine Hake observes, in the title of one of the most popular Berlin films of the 1990s, Wolfgang Becker's *Life Is a Building Site* (*Das Leben ist eine Baustelle*, 1997).[12] However, in this chapter

I will argue that representations of life in Berlin in the 1990s tend to formulate a notion of belonging which eschews any reference to anything resembling a national identity. Instead, the films examined here show characters in search of forms of identification and belonging which are largely restricted to a private sphere based primarily around the heterosexual couple and, to an extent, on makeshift families. Equally, while the one representative of the New German Cinema considered here, namely Wim Wenders, still refers to the National Socialist past and its continuities in the present, younger filmmakers show little concern with Berlin's and Germany's history.

Neither do these films refer to the oft-invoked German 'dream' of *Heimat*,[13] that largely focuses on the myth of that sense of belonging and rootedness in a community which offers an implicit alternative to the alienation of urban modernity. This was seen, for example, in the *Heimatfilm* genre of the 1950s and 1960s.[14] Nevertheless, such forms of localized belonging have historically been possible in Berlin, whether in the Berliner's identification with his or her neighbourhood (*Kiez*),[15] or in the more limited, 'studied inwardness' of the '*Hinterhof* [tenement courtyard] mentality' which Peter Fritzsche sees as characteristic of West Berlin in the 1970s and 1980s.[16] As Kevin Robbins points out, the city has never only evoked feelings of 'alienation and disorientation': 'the liberating diversity of the city has equally been associated with new possibilities for encounter and solidarity'.[17] This hope that the urban environment might be the locus of new forms of identification, liberated from the ties of tradition, can be found in discourses as diverse as Engels's writings on the working class,[18] and the attempts of postmodern architects to combat what are regarded as the deterritorializing effects of impersonal and uniform modernist style.[19] However, it is neither the public solidarity of class nor the re-assertion of the distinctive character of the neighbourhood which are foregrounded in the films to be analysed here, but rather the privatized realm of the romantic relationship and the family, the latter being to an extent redefined. As will become clear in the course of this chapter, this strategy may be regarded as one response to the condition of urban postmodernity.

WINGS OF DESIRE

Wim Wenders' *Wings of Desire* (*Der Himmel über Berlin*, 1986) is not only one of the most internationally acclaimed German films of the postwar period, but also a harbinger of the tendencies outlined above. As such, it will provide, along with its post-unification sequel *Far Away, So Close!* (*In weiter Ferne, so nah!*, 1994), a useful introduction to my analysis of Berlin films in the 1990s. David Harvey has observed that *Wings of Desire* may be read as an allegory of the postmodern condition.[20] The point of view of the angels Damiel and Cassiel represents a nostalgia for a sense of belonging and interconnectedness that the mortals they observe no longer have access to. The latter remain locked in their isolated concerns and in the discrete spaces which they inhabit. This can be seen in one of the film's early scenes in which the camera moves between the various rooms of a flat in which a confused young man, his mother and his father are all sat apart from each other, lost in their own thoughts. As they cannot hear each other's interior monologues, which form part of the angels' privileged knowledge, there seems to be little hope of communication or understanding between them. The city's fragmentation into a series of disconnected spaces is made still more apparent on Damiel's entry into the human world, when a young girl asks him for directions. The angel can recite a long and complicated set of instructions to the girl, demonstrating his abstract knowledge of the city as an interconnected whole, but this is not comprehensible to the child, who walks away frustrated, much to Damiel's amusement.

That the former angel cannot communicate his experience of the interconnectedness of the city, which is not part of the lived reality of its inhabitants, does not, however, mean that human beings are condemned to the kind of alienation witnessed in the scene in the flat described above. Redemption from alienation can be achieved, as the example of Damiel and the trapeze artist Marion demonstrates, in the heterosexual relationship. The apparent inability of human beings to find meaning in a society within which – like the city that is its metaphorical represen-tation – they lead isolated existences, can be remedied by commitment to another individual and the improvised 'story' which they create for each other in their relationship. The 'homelessness' which is associated with the post-traditional world[21] expresses itself for Marion as an absence of any 'fate' which could give individual lives meaning. However this can be compensated for by a conscious decision to commit oneself to a personal project, in this case her love for Damiel: 'This must be the end of chance! [...] I don't know if there is such a thing as fate, but there is such a thing as a decision!'[22] Whilst the figure of Homer, the aging writer, mourns the loss of a single story that could address the whole of a society in which 'one person knows nothing of the other',[23] Marion and Damiel are content with a story which makes sense for them as a couple without making any wider claim to validity for others.

The fragmentation of space observable in *Wings of Desire*, which finds a parallel in the fragmentation of human society, has another consequence in that spaces and the individuals who inhabit them become largely interchangeable. This theme is introduced by the fundamental questions of the child described in the text which Damiel is transcribing at the beginning of the film. Here the sense of place is linked with the sense of self: 'Why am I me and not you? [...] Why am I here and why not there?'[24] Without a sense of belonging to a particular place, these words suggest, we are not clearly distinguishable from other individuals. Equally, if we cannot justify our attachment to any one particular place, then our relationships with those who share that place with us become contingent, further unsettling our sense of self. As Marion observes of a previous lover: 'I was with a man, in love and I could just as well have left him standing and gone off with someone we met on the street.'[25] Her relationship with Damiel will be different, however, because of their deliberate decision to create a 'story' together, founded on an ideal of romantic love. This abandonment of nostalgia for any universally accepted 'grand narrative' (figured here as the lost belief in a 'fate' determined by a now absent God) in favour of a personal and localized story which allows these individuals to make sense of the world in their own terms is clearly a postmodern strategy.[26]

In *Wings of Desire*, the causes of the loss of the 'grand narrative', and of the fragmentation to which human society is subject as a result, are not clearly articulated. In *Far Away, So Close!*, however, money, or rather globalized capitalism, takes on a central role. Cassiel, who follows Damiel into the human world, does so in order to do good in the world, not to be with a woman and to have a family, as Damiel has done by the beginning of the second film. This desire to do good, however, is formulated in terms of his desire to overcome the distance between the human beings that he observes from his angelic viewpoint. The message he wants to carry to humanity is that of an empathy which could overcome the fragmentation of human society, represented again by the city of Berlin. As he says at the beginning of the film: 'We are messengers, bringing closeness to those who are far away.'[27] Despite initial attempts to do 'good works', Cassiel is driven to drink and desperation by the pervasive 'loneliness' ('Einsamkeit') of the city:

> ... nobody hears what is going on inside other people, nobody sees into the hearts of others. [...] Everybody creates their own world in their own hearing and seeing. And they are prisoners in it. And from their cells they see the cells of the others.[28]

Cassiel's attendance at a concert by American rock star Lou Reed crystallizes his dilemma by posing, in song form, the question 'why can't I be good?' Reed makes another appearance when Cassiel is begging, drunk on the streets, but Cassiel makes the mistake of taking Reed's offer of dollars as a response to the dilemma posed in the earlier song. The seeming illogicality of Cassiel's decision to set about making money as a possible answer to the question 'why can't I be good?', which may be mitigated by his inebriated state at the time, nevertheless leads him to discover the root cause of his failure to bring 'closeness' to the people of Berlin. The German–American gangster, Anton Becker, whose henchman he becomes, is the descendant of an escaped Nazi politician who makes a good deal of his money by trading pornography for arms in the former communist bloc. Becker provides a rather crude symbol for the exploitative and amoral characteristics of globalized capitalism. However, his business also provides an important lesson in the way in which such dealings effect the relationship between that which is 'far away' ('in weiter Ferne'), and that which is 'so close' ('so nah'). Becker takes pornography, the production of which is inherently exploitative, and swaps it for arms from another part of the world, which he then sells on to somewhere else. From inside his anonymous bunker beneath Berlin, Becker co-ordinates the harm done by human beings to others they will never meet through the mechanism of the global market: they are connected to each other by means of their transactions with Becker, yet remain ignorant of the damage they do to each other.

Becker's activities are implicitly linked to National Socialism, though the film does not provide the viewer with a clear understanding of the relationship it perceives between fascism and global capitalism. Becker's cynical belief that 'if we don't do it someone else will' certainly shows that inability to empathize with other human beings which Cassiel seeks to overcome, yet the fact of his Nazi parentage, and the revelation that the bunker he is using was built as a store for 'everything the Nazis ever photographed' suggest a link between Becker's activities and those of the National Socialists. To drive this point home, Cassiel later uses one of Becker's father's propaganda films as a fuse to blow up his video copying equipment.

Significantly, families play a key role in the sabotaging of Becker's business and the rescue of Cassiel's friends from the German gangster Patzke, who would like to muscle in on Becker's enterprises. Damiel and Marion, as well as the family-like community of the circus artists, described by their leader as 'my children' ('mes enfants'), help Cassiel to steal the contents of the weapons store. Moreover, when the barge carrying the weapons is hijacked by Patzke and his henchmen, Cassiel lays down his life to save Damiel, Marion and their daughter, as well as the circus artists and the newly reunited family of Becker, his sister and her daughter Raissa. Here Becker is apparently redeemed by his reinsertion into this family, and at one point even tries to sacrifice himself in place of Raissa, who Patzke is threatening to shoot if he does not get his own way. The final scene of the film sees all of these families huddled together on the barge as it sails out of the city into a lovingly photographed, mist-covered landscape. This evokes a space beyond the city in which, at least within the context of the family, it is possible for human beings to rediscover the empathy of what Cassiel, in his final monologue calls 'the loving look' ('der liebevolle Blick'). In this sense, Cassiel's mission to bring a sense of 'closeness' to the inhabitants of the city succeeds in a limited way: it is the intimacy of family, as a counterpart to the heterosexual couple foregrounded in *Wings of Desire*, which is presented as a site of resistance to the sense of disconnected-ness associated with the city, and now projected onto the globalized capitalist system.

The influence of Wenders' *Wings of Desire*, on a formal if not on a thematic level, can be directly observed in post-unification depictions of Berlin in the documentary films *Berlin Babylon* (Hubertus Siegbert, 2001) and Uli M. Schüppel's *The Square* (*Der Platz*, 1996). Both of these films, which deal with the reconstruction of the city, echo Wenders' master-piece: the former through its use of a camera which glides slowly over the city as if from the point of view of an angel, before descending to focus on the lives of particular inhabitants of the new capital; the latter in its use of voice-overs which give the viewer access to the thoughts of building workers on the new Potsdamer Platz, thus recalling the eavesdropping of Wenders' angels. However, the importance attached to the heterosexual romance as a postmodern refuge from the city is recalled in what may at first seem a rather unlikely context: namely, in Tom Tykwer's fast-paced box-office success *Run Lola Run* (*Lola rennt*, 1998).[29]

RUN LOLA RUN

Although often neglected by commentaries on Tykwer's film, the director himself has described those scenes in which we see Manni and Lola lying in bed discussing their relationship and their future as 'the secret heart of the film'.[30] Despite what one critic calls 'the limited intellectual depth of the conversations',[31] the questions posed recall themes already highlighted in *Wings of Desire*. In the first of these scenes, Lola asks Manni if he is sure that he loves her, since, after all, 'I could be some other woman'.[32] Here, Lola's comments echo those of Marion in *Wings of Desire* when describing her former lover. In the second, Manni asks Lola what she would do if he were to die, ultimately convinced that Lola would find a replacement for him.[33] These conversations frame questions which recall those of Damiel's text about 'the child' in Wenders' film: 'Why am I me and not you? Why am I here and why not there?', i.e. why am I this person rather than any other, and why is it me in this situation when it could be anyone else? In *Wings of Desire*, of course, Marion and Damiel actively choose their 'story', that is to say their reason for being who they are and where they are, through their love affair. In this way, as Skidmore observes,[34] they escape the kind of contingency which apparently haunts Manni and Lola's relationship. In *Run Lola Run*, the romantic partnership still contains the possibility highlighted in *Wings of Desire*, but this is now set in the context of a struggle for economic survival in capitalist society, presented in a highly stylized manner against the backdrop of 1990s Berlin.

Despite the potential disharmony which Lola's conversations with Manni express, I would argue that these two scenes represent Lola's ultimate goal. Throughout the three 'rounds' of the film she is attempting to get back into the same frame, in filmic terms, as Manni. The rapid cutting between their two faces as they talk on the phone at the beginning of the first 'run' highlights both their distance from each other, which is the challenge Lola must overcome, and their desperate need to share a single place: the rapid alternation of the shots of the young woman and her boyfriend almost seem to merge the two spaces they occupy into one. Lola's desire to be in the same frame as Manni is most evident in the moments leading up to their first two meetings outside the supermarket, where the screen is split to show Lola running towards the camera simultaneously with a shot of Manni outside the doors of the shop. In the version where Manni actually enters the supermarket to rob it, Lola appears in both halves of the split screen as she arrives, but only as Manni leaves the frame to begin his robbery. In the final happy ending, of course, the couple are caught in a freeze-frame close-up, smiling as they walk away together against the neutral backdrop of an anonymous street scene. As in the scenes in bed, Lola and Manni occupy a space apparently divorced from the city around them. However, to preserve this private realm, founded on their romantic relationship, they have to go into the city and make money, whether it be in their careers as small-time criminals or in the caricatured form of Lola's race across the city to find 100,000 DM in order to save Manni's life.

Lola has a highly instrumentalized view of the city. Her task is to follow the most efficient route to find the money and to arrive in a certain place at a certain time, as she had earlier failed to do when she was late for her appointment with Manni. She has no time to engage with those spaces she must move through or with the people she encounters. Lola's complete detachment from her environment, whose streets are reduced to a series of largely empty spaces through which she moves at speed,[35] is illustrated by the short sequences of stills which outline the fate of those people Lola passes by. These biographies may be clichéd, consisting of tales of lottery wins, drug addiction, romance and religious conversion, but the detachment with which even the unhappiest of these condensed stories is presented to the audience echoes Lola's indifference to them. After all, it is only the viewer who hangs back for these brief glimpses into these other lives, whereas Lola is already further down the street. The book which Tykwer published to accompany his film, containing the screenplay and various commentaries by the director, attempts to make good Lola's indifference to those she encounters by providing biographical notes on the these figures. Norbert the tramp, for example, turns out to be a disillusioned '68er fallen on hard times.[36] However, these texts only serve to highlight Lola's lack of engagement with these figures. They are fleshed out in the book with distinct biographies, desires and dreams but remain irrelevant to Lola's pursuit of her goal within the film.

The opening sequence, in which a large crowd of extras forms into letters which spell out the film's title, provides an appropriate metaphor for the city of Berlin as experienced by Lola. The camera wanders amongst a crowd of faceless men and women, occasionally picking out individuals whose paths Lola will cross during her three races against the clock. They do not move or speak – with the exception of Schuster, the security guard at Lola's father's bank – and their distinction from the crowd, in which they stand immobile as it moves around them, is arbitrary. It is only their chance meeting with Lola which marks them out, if only minimally, from the anonymous mass. As has already been observed, the streets of Berlin in *Run Lola Run* are never as crowded as this, but the mass presented here is not in any real sense present to Lola. For her, as the security guard suggests, the city is the space in which she must play a game, the prize taking precedence over engagement with the individuals she meets during her race.

In this sense, Lola's behaviour recalls accounts of the postmodern city proposed by theorists such as Zygmunt Baumann and Richard Senett. As Baumann observes, in analyses of the postmodern condition the notion of the subject as a 'nomad', indicating the rootlessness of individual lives, has gained a certain currency. However, Baumann argues, nomadism is an inappropriate metaphor here, since nomads move between distinct places with particular characteristics and, by staying there for limited but prolonged periods, must interact with these new environments. Rather, he suggests, postmodern subjects, especially in an urban context, are 'tourists', moving through the city whilst failing to engage either with the places or the people they encounter. Postmodern tourists are '[i]n, but not of. […] Physically close, spiritually remote'.[37] Senett writes in comparable terms of the urbanite as a 'traveller' who, 'like the television viewer, experiences the world in narcotic terms; the body moves passively, desensitized in space, to destinations set in a fragmented urban geography'.[38]

As Henri Lefebvre suggests in his seminal 1974 study *The Production of Space*, the fragmentation of the urban environment can be attributed to the workings of the capitalist system. Lefebvre argues that capitalism has a tendency to turn all places into 'abstract space', which he conceives of as simultaneously homogenized and functionalized.[39] Capitalism, Lefebvre proposes, takes hold of all space and subordinates it to the needs of the market, so that in effect each space becomes only an interchangeable building block in a global system. For the market, he argues, one space is no different from another. At the same time, these spaces become fractured and disconnected in that they can be linked together only by means of their organization by the market, rather than, for example, by their physical proximity. Seen in Lefebvre's terms, Lola has a distinctly capitalist attitude to space: first, she has a clear financial goal; second, she links together spaces which would otherwise remain incoherent in order to reach that goal; finally, each of the locations she passes through is an interchangeable element which she instrumentalizes in order to achieve her aim. This is particularly evident in Lola's final run, in which she succeeds not by running faster and beating the clock, or by being more persuasive towards her father so that he might give her the money, but by adding a new destination to her run, namely the casino. The spaces of the city thus become pieces of a puzzle which Lola rearranges as she pleases in order to achieve her own ends. This is perhaps the real sense of the motto which Tykwer ascribes to Lola in his description of her: 'I make the world as I like it'.[40]

Lola's attitude to the city is also reflected in the means employed by Tykwer in filming Berlin as a backdrop for his heroine's adventures.

Tykwer lays particular stress in interview on the artificiality of the world he creates for Lola,[41] and an analysis of the actual locations which are used in the film, such as that undertaken by Margit Sinka,[42] reveals that the director has created a montage of spaces which in the real Berlin could never be linked together in the sequence shown in Lola's journey. In this way, just as Lola rearranges the spaces which she runs through until she achieves her goal, so the director himself creates a collage of disparate locations in order to shoot his film.

The Berlin of *Run Lola Run* is thus constructed of fragmented and interchangeable spaces inhabited by anonymous individuals. As already observed, however, Manni and Lola attempt to escape these spaces and establish a sense of belonging through their love for each other. Like Damiel and Marion in *Wings of Desire*, they want to be unique and irreplaceable to each other, and to clearly belong together in a particular place by virtue of their relationship. In the scenes in bed, the romantic myth that Lola is 'the only woman' ('die einzige Frau') for Manni, is to some extent presented ironically by the red lighting, the colour used here as a conventional sign of passion. Nevertheless, it is to save this sense of belonging, as much as to save Manni's life, that Lola runs.

This over-investment in the romantic relationship as a source of identity in postmodern society is addressed by the sociologists Ulrich Beck and Elisabeth Beck-Gernsheim in their book *The Normal Chaos of Love* (1990). Beck and Beck-Gernsheim argue that the importance of the love relationship in contemporary society is directly proportionate to the extent to which more traditional forms of identification become obsolete. In an increasingly mobile, individualized and secularized society, notions of community, nation, class and so on are eroded to the point that the romantic relationship is the only thing that remains as a means for the individual to bind himself or herself to others and secure a sense of personal identity.[43] Paradoxically, however, the new importance placed on the romantic relationship as an alternative to traditional markers of identity serves only to highlight its fragility as a means of defining one's place in the world. Since heterosexual partnerships are no longer held together by the bonds of traditional values or the material considerations which were paramount in the pre-modern world, the only force capable of maintaining Manni and

Lola's commitment to each other, thus guaranteeing their unique identities, is that of love itself. As Beck and Beck-Gernsheim argue, in what could almost be a direct commentary on *Run Lola Run*:

> [Love] stresses uniqueness, promises a shared uniqueness, not by falling back on the traditions of class, on wealth, or on legal rights, but through the truth and directness of feelings, the individual belief in love and its particular personification.[44]

Love, in Beck and Beck-Gernsheim's analysis, as well as in Tykwer's *Run Lola Run* and Wenders' *Wings of Desire*, provides the last anchor of identity for individuals who would otherwise feel themselves to be interchangeable members of the anonymous mass of the city's inhabitants. Love provides the justification for their being in a particular place, i.e. with their loved one, and reveals their unique identity through the feelings they hold for each other.

OSTKREUZ

Although Michael Klier's realist film *Ostkreuz* (1991) seems far removed from Tykwer's *Run Lola Run* – which uses elements of contemporary pop culture such as cartoons and techno music — the story of Elfie, a taciturn teenage girl living with her mother in temporary accommodation for former East German refugees in Berlin, has much in common with the adventures of Lola. Elfie's driving obsession, which she pursues with a similar tenacity to Lola, is to secure for herself a place to belong within the city by establishing a permanent home for herself and her mother. The central problem which Elfie faces in this project is the fact that her mother lacks the 3000 DM deposit necessary to be able to rent a flat. Elfie becomes involved with the small-time crook Darius in an effort to raise this money, and while her various journeys across the city on foot, like Lola's, are undertaken for economic ends, ultimately Elfie aims to establish a place which can be called home within the city.

Here again, the spaces through which the protagonist passes are presented as disconnected and, by virtue of their featurelessness, largely interchangeable. Exterior shots of Berlin, focusing on the dilapidated housing developments in the east, emphasize the emptiness and anonymity of the spaces presented. Although in occasional long shots the viewer is able to see the sky and east Berlin's television tower, no other Berlin landmarks are shown, and the film's protagonist is generally presented against the backdrop of the blank facades of buildings, the edges of which the viewer cannot see. On the one hand, Elfie is apparently enclosed by the built environment around her, a fact which expresses the hopelessness of her situation. On the other, the unwilling-ness of the director to show these spaces (which are deliberately lacking in distinct architectural features) in connection with the wider city emphasizes both the interchangeability and the fragmentation of urban spaces. When Elfie is shown out in the open, the waste ground and ruined high-rise blocks through which she wanders lack any distinct sense of place and are, even more so than the streets of Lola's Berlin, almost entirely emptied of people.

Even the temporary accommodation where Elfie lives with her mother, and where most of the film's interiors are shot, suggests empty and anonymous space as opposed to the sense of place and belonging which a home might be expected to offer. The corridors which Elfie walks down and the doors which she knocks on when attempting to sell items she has acquired are white and featureless; when doors are closed on Elfie, the camera remains fixed on the blank white space in front of her. In order to further emphasize Elfie's inability to establish a sense of connection and place in this anonymous environment, the camera often remains trained on the spaces which Elfie passes through after she has walked out of shot, as in the repeated images of Elfie returning to her temporary accommodation in the evening.

Klier's tactic here is to film the city of Berlin as a series of what Gilles Deleuze would term 'any-spaces-whatever'. In discussions of early film, it has frequently been observed that the medium itself proved to be especially suited to representations of the modern city, as the technique of montage could reproduce the disorientating speed and mobility of the urban experience.[45] From my discussion of the experience of the postmodern city thus far, however, it will be clear that Deleuze's description of the cinematic image as 'any-space-whatever' is more productive in establishing a link between the characteristics of the cinema and the city which it represents. For Deleuze, the cinematic image can represent real spaces in such a way that they are removed from their context in the world and their 'human co-ordinates',[46] thus creating *'deconnected or emptied spaces'*.[47] One way in which such an effect can be achieved is through a *mise-en-scène* which makes use of the wastelands of 'undifferentiated urban tissue', that is to say blank and empty spaces against which human beings must attempt to create their own meanings in a void.[48]

The spaces filmed by Klier are clearly 'any-spaces-whatever', but, as in *Wings of Desire, Far Away, So Close!* and *Run Lola Run*, it is the private sphere, defined by the establishment of the heterosexual couple and/or the family, which offers redemption and the possibility of a sense of belonging and attachment to a specific place. Elfie's pursuit of this dream, however, is figured, like Lola's, as a search for the financial means which will make the creation of this private refuge possible. Elfie is also therefore required to instrumentalize the spaces that she passes through and the people she finds in them, thus mimicking the attitude of the capitalist system to space as described by Lefebvre and exemplified by Lola. Both Lola and Elfie might be described as 'anti-flaneurs', in that they traverse urban space without making any attempt to resist its alienating effects.[49] Lola is simply moving too fast and too purposefully to identify with the spaces she traverses and the people she encounters. Elfie too, although moving at a much slower pace, does not accept the notion that she might be moving through the city in order to become familiar with it and somehow engage with it. Her friend Edmund, for example, asks her: 'Are you just looking around … just like that, in the city?'[50] Elfie is puzzled by the question, since, I would argue, she has no interest in the city itself. In a later conversation with Edmund, she even goes as far as to claim, 'I am not on the move' ('Ich bin nicht unterwegs') despite the fact that she has hardly come to rest throughout the course of the film. The actual experience of being in and moving through the city, however, is of no consequence to Elfie, whose ultimate goal is to retreat into a private space of belonging, within but not of the urban environment.

When she abandons Elfie for a new life with her lover, Elfie's mother's attitude demonstrates that even the bonds of family are fragile as a means of securing a sense of belonging in capitalist postmodernity. Elfie overhears her mother, for example, telling her lover that it would be easier for her if her daughter 'wasn't there' ('nicht da wäre'), and the mother is eventually willing to leave her daughter behind in order to gain access to the financial security which seems to be the main attraction of her new partner. It is indicative of the private sphere's status as a last bastion of identity and belonging in the postmodern urban environment that Elfie nevertheless clings to the notion of the family in order to secure for herself a sense of place in the city. Using the 3000 DM she has earned during the course of the film, she sets up a squat with Edmund and the film ends with them bedding down for the night in a dank, derelict room. Again Klier chooses to place his characters in front of blank, anonymous facades, against which their only defence is to stick a kitsch image of a kitten to the wall behind them in an attempt to invoke the aura of place and belonging. Here more than in any of the films examined so far, the viability of a retreat into the privatized sense of belonging represented by the heterosexual couple and the family is clearly called into question as a defence against the alienating effects of the urban environment.

BREAK EVEN

Eoin Moore's first feature *Break Even* (*Plus minus null*, 1998) also incorporates a search for a place to belong in Berlin centred around the heterosexual couple and framed within a clear economic context. Of all the films discussed in this chapter so far, *Break Even* offers the most direct depiction of the city under reconstruction, since Alex, the central male figure, is an unskilled building worker employed on one of the city's many construction sites. Alex is strongly identified as a representative of the typical Berliner, with his distinct accent and his close associations with the geography of the city: when introducing himself, for example, he tells people that he is called Alex, 'like the square', and Moll, 'like the street'. Like Elfie, Alex's home is a prefabricated building, a temporary and de-individualized dwelling, in this case situated on one of the building sites where he works. Divorced from his wife and separated from his child, Alex is now homeless in more than the literal sense of having no permanent roof over his head. However, his ambition to pay his wife the child maintenance he owes her is symbolic of his desire to regain his family and thus his sense of belonging. Here again, economic success or failure is intrinsically bound up with the ability of the film's protagonist to experience a sense of home in the city. Yet Alex's petty thievery from his boss, which is eventually discovered, is such a precarious strategy that Alex's capacity to achieve this is in question from the start.

The unfinished character of the night-time Berlin through which Alex moves reflects his situation, in that he is shown in spaces which seem to lack clear definition. They city's contours are mainly visible by means of the lights on the scaffolding and the cranes, as well as by neon signs and the headlights of passing cars. Shots of Alex travelling around Berlin in his shabby Trabant are often in slow motion. Here the coloured lights blur, reducing the Berlin streets to a confused mass of streaked electric light against a background of darkness. This can be seen during the prostitute Svetlana's first drive with Alex through the streets of the city, in which the camera twists and turns to show the viewer Svetlana's point of view as she hangs with her head out of the car window. Again, in this sequence the streets outside become indistinguishable as they dissolve into a confusion of coloured light and darkness. This may be regarded as another means of creating images of the 'any-space-whatever' already discussed above in relation to Klier's *Ostkreuz*.

Although daytime exteriors occasionally include Berlin landmarks, Alex and his friends are generally creatures of the night, where Berlin as a distinct place appears to lose its contours. Equally, they are all also marginal figures in terms of their economic and familial status. Alex, as has already been mentioned, has lost his wife and daughter, and is unable to earn enough money either to support his child or find himself a permanent address. Ruth and Svetlana, the two prostitutes whom he befriends, are an east German and a Yugoslav woman respectively, who both feel they have lost their families. Ruth, a former childcare worker in a GDR state nursery, reminisces, for example, about the children who used to be in her care and whom she regarded as her own, whereas Svetlana has been forced to leave her home because her father and mother came from different ethnic groups. The new Berlin which Alex is helping to construct, however, seems to offer little hope of integration into a sense of belonging in the city, as Ruth points out whilst Alex is showing her (again, at night), one of the construction sites in the centre of Berlin. Whilst the work is still underway and the site is in chaos, their presence is still at least a possibility. However, when the work is finished and everything is 'big and clean' ('groß und sauber'), she doubts whether the likes of herself and Alex will ever be allowed to enter the buildings being created here.

This affinity between the night and exclusion from a sense of belonging is re-emphasized at the end of the film when the camera pulls away from Alex on a night-time street somewhere in Berlin as he prepares to move his belongings into a new prefabricated building on another building site. Alex slowly disappears from view as he is swallowed up by a darkness in which only the coloured lights of the cityscape remain visible. Alex's failure throughout the film to establish himself in a heterosexual partnership is the ultimate cause of his symbolic disappearance. His initial lack of success in winning back his wife, his inability to provide Svetlana with the marriage certificate she needs in order to stay in Germany, and then his break-up with Ruth after she refuses to sink her savings into one of his money-making schemes, all mean that by the end of the action he has lost his chance to become a husband and father again. As he himself admits: 'I'm not a family man' ('Ich bin kein Familienmensch'). In the film's final shot, as Alex recedes into the distance, he is exiled into the blankness of an 'any-space-whatever', rather than being released into the new experience of belonging he would prefer.

A FINE DAY AND *SILVESTER COUNTDOWN*

The depiction of capitalist society to be found in *Break Even* is reminiscent of that seen in *Ostkreuz*, in that the struggle to establish a sense of belonging within the context of the heterosexual couple or the family is called into question by the harsh economic realities facing the excluded in new Berlin. In Turkish–German director Thomas Arslan's third film, *A Fine Day* (*Der schöne Tag*, 2000), the city as a site of the struggle for economic survival is entirely neglected in favour of a foregrounding of the search for identity and belonging through the heterosexual partnership which has been central to my discussion so far. *A Fine Day* presents a long, slow summer day in the life of Deniz, a Turkish–German actress employed as a voice-over artist in Berlin. Deniz's personal life is characterized by an inability to communicate (she only rarely speaks, despite occupying the screen throughout), and frustration at her inability to find a suitable partner. In the course of the day depicted, she leaves her current boyfriend of three years and meets another young man, who lives in her neighbourhood, by chance on a train.

Like Lola, Elfie and Alex, Deniz is constantly on the move within the city and, like them, her ultimate goal is to establish a place of belonging through a heterosexual partnership. Although there are no economic conditions which have to be met to achieve this aim, *A Fine Day* could accurately be described as a *film-à-these* which seeks to illustrate the problems of postmodern romantic attachments as outlined by Beck and Beck-Gernsheim. Like these two real-life sociologists, the fictional academic whom Deniz meets towards the end of a film in a café describes the way in which contemporary relationships are held together 'almost only by feelings' ('fast nur über Gefühle') and the subsequent fragility of these relationships. Deniz, on the other hand, complains that the frequency with which individuals change their partners is 'arbitrary' ('beliebig'), thus recalling Lola's fear that 'I could be some other woman'. Again, the fragility of the heterosexual relationship leads potentially to a loss of identity, in that each partner has no guarantee of their uniqueness in their lover's eyes and thus of the necessity of their being together. This theme is also taken up in the scene from Eric Rohmer's film *A Summer's Tale* (*Conte d'été*, 1997) which Deniz is dubbing at work in the studio. Here, the words of Rohmer's figure, a young woman addressing the film's male protagonist, can be regarded as an expression of Deniz's own fears: '… if it doesn't work out with one girl, there's always another. [...] For you, all girls are basically interchangeable.'[51]

As Beck and Beck-Gernsheim observe, this sense of vulnerability is heightened when individuals no longer have access to other means of defining their identity outside of the romantic relationship. This loss of identity, experienced as an inability to achieve a sense of belonging within the city, is expressed in Arslan's film through aspects of the *mise-en-scène* which recall again Deleuze's notion of 'any-space-whatever'. First of all, Deniz never stays even in her own flat for long, and this interior is itself characterized by a blank whiteness. Deniz has very little furniture and the white walls of her flat are largely undecorated. In this way, the inside of her flat recalls the outside of the building in which it is housed, which also has largely featureless white walls. Other exteriors are carefully chosen for their anonymity: the interior of the underground station near Deniz's flat, for example, is covered with plain tiles in pale blue and white, unbroken by any detail which might assert the distinctiveness of this location. The other buildings Deniz passes by and the parks which she frequently passes through, equally lack any features which would allow the viewer to situate them as particular places within the real Berlin. Not only do the physical spaces themselves resist the establishment of any sense of place, but the marked absence of people in the streets and stations of Berlin presented here, as in Lola's and Elfie's journeys across the city, indicates her inability to engage with the other inhabitants of Berlin. The emptiness of the city created by Arslan is particularly evident when Deniz meets her sister at the almost entirely deserted Zoo Station (*Bahnhof Zoo*), and walks through nearby streets (normally some of the busiest in the capital) to a restaurant.

Deniz's detachment from the spaces through which she passes is suggested, as one reviewer points out, by her expressionless demeanour,[52] yet it is also reflected in the equal detachment practised by Arslan's camera. The standard method employed by the director for filming Deniz as she walks about the city is to have her move towards and then away from the camera as it pans round to follow her moving slowly away; in other words, it takes on the point of view of a disinterested bystander watching Deniz pass by. This non-engaged observation is also typical of Deniz's own attitude to the people she encounters during her many bus and train journeys during the course of the film. However, her gaze can become interested, as shown during her attempts to flirt with the young men she encounters. One such instance leads to a meeting with Diego, who turns out to already have a girlfriend, but Deniz is obviously not discouraged by this experience, as the final scene of the film finds her exchanging glances with another man in a train. Deniz clearly desires to transform the chance meetings of the city into relationships which could provide an escape from her nomadic, or rather in Baumann's term 'touristic' existence. Nevertheless, the viewer may well harbour serious doubts as to whether these attachments will provide the sense of belonging within the city which she seeks. After all, her relationship with her boyfriend seems, to a great extent, to have failed because the sense of attachment and identity to be found in the romantic relationship proved to be somehow tenuous and unconvincing from Deniz's point of view: she leaves her boyfriend largely because he cannot answer the question: 'What do I mean to you? And why?' ('was bedeute ich dir? Und warum?').

Although very different in style from Arslan's film, Oskar Roehler's *Silvester Countdown* (1996) portrays the pitfalls of securing identity within the context of the heterosexual relationship, against the backdrop of the metropolis. The main figures portrayed here, the significantly named Romeo and Julia, are members of that bored young generation of pleasure-seeking, 20-something Berliners familiar, for example, to readers of Judith Hermann's best-selling volume of short stories *Summerhouse, Later* (*Sommerhaus, später*, 1998).[53] Unlike the figures examined so far in Berlin films of the 1990s, the retreat from the city into the private sphere has already taken place in *Silvester Countdown*, as we observe Romeo and Julia not in the process of trying to form a relationship, but in the throes of its collapse. They have already removed themselves from the urban spaces of the city into a private space defined by their relationship, and much of the action therefore takes place in their flat. Here again the lovers find that their feelings for each other – which they try to keep alive through experiments in sexual role-playing – are not permanent enough to secure this place of belonging within the city.

The blank walls of the largely empty rooms which they inhabit echo the featurelessness of the exteriors which I have already observed in other filmic depictions of Berlin. In this sense, Romeo and Julia have only displaced the problems facing the other protagonists discussed in this chapter onto the domestic interior which others regard as offering an alternative sense of belonging and thus as an escape from the alienation of the city and of postmodern society. Significantly, one of the two shots which do show either of the protagonists against the backdrop of Berlin positions Romeo looking directly into the camera in front of one of many building sites to be found in the capital during the 1990s. This shot is seen after Julia has already left the flat and indicates that Romeo's identity remains uncertain and in progress like the cityscape behind him now that he has failed to secure that identity in his relationship with Julia.

LIFE IS A BUILDING SITE

An altogether more positive take on these themes is to be found in Wolfgang Becker's mainstream success *Life Is a Building Site*, which was co-scripted by Tykwer. Here the 'arbitrariness' which Deniz fears in moving from partner to partner in *A Fine Day* takes on an altogether more deadly aspect. Jan Nebel, the hero of Becker's film, is clearly in the habit of entering into non-committed sexual relationships with a number of women, yet the opening scene of the film, which intercuts images of Jan making love to a friend of his sister and a riot taking place in the streets below, makes clear how little satisfaction he achieves in this way: Jan's face remains impassive throughout and he eventually decides to leave. Furthermore, when he later discovers that one of the women he has slept with may be HIV positive, his inability to establish a stable heterosexual partnership may have become the cause of his imminent death.

Jan's alienation from the family, as well as from the romantic partnership on which it is based, is exemplified by his relationship to the nuclear family of his sister, brother-in-law and niece. His sister and brother-in-law are far from an ideal couple and neglect their daughter. Furthermore, when Jan's father dies, it becomes clear that his own home life as a child was also unhappy. Jan comes from a 'shitty family' ('Schießfamilie'), his sisters observes, but 'we're not doing any better' ('wir machen es auch nicht besser'). Initially at least, *Life Is a Building Site* does not idealize the nuclear family as a refuge from the anonymity of the city. However, the alternative is Jan's detached wandering, portrayed here in terms of the erotic conquests which are potentially as deadly as the 'being alone' ('Alleinsein'), which he imagines was the cause of this own father's death. Jan's unusual name ('Nebel' literally means 'fog'), which draws considerable comment from other characters in the film, is both a reminder of the epileptic fits to which he is prone (sufferers often see a fog before the eyes), and the way in which he moves through life as if in a fog which isolates him from those around him.

Vera, whom Jan falls in love with during the course of the film, represents a very different attitude to the city. As a jobbing singer and occasional busker, she has a habit of appearing in the most unlikely places. However, she seems to make herself instantly at home in any surroundings, and to enter easily into personal relationships with anyone she encounters by chance, notably with Jan himself. This can also be seen in the scene where she is waiting on a railway platform for Jan: since he is late, she spends her time befriending the signalman and smoking his cigarettes. Perhaps more importantly, she offers Jan the promise of achieving a secure identity through their relationship. This is suggested by the tape recording she makes for Jan of passers-by responding to the question 'who is Jan Nebel?' ('wer ist Jan Nebel?'). Jan's lack of a distinct identity in the crowd of the city, evidenced by the confused answers on the tape recording, is not important to Vera since, even if nobody else knows who Jan Nebel really is, she claims, 'I know' ('ich weiß es'). Vera's confidence in her own identity and in her ability to help Jan achieve a similar confidence through their relationship also allows her to experiment with the anonymity which life in the city allows the individual without feeling it to be a threat. For example, she shows Jan how easy it is to bluff one's way into functions simply by pretending to be someone else or, in another instance, to get away with occupying a hotel room one has not booked.

Most importantly, however, Jan is eventually able, through Vera and his friendship with ageing rocker Buddy, to find a home within the city. He participates in the creation of an alternative family which includes the couples of Jan and Vera, and Buddy and the Greek immigrant Kristina, as well as Jan's niece Jenny. They renovate Jan's father's flat and thus make good the failure of the family which this place represents. The final success of the heterosexual partnership (and of the family associated with it) as a haven from the city is driven home for the audience by the final image of Jan, Vera, Buddy, Kristina and Jenny skating on a frozen lake in the countryside, the only scene in the film which allows the characters to leave the alienating environment of the city.

NIGHT SHAPES

The final film I will examine in this chapter is Andreas Dresen's *Night Shapes* (*Nachtgestalten*, 1999), which manages to combine elements of the affirmation of the family as a source of belonging with a critique of capitalism as a force undermining that possibility. Nevertheless, the basic tone of Dresen's film, which presents the adventures of a variety of Berliners and visitors to the city on one night, is perhaps more optimistic than all of the films discussed here. Dresen presents the city of Berlin not as a series of fragmented spaces, but as a fundamentally interconnected whole.

Five main narratives are interwoven in the film: the search of Hannah and her boyfriend Victor, both homeless, for a hotel room, which they intend to pay for with a 500 DM note which Hannah finds in the film's opening scene; the quest of Jochen, a farmer from Mecklenburg, for a good time in the big city and his subsequent meeting with the teenage prostitute, Patty; businessman Henrich Peschke's attempts to find the uncle of a lost African boy, Felix, whom he meets by chance at the airport; the efforts of Felix's uncle to track the boy down after arriving late to meet him; and finally, the adventures of a gang of teenagers who steal and beg on the streets.

The extent to which these figures inhabit a common universe, even if they are not directly aware of it themselves, is most clearly expressed in the motif of the Pope's visit which is mentioned repeatedly throughout the film and which can be seen on newspapers, heard on the radio and seen on television in scenes involving all of the main characters. The Pope takes on a particular significance because of the message which he has evidently come to Germany to preach: namely, to warn that humankind has become 'torn apart' ('zerissen'). Here, religion becomes a metaphor for the hope of overcoming the alienation of postmodern society, much in the same way that it is an angel, Cassiel, who proclaims himself an apostle of 'closeness' in *Far Away, So Close!* The interconnectedness of all of the lives in the city is further suggested by the fact that figures often pass through the same places and encounter the same minor characters, such as the taxi driver whose passengers include Jochen, Hannah and Victor, and Peschke. Other connections of this kind are provided by the gang of street children, who rob Jochen of his bag on his arrival in Berlin, steal Peschke's car and assist Hannah after a violent argument with Victor, or by the figure of Zombie, a homeless man who crosses the paths of a number of the main characters before his death alone on the street. This deliberate interweaving of apparently disconnected biographies is symptomatic of what Fredric Jameson has called 'synchronous monadic simultaneity', a form of plotting which he regards as modernist in intent. By presenting 'isolated subjects together' in this way, he argues, the filmmaker reassures the audience of 'the ultimate unity of the social totality', as opposed to presenting the audience with the irredeemable fragmentation which Jameson associates with the postmodern.[54]

Despite the assertion in *Night Shapes* of the interconnectedness of all the individuals it presents, the film cannot propose any new means of mediation between the individual and the rest of society in order that human beings can secure a sense of belonging. Religion, although used as a metaphor for a desire to end the fragmentation of society, is clearly not a practical solution in terms of its practice as a doctrine, since it tends to judge and exclude others – as Hannah and Victor discover when they are denied a place to sleep in a Christian hostel because they are not married.[55] Once again, the family, often centred around the heterosexual partnership, must serve as a replacement for that wider sense of meaning and community which religion offered to a pre-modern world.

Hannah and Victor are very much a case in point, of course, with their desperate search to put a roof over their heads, and thereby create, if only for one night, a home for themselves and their unborn child in the city. Jochen, on the other hand, fails in his attempt to romance Patty, who sees in him only an opportunity to earn easy money and feed her heroin habit. Jochen's origins in the country show that isolation is not just a condition of city dwellers, but his belief that romantic love can overcome the distance between himself and Patty is clearly misplaced. This is never more evident than in the nightclub scene in which Jochen is seen gazing at Patty through a wire fence, holding the red rose which he has bought for her in an attempt to awaken her romantic interest in him. Peschke's obsession with his position in his firm and the wishes of his boss, Dr Schneider, is the force that blinds him to the developing affection between himself and Felix as the two of them search for Felix's uncle. Whilst obviously not a romantic relationship, the hope is held out here that Peschke might escape his lonely bachelor existence by assuming a paternal role. However, at the end of the film, Peschke is too busy complaining about his life in the rat race to see Felix waving to him as his taxi drives away.

As will be evident from the above summary, it is very often money which is portrayed, as so often in the films examined here, as the root cause of the distance which exists between the figures portrayed. In the cases of Jochen and Patty and Peschke and Felix, the pursuit of money, for whatever reason, sabotages the possibility of building new romantic or family-like relationships with others. Yet the picture is not entirely pessimistic in this respect. Although the strain of trying to secure a hotel room with the money they have found nearly leads to the break-down of Hannah and Victor's relationship, they nevertheless defy the demands of the capitalist economy by refusing to leave their room at the prescribed time. Instead, they continue to make love, oblivious to the noise of the city outside. Another sign of hope is to be found in the figures of Felix's uncle and a woman he encounters at the airport who works in one of the fast-food kiosks. Whilst both are clearly part of an economic underclass working in menial jobs, their blossoming romance provides a counterbalance to those other relationships which appear to collapse under the pressure of financial necessity.

This emphasis on the family as a potential site of belonging is tempered to an extent by the film's penultimate shot, in which the camera pans in close-up across the faces of the teenage gang which has stolen Peschke's car and driven it to a beach. The children watch fascinated as Peschke's car burns, but the final boy we see suddenly turns his eyes towards the camera as if to acknowledge its presence. This shot is reminiscent of the final moments of Frederico Fellini's *La dolce vita* (1960), in which the film's protagonist encounters a young girl on a beach who has earlier been described as being 'like an angel in an Umbrian church'. Like Fellini's film, *Night Shapes* works with a central religious metaphor, with the arrival of the Pope from the skies over Berlin replacing the statue of Christ being flown over the city of Rome by helicopter at the beginning of *La dolce vita*. Fellini's protagonist Marcello fails to recapture the sense of a meaningful existence which is the promise of religion, having been deafened to that meaning by his life amongst the glamorous socialites of the metropolis. Similarly, when the child/angel speaks he is unable to hear her because of the roar of the sea. As in *La dolce vita*, it is the audience in Dresen's film who are finally confronted with an image of the enigmatic face of a child, his expression in *Night Shapes* possibly suggesting indifference, sadness, disorientation or perhaps a combination of all of these feelings. The gang of street children, unlike the other central characters in the film, never experience the possibility of integration into a private space of belonging within the city through the family. Rather, they represent those who would remain excluded, even if the other figures succeeded in establishing relationships upon which they could build a private sense of belonging within the city. In this sense, the gaze of the child at the end of *Night Shapes* may be read as a challenge to think beyond such forms of belonging, and to recognize those who are excluded from them.

As the examples I have analysed in this chapter demonstrate, Berlin as a microcosm of, and metaphor for, post-unification society is portrayed as an alienating environment in which a sense of belonging can no longer be attained, except by means of a retreat into the private sphere. *Run Lola Run* to an extent celebrates the triumph of the private and its ability to reinforce identity. However, films such as Arslan's *A Fine Day*, Klier's *Ostkreuz* or Roehler's *Silvester Countdown* point to the fragility of the heterosexual partnership and the dangers of its over-investment as a site of belonging. While Wenders' *Far Away, So Close!* attempts to address the conditions of capitalism which contribute to the pervasive sense of 'loneliness' which characterizes the society experienced by the angel Cassiel, this film, like Dresen's, continues to valorize private relationships, whether romantic or familial, as a means of resistance to that loneliness. However, the questioning gaze of the teenage boy shown at the end of *Night Shapes* serves as a timely reminder of the dangers of such a strategy and the exclusions on which it is founded.

Notes

1 Anthony Read and David Fischer, *Berlin: The Biography of a City* (London: Pimlico, 1994), p. 136.

2 See so-called 'rubble films' such as Wolfgang Staudte's *The Murderers Are among Us* (*Die Mörder sind unter uns*, 1946), Gerhard Lamprecht's *Somewhere in Berlin* (*Irgendwo in Berlin*, 1946) and Roberto Rossellini's *Germany, Year Zero* (*Germania, anno zero*, 1949).

3 For examples in German cinema, see Helke Sander's *The All-Round Reduced Personality – Redupers* (*Die allseitig reduzierte Persönlichkeit – Redupers*, 1977), Reinhard Hauff's *The Man on the Wall* (*Der Mann auf der Mauer*, 1982), or, most famously, Wim Wenders' *Wings of Desire* (*Der Himmel über Berlin*, 1986).

4 Frank Trommler, 'Introduction' in Trommler (ed.), *Berlin: The New Capital in the East: A Transatlantic Appraisal* (Washington: American Institute for Contemporary Germanic Studies, 2000), pp. 1–5 (p.1).

5   Brian Ladd, *The Ghosts of Berlin: Confronting German History in the Urban Landscape* (Chicago: University of Chicago, 1997), p. 225. See also Michael Sontheimer, *Berlin, Berlin: Der Umzug in die Hauptstadt* (Hamburg: Spiegel, 1999), pp. 29–45. Berlin had already been made the official capital in the Unification Treaty (*Einigungsvertrag*) of 1990.

6   Régine Robin, *Berlin chantiers: Essai sur les passés fragiles* (Paris: Stock, 2001).

7   Ladd, *The Ghosts of Berlin*.

8   See Ladd, *The Ghosts of Berlin*, pp. 196–9 and pp. 59–63, and Bill Niven, *Facing the Nazi Past: United Germany and the Legacy of the Third Reich* (London: Routledge, 2002), pp. 194–232. Controversy still continues over the monument to German communist leader Ernst Thälmann in the Prenzlauer Berg district. See Peter Moneath, 'Ein Denkmal für Thälmann' in Moneath (ed.), *Ernst Thälmann: Mensch und Mythos* (Amsterdam: Rodopi, 2000), pp. 179–201 (pp. 196–7).

9   See Heinz Bude, *Generation Berlin* (Berlin: Merve, 2001).

10 As in Christoph Stark's film *Julietta* (2001).

11 'die Hauptstadt der Vereinigung'. Bodo Mohrshäuser, *Liebeserklärung an eine häßliche Stadt: Berliner Gefühle* (Frankfurt/Main: Suhrkamp Taschenbuch, 1998), p. 135.

12 Sabine Hake, *German National Cinema* (London: Routledge, 2002), p. 191. For release in Great Britain and the United States, the film was given the title *Life Is All You Get*, but I will use the literal translation in the rest of this chapter.

13 The term *Heimat* may be translated as 'homeland', but has a specific meaning within German culture which is not completely rendered in this English word.

14 For an analysis of the notion of *Heimat* in German literature and film, see Elizabeth Boa and Rachel Palfreyman, *Heimat: A German Dream: Regional Loyalties and National Identity in German Culture, 1890–1990* (Oxford: OUP, 2000).

15 For a recent celebration of the *Kiez* as a form of *Heimat*, see Günter de Bruyn, *Deutsche Zustände: Über Erinnerungen und Tatsachen, Heimat und Literatur* (Frankfurt/Main: Fischer, 1999), pp. 98–9.

16 For Fritzsche, the *Hinterhof* (tenement courtyard) in this period was an 'interior of comfort, familiarity and stillness in which neighbourhood is set against the "outside" of the city'. Fritzsche, 'A City of Strangers or a City of Neighbours?: Berlin Confronts Metropolis' in Trommler (ed.), *Berlin*, pp. 23–35 (p. 25).

17 Kevin Robbins, 'Prisoners of the City?: What Could a Postmodern City Be?' in Erica Carter *et al.* (eds.), *Space and Place: Theories of Identity and Location* (London: Lawrence and Wishart, 1993), pp. 303–330 (p. 323).

18 Raymond Williams, 'The Metropolis and the Emergence of Modernism' in Edward Timms and David Kelley (eds.), *Unreal City: Urban Experience in Modern Literature and Art* (New York: St. Martin's Press, 1985), pp. 13–24 (p. 18).

19 For a discussion of these debates, see Nan Ellis, *Postmodern Urbanism* (Oxford: Blackwell, 1996).

20 For Harvey's reading of the film, see David Harvey, *The Condition of Postmodernity: An Enquiry into the Origins of Cultural Change* (Oxford: Blackwell, 1990), pp. 308–23.

21 See Peter Berger *et al.*, *The Homeless Mind: Modernization and Consciousness* (Harmondsworth: Penguin, 1973).

22 'Mit dem Zufall muß es nun aufhören! [...]. Ich weiß nicht, ob es eine Bestimmung gibt, aber es gibt eine Entscheidung!' Wim Wenders and Peter Handke, *Der Himmel über Berlin: Ein Filmbuch* (Frankfurt/Main: Suhrkamp, 1989), p. 161.

23 'einer weiß nichts vom anderen'. Wenders and Handke, *Der Himmel über Berlin*, p. 30.

24   'Warum bin ich Ich und nicht du? [...] Warum bin ich hier und warum nicht dort?' Wenders and Handke, *Der Himmel über Berlin*, pp. 14–15.

25   'Ich war mit einem Mann, war verliebt und hätte ebensogut ihn stehenlassen und mit dem Fremden, der uns auf der Straße entgegenkam, weitergehen können.' Wenders and Handke, *Der Himmel über Berlin*, p. 160.

26   See Jean-François Lyotard, *The Condition of Postmodernity: A Report on Knowledge*, tr. Geoff Bennington and Brian Massumi (Manchester: Manchester University Press, 1986; originally 1979), p. 41: 'This is what the postmodern world is all about. Most people have lost the nostalgia for the lost narrative.'

27   'Wir sind Boten, die Nähe zu tragen zu denen in der Ferne.'

28   'keiner hört, was im anderen vorgeht, keiner sieht dem anderen ins Herz. [...] Es schafft sich jeder in seinem eigenen Hören und Sehen seine eigene Welt. Und darin ist man Gefangener. Und aus seiner Zelle sieht man die Zellen der anderen.'

29   James M. Skidmore also notes striking the similarities between these two films, but interprets those similarities in a different context, seeing both works as narratives about the possibilities of the city as a site of new beginnings and self-creation. Skidmore, 'Berlin, the Unchanging Symphony of a Big City: Determining Story in *Der Himmel über Berlin* and *Lola rennt*', *German as a Foreign Language*, 1 (2003), 17–29, http://www.gfl-journal.de/1-2003/skidmore.pdf.

30   'das heimliche Herz des Films'. Tom Tykwer, 'Generalschlüssel fürs Kino' in Michael Töteberg (ed.), *Szenenwechsel: Momentaufnahmen des jungen deutschen Films* (Reinbek bei Hamburg: Rowohlt Taschenbuch, 1999), pp. 17–33 (p. 22).

31   'der geringe intellektuelle Tiefengrad der Gespräche'. Guido Rings, 'Zwischen "Schicksal", freiem Willen und instinktivem Verhalten: Hybriditätsaspekte und Ansatzpunkte zu deren Vermittlung in Tom Tykwer's *Lola rennt*', *German as a Foreign Language*, 1 (2002), 1–28 (p. 3), http://www.gfl-journal.de/1-2002/rings.pdf.

32   'ich könnte auch irgendeine andere sein'. Tom Tykwer, *Lola rennt*, ed. by Michael Töteberg (Reinbek bei Hamburg: Rowohlt Taschenbuch, 1998), p. 58.

33   Tykwer, *Lola rennt*, pp. 92–93.

34   Skidmore, 'Berlin, the Unchanging Symphony of a Big City', pp. 17–18.

35   The lack of crowds which Margit Sinka observes in the Berlin streets Lola uses is, as will become clear, a common feature of the filmic depictions of Berlin to be discussed here. Margit Sinka, 'Tom Tykwer's *Lola rennt*: A Blueprint for Millennial Berlin', *Glossen*, 11 (2000), http://www.dickinson.edu/departments/germn/glossen/heft11/lola.html. See also Tykwer's own comments: 'The streets are emptied for Lola – she is running alone against the rest of the world' ('Die Straßen sind leer gemacht für Lola – sie rennt einsam gegen den Rest der Welt'). Tykwer, *Lola rennt*, p. 135.

36   Tykwer, *Lola rennt*, p. 127.

37   Zygmunt Baumann, *Postmodern Ethics* (Oxford: Blackwell, 1993), p. 243.

38   Richard Senett, *Flesh and Stone: The Body and the City in Western Modernity* (London: Faber and Faber, 1994), p. 18.

39   Henri Lefebvre, *The Production of Space*, tr. Donald Nicholson-Smith (Oxford: Blackwell, 1991), p. 355.

40   'Ich mach mir die Welt, wie sie mir gefällt.' Tykwer, *Lola rennt*, p. 118. This motto is borrowed from children's author Astrid Lindgren's character Pippi Longstocking, with whom Lola also shares her red hair.

41   Tykwer, *Lola rennt*, pp. 135–6.

42   Sinka, 'Tom Tykwer's *Lola rennt*'.

43   Ulrich Beck and Elisabeth Beck-Gernsheim, *Das ganz normale Chaos der Liebe* (Frankfurt/Main: Suhrkamp, 1990), p. 49.

44   '[Die Liebe] betont die Einzigartigkeit, verspricht die Gemeinsamkeit der Einzigartigkeiten, nicht durch Rückgriff auf ständische Überlieferungen, Geldbesitz, rechtliche Ansprüche, sondern kraft Wahrheit und Unmittelbarkeit des Gefühls, des individuellen Liebesglaubens und seiner jeweiligen Personifizierung.' Beck and Beck-Gernsheim, *Das ganz normale Chaos*, p. 239.

45   On this point, see Mark Shiel, 'Cinema and the City in History and Theory' in Mark Shiel and Tony Fitzmaurice (eds.), *Cinema and the City: Film and Urban Societies in a Global Context* (Oxford: Blackwell, 2001), pp. 1–18 (p. 1); Hanno Möbius and Guntram Vogt, *Drehort Stadt: Das Thema "Großstadt" im deutschen Film* (Marburg: Hitzeroth, 1990), p. 9; Michael Minden, 'The City in Early Cinema: *Metropolis*, *Berlin* and *October*' in Timms and Kelley (eds.), *Unreal City*, pp. 193–212 (p. 203).

46   Gilles Deleuze, *Cinema 1: The Movement-Image*, tr. Hugh Tomlinson and Barbara Habberjam (London: Athlone Press, 1986), p. 122.

47   Deleuze, *Cinema 1*, p. 120. Italics in original.

48   Deleuze, *Cinema 1*, p. 120.

49   See Walter Benjamin's discussion of the 'flaneur'. Benjamin, 'Das Paris des Second Empire bei Baudelaire' in Benjamin, *Walter Benjamin: Ein Lesebuch*, ed. by Michael Opitz (Frankfurt/Main: Suhrkamp, 1996), pp. 500–91 (pp. 524–56).

50   'Siehst du dich um ... nur so, durch die Stadt?'

51   'geht es nicht mit der einen, ist da noch die andere. [...] Für dich sind im Grunde alle Mädchen austauschbar.'

52   Stephanie Maeck, 'Die Entdeckung der Langsamkeit', *taz* (Hamburg edition), 28 November 2001, p. 23.

53   Judith Hermann, *Sommerhaus, später: Erzählungen* (Frankfurt/Main: Fischer Taschenbuch, 2000).

54   Fredric Jameson, *The Geopolitical Aesthetic: Cinema and Space in the World System* (London: BFI, 1992), p. 115.

55   The criticism of institutionalized Christianity here is heightened by the fact that, as Alexandra Ludewig suggests, Hannah (who is pregnant) and Victor may be regarded as counterparts to the biblical Mary and Joseph, who were also in search of a 'room at the inn'. Ludewig, '*Heimat*, City and Frontier in German National Cinema', *Debatte*, 9.2 (2001), 173–86 (p. 181).

Chapter 7

Women amongst women: the New German Comedy and the failed romance

Dickon Copsey

In terms of domestic audience popularity, 1996 was a high point for the German film industry. Less than three years after the 8.4% slump of February 1993, the industry's domestic market share had risen to an unprecedented 21.9%, its highest level for twenty years.[1] The psychological significance of this popular revival can best be measured by subsequent film industry and media speculation on a return to the golden era of 1950s 'Papas Kino' (literally, 'Dad's Cinema').[2] Forty years on from the avant-garde renaissance of the New German Cinema, this reference to an earlier era of 'conventional' filmmaking is pointedly ironic.

The roots of this apparently rejuvenated narrative entertainment cinema[3] can be traced back to the early 1990s and the success of films such as Detlev Buck's *Little Rabbit* (*Karniggels*, 1991), Sönke Wortmann's *Alone Amongst Women* (*Allein unter Frauen*, 1991) and *Little Sharks* (*Kleine Haie*, 1992), and Katja von Garnier's *Making Up* (*Abgeschminkt*, 1993). These films inspired a stream of comic features ranging from slapstick 'proletarian comedies' (*Prolkomödien*)[4] to male and female buddy movies, but were dominated by a series of star-lead, relationship comedies obsessively reworking the themes of gender and sexuality for an affluent, post-1968 generation.[5]

Drawing on such earlier successes as Doris Dörrie's *Men* (*Männer*, 1985) and Peter Timm's *A Man for Every Situation* (*Ein Mann für jede Tonart*, 1992), von Garnier's film set a trend for a revival of the romantic comedy genre within German cinema. This trend has continued with such domestic box-office hits as Wortmann's *Maybe, Maybe Not* (*Der bewegte Mann*, 1994) and *The Superwife* (*Das Superweib*, 1996); Rainer Kaufmann's *Talk of the Town* (*Stadtgespräch*, 1995); Dörrie's *Nobody Loves Me* (*Keiner liebt mich*, 1996); Sharon von Wietersheim's *Workaholic* (1996); and Sherry Horman's *Women Are Something Wonderful* (*Frauen sind was Wunderbares*, 1994) and *Doubting Thomas* (*Irren ist männlich*, 1996). Focusing on issues of identity, gender and sexuality, these films represent a significant sub-genre of what critics have dubbed New German Comedy,[6] which foregrounds women as both the subjects of representation and of consumption.

In 1996, Brad Hagen acknowledged this industry-wide shift in an article in *Variety* stating that, 'two-thirds of the other biggest hits of the first half of the year were German productions with a decidedly femme-appeal slant'.[7] The presence of such films and associated female directors, such as Hormann, Dörrie and von Garnier, has been linked to an increasing visibility of women and issues of relevance to women within the German film landscape of the 1990s.[8] After a decade in which male audiences and consequently male-orientated action films dominated, the early 1990s saw a shift towards 'softer' films with a strong female presence. Despite a general down-turn in the crucial under-25 cinema-going market, many films of this period were attracting audiences that were more than 75% female.[9] Whatever the reasons, women have been recognized as an extremely important market for the German film industry, and this is reflected in film production and marketing strategies.[10]

This move towards a more audience-orientated filmmaking practice, even one with a clear gender bias, is itself nothing new within the context of German film history.[11] Institutional changes within the German film industry, such as the growth of 'economically-orientated' film funding, have augmented this trend, encouraging the replication of financially successful projects which offer mass appeal and clearly defined target audiences. The female-centred[12] romantic comedies with their pacey narratives and contemporary urban settings would appear to fit this bill. Historical precursors and economic conditions alone, however, can never fully address the issue of audience popularity.

David Coury argues that common to all of the New German Comedies is a structural reliance on the traditional elements of classic cinema: namely, 'causality, linear narrative, closure and the most necessary element of all, a happy end'.[13] To analyse and explain this structural commonality clearly requires a move away from theories of production towards an understanding of consumption and, more particularly, the audience. In an attempt to explore the social and psychological significance of this sub-genre of woman-centred romantic comedies in their representation of self-determining female identities, and the apparently pleasurable romantic narratives they construct for their female audiences, I intend to ask three central questions.

Firstly, to what extent is it possible to argue for the existence of a discourse of resistance within the conformity of this classically normative cinematic genre? In her seminal work on women's consumption of popular romantic fiction, *Reading the Romance*, Janice Radway constructs a model of the ideal romance.[14] According to Radway, the reactionary core of the ideal romance, based as it is upon the quest for the ideal (male) partner and resolution of all problems in the consummation of this relationship, is imperative for the reassurance of its readers that a utopia of 'successfully managed heterosexual relationships' can exist.[15] Clearly, the centring of women as the subjects of representation and of consumption is as relevant to the work of popular romantic fiction as it is to the new wave of romantic German comedies.[16] In terms of narrative structure both genres revolve around a female lead's quest for the ideal (heterosexual) relationship. Invariably, the narrative opening involves a questioning of the heroine's identity, which is then linked to her lack of a suitable partner. A meeting and moment of (mis)recognition with her lover/husband-to-be typically follows and closure is achieved only after all initial differences have been reconciled. So, in the context of this narrative commonality, is the 'vicarious nurturance and enjoyment'[17] that Radway's romances provide their readers equally essential to the operation of the German romantic comedies, or do these cinematic romantic narratives offer a more problematized and critical approach to gender and sexual identity in 1990s Germany?

Temby Caprio's argument that the 1990s saw a shift of emphasis from the socially critical women's film (*Frauenfilm*) to the politically correct women's comedy film (*Frauenkomödie*) should be viewed with a certain degree of caution.[18] Clearly, the films' positioning of these new anti-patriarchal heroines (such as the archetypal strong, blonde role model, Katja Riemann) within the genre of (heterosexual) relationship comedies must be treated with a certain amount of scepticism. However, I shall argue, in the second part of my discussion that the political significance of this positioning may be offset by the films' reclamation of a hetero-sexual desire that both patriarchy and an idealist feminist matriarchy have historically denied to women.

Aware of the importance of this historical context, Caprio sets out to evaluate this genre of woman-centred romantic comedies as a new brand of entertainment cinema for women, which combines both pleasure and politics in its articulation of a specifically female desire. Focusing on Katja von Garnier's popularly acclaimed graduation film *Making Up*, she cites Claire Johnston's call for a filmic response to both the over-politicized feminist-centred film,[19] and the equally extreme ideological positioning of mainstream cinematic representations of women. Consequently, my final question will focus upon the extent to which the success of women's filmmaking in the 1970s in 'represen-ting and foregrounding the authentic experiences of women', and representing the 'particular aspects of women's reality that have been traditionally excluded from the public sphere' can be seen as part of a tradition that has been continued into the 1990s.[20]

THE PROMISE OF PATRIARCHY

As with many of this decade's most successful young German directors, Katja von Garnier seems uncomfortable with comparisons between her work and that of the auteurist filmmakers (*Autorenfilmer*) of the 1960s and 1970s, declaring that, 'there is so much to say about women today that is funny and ironic. A funny "women's film" – it sounds like a contradiction in terms – has been a rare thing in Germany up until now. In the past everything was so dreadfully serious'.[21]

The move away from the explicitly foregrounded gender politics and socio-political critique of the 1970s women's film has been well documented in the German context, with female directors increasingly keen to avoid being put in the 'women's corner'.[22] Consequently, von Garnier's aim is to portray female characters from the 1990s who share neither the career obsessions of the 1980s nor the feminist hang-ups of the 1970s. However, while rejecting the title of women's film she has no doubt as to the reason for the success of her debut film *Making Up*, stating that, 'women can recognise themselves and men can learn something'.[23] This acknowledgement of both specifically female-orientated themes of identification and a pedagogy directed towards men seems to somewhat contradict this anti-feminist stance. Clearly, the film adheres in terms of narrative, casting and subject matter to the norms of a classical, mainstream cinema. However, its female authorship, its focus on issues of female gender and sexuality, so symptomatic of the 1990s German comedies, and its commodification as a product designed to appeal to a predominantly young and female audience, all combine to position it within a wider tradition of feminist filmmaking and the contemporary sociological feminist debate.[24]

As is the case with all of the woman-centred New German Comedies, *Making Up* traces a path from middle-class identity crisis to ultimate conflict resolution. As is invariably the case in the 1990s 'Comedia Sexualis',[25] these somewhat premature mid-life crises are expressed in terms of relationship difficulties: in other words, the lack or unsuitability of a partner. In *Making Up* the identity crisis which faces the central female protagonist Frenzy (Katja Riemann), and which articulates itself in her artistic block, is ultimately resolved through her relationship with the German–American soldier, Mark. This reactionary structural core of conflict resolution through traditional heterosexual romantic involvement is as integral to the new German romantic comedy film as it is to the narrative development of Radway's ideal romances. Frenzy's initial resistance to this involvement is as typical of Riemann's archetypal portrayal of the strong, aggressively independent careerist as it is of the ideal heroine of romantic fiction. Indeed, as will be seen from her portrayal of the central female protagonists in *Making Up, Maybe, Maybe Not, A Man for Every Situation* and *Talk of the Town*, Riemann corresponds to the model of the ideal heroine of romantic fiction in almost every respect.

These characters are invariably coded as displaying the 'male' characteristics of independence (from male financial support), professional aptitude (in the traditionally male-dominated public sphere of work and business), and a spunky tomboyishness, suggestive of the possibility of an autonomous, potentially aggressive sexuality. However, in the films as in the works of fiction, the initial strength and independence attributed to these female protagonists is ultimately compromised. Frenzy's capitulation to the powers of the patriarchal status quo in *Making Up* would appear to be twofold. Subsequent to her meeting with Mark, she not only compromises her sexual integrity by abandoning her 'male' characteristics of bad-tempered tomboyishness (in favour of a decidedly patriarchal concept of femininity), but also her professional and artistic integrity, as she willingly transforms the acerbic 'mosquito woman' of her cartoon strip into an almost porno-graphic male sexual fantasy.

REBELS, REACTIONARIES AND RELATIONSHIP CRISES

This rebel-to-reactionary transformation clearly reproduces gender stereotypes through its advocation of a changed sense of female self within an unchanged social arrangement. In Rainer Kaufmann's *Talk of the Town* Riemann plays Monika, a 30-something radio presenter and agony aunt who hosts an early morning radio show. Creative jobs are key to the romantic comedies, both as markers of middle-class status and character individuation. Such themes are clearly integral to the identifi-cation and reassurance which the films offer the aspirationally bohemian, yet financially secure, elites at which they are aimed. Interestingly, such professions are also cited by Radway in relation to the ideal heroines of romantic fiction. Literary and media jobs, such as those occupied by Frenzy, Monika, Rhoda in *Workaholic* and Franziska in *The Superwife* are especially favoured by the authors of the ideal romances. On the one hand, these television and radio presenters, graphic designers and novelists all occupy particular positions of power and cultural capital vis-à-vis the culturally mediated use and manipulation of language.[26] However, in their career choices these female protagonists would also appear to engage with the more general feminist debate surrounding the visibility and representation of women within the public sphere. In this respect, their presence as successful, independent and culturally visible women offers a fictional counterpoint to Gaye Tuchman's seminal critique of the 'symbolic annihilation of women'[27] within the mass media.

Exhorting her female listeners to emancipate themselves from their inadequate male partners, Monika's potentially radical socio-sexual stance and self-sufficiency in Kaufmann's *Talk of the Town* is, however, quickly subsumed within the much larger generic concern of the relationship crisis. Like Frenzy, she is 30 and partnerless; 'a biological time-bomb'[28] just waiting to explode, according to her mother. As with all romantic heroines, the greater her initial resistance to the notion of romantic involvement ('a man is really the last thing that I need'),[29] the greater the significance of her ultimate transformation. Monika's subsequent overnight transformation from apparently strong, independent career woman to gooey-eyed, lovesick teenager mirrors the feminization process that Frenzy undergoes in *Making Up*. Significantly, she is ultimately attracted to Erik, the older, professional, patriarchal figure and the epitome of bourgeois respectability and conservatism.

SEX, MARRIAGE AND AGEING PATRIARCHS

In Timm's *A Man for Every Situation*, Riemann's initial romantic suitor, Klaus Klett is hardly less reactionary in his machismic representation. Appearing out of the night in a screech of ABS brakes and exhaust fumes, the suited, cigar-smoking 'Dr Porsche' makes clear the power imbalance of this particular damsel-in-distress scenario, as he whisks Pauline Frohmuth (Riemann) away from her broken down VW Beetle and speeds her to her opera recital. Klett's power is defined in terms of professional success, material affluence and sexual prowess. This is in contrast to Pauline's junior status, uncertain career prospects and apparently inferior socio-economic standing. Immediately categorized in terms of his chauvinism and predatory sexual nature, he mocks Pauline for her career ambitions while unashamedly gazing on her exposed flesh as she changes out of her wet clothes in the passenger seat.

The foil to Klett's hyper-masculinity comes in the shape of the romantically attentive and sensitive culture critic Georg Lalinde. Klett's aggressive, patriarchal seduction of Pauline is problematized by her parallel and very different love affair with Georg. However, it is ultimately the arrogant and promiscuous misogynist Klaus who proves to be both the father of Pauline's unborn twins and the ultimate source of romantic fulfilment and patriarchal support. The feminized, impotent

Georg, tyrannized by his wife and rejected by Pauline, returns to the opera stalls and to his role as critic, a role that precludes all but vicarious involvement with the (melo)dramatic narratives of life. The ideal romance's citation of patriarchal aggression and arrogance as a moment of female *mis*recognition is clearly evoked here and Pauline is left to set up home with the shameless, lousy, arrogant show-off'[30] she once so fiercely berated.

In Sönke Wortmann's 1996 hit comedy *The Superwife*, this model of female transformation from rebellion to conformity appears to be inverted. As its title suggests, this film arguably engages more directly than any of the other films discussed here with the question of women's rights and women's position in a male-dominated society and, more particularly, with the 'personal costs hidden inside the role of wife and mother'.[31] Thomas Heinze, the typecast male chauvinist pig of the New German Comedy film, is Will Groß, an exploitative and unfaithful husband, as well as an entirely inadequate father. This character functions to expose any fantasies still remaining with regard to the institution of bourgeois family life. His systematic exploitation of Franziska leaves little doubt as to the uncomfortable reality behind the ideal romance's reassuring assertion (to its predominantly married readers) that the institution of marriage is ultimately 'protective of women's interests'.[32]

The cultural representation of family as a social system 'whose basic rightness must not be challenged'[33] is brought under equal pressure, reconfigured from a *locus* of support and solidarity to one of female oppression and patriarchal domination. This destabilization of reactionary notions of masculinity through the rejection of patriarchal support systems is a theme common to all of the woman-centred relationship comedies. Contrasting the weaknesses and general negative influence of the patriarchal figure with the strength and hidden potential of the matriarch, *The Superwife* is typical in this respect. Franziska's success in both public and private spheres of work and family is assured, but only after her divorce.

Traditionally, the institution of marriage constituted the founding social norm of the mainstream romantic comedy.[34] In other words, the comedy revolved around relationship difficulties which were ultimately resolved through marriage. In this way marriage was mysticized through its link with romantic love and the bourgeois status quo was maintained. According to David Shumway the traditional romantic comedy constructs the illusion that both complete desire and complete satisfaction are obtainable and that it is through marriage that they can be obtained.[35] In the contemporary German romantic comedy, however, marriage is either rejected as an institution ultimately exploitative of women (as in *Talk of the Town* and *The Superwife*), or simply ignored as an obsolete relic of a parental generation (as in *Making Up*). In view of this demystification of marriage, where, then, is the 'romance' of these apparently 'romantic' comedies posited and how are the desires of their largely female audiences negotiated?

FANTASY, FEMINISM AND GIRL POWER

In the case of Franziska, the relationship of desire constructed between performer and spectator would appear to revolve around a tripartite amalgamation of independence, empowerment and glamour. From the outset the progressive qualities of this female heroine are relativized by the accidental nature of her divorce. There is also the problematic issue of the representation of male/female relationships as existing solely on a sexual level.[36] Indeed, as with all of the New German Comedy women, Franziska is as incapable of forming platonic relationships with hetero-sexual males as they are of viewing her as anything other than a sex object. This view of relationships between men and women as existing only on a sexual level, 'cancel[s] out completely the possibility of any relationship other than the romantic one between boy and girl',[37] and can only work in favour of a patriarchal ideology, which seeks to place women in the role of wife and mother and prevent any meeting of the sexes on equal terms.

The dream of empowerment represented by Franziska's overnight transformation from downtrodden housewife to best-selling author is equally questionable, both in the choice of the glamorous actress Veronica Ferres to play this role and the film's narrative reliance on chance and luck.[38] Furthermore, it is doubtful whether Franziska has truly escaped a patriarchally defined femininity. In her single-minded pursuit of commercial success, her aggressive seduction of two passing acquaintances, and her excessive bout of drinking (followed by a hefty session of throwing up), Franziska is clearly out to prove that she can beat the boys at their own game. The paradox is that in spite of this wholesale adoption of apparently male qualities, she never loses a certain 'girlier-than-girliness'.[39] Remaining sweetly and prettily naïve throughout, Franziska dutifully fulfils her role of mother, whilst retaining an overtly raunchy sex appeal.[40] In other words, while having pretensions to the accolade of *Superwife*, she simultaneously fulfils all of the demands placed upon her by a demanding and exploitative patriarchy.

Conforming to Radway's model of the ideal heroine, the New German Comedy women are never vain but always beautiful, tending almost to neglect their bodies in their rejection of cosmetic artificiality. Riemann is the prime exponent of this particular 'natural look'. Refusing Maischa's lipstick in *Making Up*, she requires the help of her brother to 'feminize' her in *Talk of the Town*, and displays a consistent preference for the androgynous look of jeans, tie and waistcoat in *A Man for Every Situation*. However, this initial challenge to stereotypes of traditional feminine behaviour is given the lie by the widespread media dissemination of these actresses as sex objects. Physical attractiveness is clearly a key signifier in the audience's scopophilic fantasy of identification with these stars, and in the case of the heroines of our ideal romances and romantic comedies, outward appearance is explicitly connected to traditional conceptions of a 'natural' femininity. Indeed, the fears and dangers of even short periods of female sexual unattractiveness are constantly reinvoked in the New German Comedies. Whether they have to battle against flabby arms (Monika in *Talk of the Town*), spots (Maischa in *Making Up*), or a bloated stomach (Rhoda in *Workaholic*), the women of New German Comedy must always remain sexually attractive if they want to prevent their men from wandering. Ultimately, it is the recognition of this uncomfortable reality which precipitates the pivotal glamorous transformation scenes integral to all of the films examined here.

According to Naomi Wolf, the mass dissemination of images of overtly sexualized women (as well as the mass neurosis inspired by it) constitutes a form of social control emanating from 'a violent backlash against feminism that uses images of female beauty as a political weapon against women's advancement: the beauty myth'.[41] Clearly, such images would appear to perpetuate the patriarchal bias of 'the look' in cinema; women are defined by appearance and ultimately attractiveness to men. However, this interpretation fails to take into account the portrayal of female camaraderie and support which remains a defining feature of the woman-centred New German Comedies. Indeed, both in the context of a romance between women (an aspect of the films I shall examine shortly) and the representation of Riemann as embodying a 'natural', make-up-free attractiveness, there is a space for a reconfiguration of the 'look' from male to female gaze.

WOMEN AMONGST WOMEN

The women are single, career-minded and almost always childless. The spiritual balance is no longer held in place by the 'dream man' but rather the girlfriend, mother or like-minded best-friend.[42]

Making Up's exploration of female camaraderie, as embodied in the relationship between Frenzy and Maischa, is a significant point of departure from Radway's model of the perfect romance. Believing that all romantic fiction originates in the failure of patriarchal culture to fulfil its female subjects, Radway draws on Nancy Chodorow's socio-psychoanalytic deconstruction of female identity formation.[43] Of particular relevance to the comedies examined here is the way in which Chodorow's feminist revisions of Freud impact on the tripartite daughter–mother–father relationship. For Chodorow the socio-historical positioning of women as mothers results in the constitution of female children with an ongoing need and desire for their primary parent, the mother. Consequently, a tension arises in the mature female identity between Oedipal and pre-Oedipal objects of desire. Drawing on this, Radway is able to hypothesize that the reader of the romance attempts, through the nurture and security provided by the ideal romance, to return to a pre-Oedipal state of maternal nurture. Ultimately, this pre-Oedipal mother figure represents a state of fulfilment which cannot be achieved within the traditional system of patriarchal, heterosexual relations. In this respect, the goal of all romances can be seen as the symbiotic reunion of the child/reader and mother/pre-Oedipal, non-patriarchal figure. The romance reader, like all women, must achieve two objectives to overcome the sense of loss engendered by this separation from the pre-Oedipal figure of nurture: firstly, she must recognize the unsatisfactory nature of the patriarchal society which initially engendered this lack; secondly, she must find someone to replace a patriarchal figure who, within the existing system of societal relations, can never realistically fulfil her needs. Paradoxically, the security, reassurance and fulfilment provided in the fantasy world of the ideal romance depend upon precisely these two realizations never coming to light.

In von Garnier's *Making Up*, as in all of the woman-centred New German Comedies, this utopian promise of successfully managed heterosexual relations is explicitly challenged. From the outset, in which the two friends compete to invent 'the biggest lie in the world' ('die größte Lüge der Welt'), the scene is set for a playful exploration of an intimate and mutually supportive female camaraderie, and this in the face of a general male inadequacy. Initially, the character of Maischa appears to conform to the ideal romance's stereotype of the predatory femme-fatale foil, who dresses to kill and feels no compunction in pursuing and taking a new lover when her boyfriend's back is turned. In contrast, Frenzy is coded as embodying a 'natural' sexual innocence, hiding behind a facade of cynical men-weariness. Her continued advice to Maischa, 'that life is about more than just men'[44] is, however, ignored.

Maischa's positioning as an object of male sexual fantasy is asserted from the very beginning of the film, when the semantic link is made to her job as a nurse by the fact that an elderly male patient constantly tries to grope her. The scene of her petulant deception of her boyfriend operates on several levels. On the one hand, Frenzy's aiding and abetting of the lie reinforces the film's theme of female collusion in the face of an inadequate and unimaginative male population, as embodied in Maischa's boring boyfriend, Klaus. However, this initial act also marks Maischa out as a potential threat to the idyll of patriarchy. This 'made-up' vamp not only lies to her boyfriend, but in her pursuit of René displays a promiscuity and an aggressive sexuality which represent a direct threat to patriarchal order.[45]

According to the norms of dominant classical cinema, as well as those of the ideal romance, such a female must eventually be punished. The punishment is summarily delivered by the lover that she has so aggressively pursued. Within a patriarchal society, women who step outside the bounds of the traditional monogamous heterosexual relationship run the risk of losing all recourse to the respect and protection that this institution apparently affords. In the world of the ideal romance this new morality of female promiscuity is unambiguously condemned, because it threatens both the patriarchal institution of marriage and traditional (patriarchal) notions of female sexuality. In contrast, the romantic history of our single, independent heroine, Frenzy, remains unelaborated. Consequently, her sexuality retains an aura of both innocence and ambiguity.

The apparently reactionary nature of this tale of good femininity versus bad femininity is, however, far from straightforward. The first problem lies in the sex scene between Maischa and René. Having attained her long-sought-after goal of seduction, Maischa realizes that for René she represents nothing more than a workout machine on which to expend his sexual energy and physical vanity. This investigation of the possibility of an abusive system of male/female relationships is of equal consequence to the ideal romance. The romantic hero's initial behaviour is normally presented as highly ambivalent or at least ambiguous, a fact which the heroine invariably interprets as evidence of his purely sexual interest in her. However, the utopian promise of patriarchy that Radway sees the ideal romance as providing for its readers dictates that this recognition of men's treatment of women as purely sex objects is ultimately coded as a moment of misrecognition. This is achieved through a transformation of the hero's aggression into tenderness, the implication being that his initial behaviour must have been the result of a previous hurt, suffered at the hands of a bad woman. The ideological message is clear. Firstly, male aggression towards women is natural and should, therefore, be forgiven, as it is merely a defence mechanism to protect men from being repeatedly hurt at the hands of women. Secondly, this socially unattractive character trait hides a much more profound nature of tenderness and respect. And finally, male objectification and fetishization of the female form is a myth, a myth which the heroine must eventually recognize as such.

Maischa's relationship with René challenges all of these assumptions.

René's initial display of complete self-obsession and egotism in his dinner conversation with Maischa is shown to hide not tenderness but merely a deeper level of self-interest and vanity. The abusive nature of the sex is reinforced both by Maischa's detached observation of the ceiling during intercourse, and her subsequent traumatized scrubbing of her unclean, abused body. In terms of the ideal romance, this direct semantic link with rape comes far too close to exposing the uncomfortable truth about the myths of patriarchal tenderness and respect. This combination of patriarchal abuse and sexual predation is cited directly by Radway's romance readers as a clear indication of a failed romance.[46] Indeed, one of the key functions of the ideal romance is the diffusion of women's fear of male aggression. In this case the opposite is achieved. In addition, Maischa, the punished, femme-fatale foil, is reinstated as a positive role model by virtue of her new-found independence (indicated, albeit somewhat superficially, by her single-handed construction of her own bookshelves) and her association with Frenzy.

In contrast, the juxtaposed relationship of Frenzy and Mark would appear to be directly implicated in the promotion of the utopian promise of patriarchy. This relationship conforms in almost every respect to the ideal romance's ideal of heterosexual relations, from the questioning of identity arising from relationship difficulties (common to all the woman-centred New German Comedies), to the ultimate promise of the validity of the patriarchal norms of femininity and heterosexual relations. There is now a debate surrounding the validity of these norms in a pluralist, postmodern society where heterosexuality is now merely a choice amongst other choices and the nuclear family is becoming increasingly exceptional. Such a situation is explicitly cited as Frenzy and Maischa discuss the predominance of homosexual behaviour amongst animals and the rigidity of Frenzy's father's opinion of women's societal roles, as defined by the boundaries of 'marriage, kids and so on'.[47]

ROMANCE BETWEEN WOMEN

The suggestion of a sensual, almost sexual dimension to the two friends' relationship is toyed with in several scenes of the film. The first comes as

Frenzy hovers over the sleeping-beauty form of Maischa, tempting her lips with various delicacies designed to arouse her from her slumbers. The sexual connotations of the final spoonful of chocolate, with its contemporary semantic links as the female aphrodisiac and 'better-than-sex', suggest another layer of intimacy than that already indicated by their sharing of the marital bed. The calm of this gentle awakening is immediately countered, however, as Maischa remembers her forth-coming date and throws herself into a desperate hunt for the ideal outfit. The performative aspects of this *Pretty Woman* scene, replicated in Rhoda's and Elly's shopping spree in Wietersheim's *Workaholic*, represent a microcosm of the film as a whole, as it playfully explores issues of female identity and sexuality.

Of greater significance, however, is the inversion of the traditional cinematic male gaze, as Frenzy observes Maischa dressing and un-dressing. The dichotomy of personality is extended into the realm of clothing as Frenzy rejects the sex object connotations of Maischa's tight-fitting, sexy little number, in favour of baggy jogging pants, hooded top and a generally *abgeschminkt* ('un-made-up') appearance. While Maischa expends her energy on rote-learning football scores in the hope of impressing her date, Frenzy concentrates on her artwork, thus reiterating the division between private and public realms as potential *loci* of female individuation. The physical intimacy of their friendship, as they uninhibitedly share bathroom and toilet space in this partition-less converted warehouse, is further emphasized by their playful cheek to cheek waltzing and frank discussion of each others' bodies: thus Frenzy tells Maischa, 'I thinks your breasts are beautiful'.[48]

Echoes of this woman-to-woman sensuality can also be seen in the relationship between Monika and Sabine in *Talk of the Town*. This is particularly apparent in their first meeting which takes place in the fitness studio that both women have unwittingly joined. In an attempt to maintain their physical attractiveness to their men (or *man*, wherein lies the comic irony of their meeting), both women submit themselves to strenuous workout regimes. Undercutting the patriarchal conformity of this obsession with physical appearance, however, is the suggestion of a sensual or even sexual attraction as part of their initial friendship. When a fight breaks out between two women in the gym Monika and Sabine enjoy a shared smile of understanding before rushing to break up the warring parties. Back to back they hold the women apart before turning to face each other flushed and excited. Sabine's coy smile instantly results in a self-conscious patting into place of her hair on the part of Monika.

As if in denial of the sexual/sensual space duly opened, the next scene sees a starry-eyed Monika hovering over Erik's romantic answering phone message, which she remotely accesses from the gym payphone. However, catching up with Sabine on their way out of the gym Monika suggests hesitantly, 'Of course, you don't have any time just now, do you?'[49] This then instigates a dinner engagement which closes with the two women walking intimately arm in arm, as they discuss their respective lives and the perfect existence which each sees the other as leading. Monika's bashful closing comment, 'that was really lovely',[50] completes the romantic imagery of this first-date scenario. This initial meeting sets the scene for the couple's ultimate togetherness which, although never overtly developed on a sexual level, is shown to be much deeper and stronger than any of the heterosexual relationships they subsequently pursue.

In her gender analysis of Michael Crichton's *Coma* (1977), Christine Gledhill recognizes the significance of the single-sex fitness studio as a subcultural social space suggestive of an order outside of the parameters of conventional heterosexual self-definition.[51] In this space where women meet, talk and take pleasure in physical being and membership of an exclusively female community, there exists scope for a gendering or repossession of the cinematic look as women watch women and women interact with women. This repositioning of the pleasure of looking at female bodies, suggestive of a gendered complicity or social solidarity at odds with the foundational narrative imperative of the gender comedy is present in the scenes between Frenzy and Maischa, and Monika and Sabine.

David Shumway suggests that this contemporary reworking of the screwball or romantic comedy genre to include the possibility of romance between women is of potentially political significance. Citing the example of Susan Seidelman's *Desperately Seeking Susan* (1985), he writes of the 'romance of identification' between the two female protagonists, which 'given the lack of female identification by women in screwball comedies or other Hollywood films [...] must be regarded as a politically significant reversal of convention'.[52] This relationship between Roberta and Susan is mirrored in both *Talk of the Town* and *Making Up*, in which both female couples find female identification to be far more fulfilling and reliable.

In Chodorow's terms, the exploration of female camaraderie, sensuality and the possibility of alternatives to traditional patriarchal support systems, as embodied in the relationships between Maischa and Frenzy (*Making Up*), Monika and Sabine (*Talk of the Town*), Pauline and Uschi (*A Man for Every Situation*), and Rhoda and Elly (*Workaholic*), can be read as an investigation of a pre-Oedipal wish for a non-patriarchal figure of nurture and, as Radway suggests, 'all that it implies – erotic pleasure, symbiotic completion and identity confirmation'.[53] In this respect, Eve Sedgwick's concept of the 'homosocial bond', developed to account for the nature and significance of male/male relationships as represented in the mid-eighteenth- to mid-nineteenth-century novel, can be reconfigured to an exclusively female setting.[54] In these romantic comedy films it is women, and not men, who ultimately promote the interests of women, thereby occupying the position of provider (*Versorger*) traditionally attributed to the patriarchal male.

UNAMBIGUOUS ENDINGS?

As the misdemeanours of the *Talk of the Town*'s Erik are gradually exposed, it becomes clear that the bond of female camaraderie between Monika and Sabine will be tested to the full. However, their consequent rejection of Erik allows them to recement their relationships in the face of general patriarchal inadequacy. The best (girl)friend, the non-patriarchal male and the sympathetic mother (in other words, the bonds of homosociality and homosexuality) prove to be the most reliable support systems. Monogamy, already discredited by the unequal burdens of chastity it has been shown to place on its subjects, is further brought into question by Monika's and Sabine's implied continued carefree promiscuity. The film plays out to the song 'It's So Nice to Have a Man about the House', providing the ironic backdrop for yet another literal and metaphorical kicking out of the heterosexual, patriarchal male.

At the end of *The Superwife*, Franziska basks in the material comforts that her new-found literary acclaim have won her, albeit in the somewhat compromised setting of capitalist Hollywood. This compromise, ultimately integral to her success, is initially foregrounded by her ex-husband's bastardization of her first novel to conform to the demands of a male-orientated, commercial cinema industry. In spite of this, however, Franziska's transformation from demure and dependent wife and mother to feisty, autonomous career-woman leaves us in no doubt as to the winners and losers of this particular metamorphosis scenario.

In contrast to the ideal romance, the final credits of *Making Up* do not roll to an enjoyable and nurturing invocation of a consummated male/female togetherness but rather to an explicitly female-directed address of female/female camaraderie and fulfilment. Again the bonds of homosociality are shown to be infinitely preferable to those of heterosexuality. The goal of Chodorow's search for the mother has been achieved and made flesh. In the face of an obsolete parental generation, and abusive or feminized patriarchs, the best female friend represents the only suitable carer. Frenzy may have found a boyfriend, and in so doing overcome her writer's block, but it is a boyfriend whose absence renders him just as inadequate as every other man in *Making Up*, from Frenzy's sexist, leering boss who ultimately forces her to an artistic compromise, to Maischa's boring boyfriends and abusive lovers. The final broken frame shot in which Frenzy and Maischa turn to the camera and introduce themselves directly to their female audiences is extremely significant in this respect. Clearly, it is women who represent the true brokers of women's pleasure – just as it is women (Katja von Garnier and Katja Riemann among them) who stand to make a commercial killing out of this process of pleasure-brokering.

SELF-REFLEXIVITY AND GENERIC SUBVERSION

The self-reflexive nature of *Making Up*'s final address is significant on several levels. As an explicit point of rupture or distanciation it demonstrates the film's awareness of its role as a woman's film, thus paying lip service, at least, to the feminist filmmaking tradition that lies behind it. In so doing, it exposes the narrative conventions of the romance genre to which it belongs and which it is in the process of subverting. It is in the context of the film's 'reflexive, deconstructive relation to what is recognized as the standard classic text'[55] that the location of a potentially progressive textual politics becomes possible.

Shumway sees metaphors for sexual consummation in the endings of all romantic comedies. Such an interpretation adds an extra, sexual level of signification to the positing of female/female relationships as the point of closure in both *Making Up* and *Talk of the Town*. The problem with such a radical reading of the films from a feminist perspective, however, is that it ignores the norm of heterosexual relations which all three ultimately reproduce. This represents the fundamental contradiction upon which all of the films are built. The ideal romance's positing of the patriarchal male as the path to the 'symbolic fulfilment of a woman's desire to realize her most basic female self in relation to another'[56] has been unambiguously rejected. The films are not concerned with the ideal romance's 'imaginative transformation of masculinity to conform with female standards',[57] but rather with the rejection of the masculine altogether. And yet, the implication with which all three of the films conclude is that our heroines will continue to pursue an aggressive, 'girl-power' heterosexual promiscuity, despite the process of demystification of the male/female romantic myth to which they have been party. However, this apparent contradiction can itself be politicized when we read it as a refusal of closure.

According to Shumway the ending of the traditional romantic comedy represents 'an absolute point, an eternal moment in which all contradictions are resolved under a force that allows no differences, no excess'.[58] In contrast, these German romantic comedies fail completely as romances in that they can never convincingly resolve their representation of female independence, solidarity and recognition of patriarchal inadequacy with the sexual norms their generic form historically dictates. Adopting the interpretation of genre as a set of rules for the production of meaning which operate through both reading and writing, this display of 'difference from the environment of conventions within which these films exist',[59] and its apparent resonance with its female audience would appear to establish a claim to a certain generic progressivity. Making explicit the inherent tensions between 'feminism as an emergent ideology and romance as a residual genre'[60] this notion of generic subversion remains central to any political, cultural studies reading of the woman-centred New German Comedies.

This subversion is typical of the contemporary use of genre conventions not 'as a blueprint for the production of a popular commodity, but as a historical form to be self-consciously used as needed: transformed, parodied, played off against, and so on'.[61] In other words, even if we accept the historical mutability of the genre form recognized within film studies from André Bazin onwards, and the dangers in ascribing progressivity to a structure which relies upon the disruption of historically received norms, these comedies still embody a clear reconfiguration of the relationship between film, filmmaker and audience. In *Making Up*, *The Superwife* and *Talk of the Town* romantic closure is resisted and thus the endings are never sufficient to contain the 'excess of meaning produced in the course of the film'.[62] They unambiguously reject the vicarious nurturing of the ideal romance while at the same time offering a tantalizing glimpse of a future alternative object of desire. Merchants in the brokering of women's pleasure themselves, they nevertheless make explicit the 'temporality of satisfaction'[63] that the romantic consummation of the traditional romantic comedy is at such pains to conceal.

However, by its very definition the consummation of the romance must question the goal of its own narrative trajectory. In other words, a romantic fantasy that constructs itself around the pursuit of an idealized object must, with the attainment of this object, cease to be romantic. I would argue that by avoiding this death of desire these New German Comedies ultimately broker pleasure to their female audiences. As failed romances, which reaffirm the female homosocial bond while questioning the 'postmodern cult of Eros'[64] and its idealized conceptions of love and intimacy, these films resist the fixing of desire, thus resisting the consummation of the narrative for their female audiences. According to Gledhill, the narrative organization of the classic mainstream cinematic text functions to hierarchize the 'different aesthetic and ideological discourses which intersect in the processes of the text, to produce a unifying, authoritative voice or viewpoint'.[65] The woman-centred New German Comedies, however, resist the 'complete reading' which such classic narrative organization and closure offers to its audience. This allows the 'ambiguities' and 'enigmatic false trails'[66] generated by the processes of the text to remain ambiguously open.

For Frenzy, Monika, Franziska, Rhoda and Pauline the romantic fantasy is maintained by consciously playing with the idea of the ideal romance while never quite subscribing to the stasis of its ultimate consummation. With the exception of Pauline, all of these female protagonists appear to acknowledge that emotional intensity can only be maintained by the avoidance of 'love that has been besmirched by the mundanities of marriage and family'.[67] In this respect, Pauline's ultimate acceptance of marital union is problematic. Drawing on overtly reactionary bourgeois notions of motherhood and family, the narrative logic of the film would appear to suggest that for pregnant women there remains little (socially) acceptable alternative other than that of marriage. Pauline shows an initial resolution to retain her independence and integrity by adopting the more socially ambiguous role of single mother and careerist. Ultimately however, Pauline's future happiness is only assured after marital union and the financial security which this brings. This would appear to tie in with Steve Neale and Frank Krutnik's model of the romantic comedy which allows for the treatment of conflicting tendencies in the desires of the woman, but only if they are 'made meaningful in regard to her eventual, and inevitable, integration within heterosexual monogamy'.[68]

And yet, this reading of the ending of *A Man for Every Situation* as politically reactionary is far from simple. The inversion of traditional gender roles, which places Pauline in the public sphere and at the height of her professional success and Klaus in the domestic role of carer and male figure of support, leaves the audience with no doubt that traditional gender inequalities have been effectively redressed. In addition, the fantastical nature of Klaus' unexplained transformation from arrogant, promiscuous macho man, to loving, supportive and domesticated carer questions the narrative veracity of this gloriously optimistic ending. In this respect, the film's conclusion would appear to conform to Klinger's construction of the progressive genre in which the traditional narrative form is exaggerated to such an extent that it exposes the irony, or excess of meaning, which must lie at the heart of its reinstatement of narrative equilibrium.

Whatever the processes involved, the 'competencies' articulated by

Radway which 'prepare certain women to recognize romances as relevant to their experience and as potential routes to pleasure'[69] would appear to have undergone a radical reconfiguration. In their playful, if not parodic, engagement with key culturally and discursively defined constituents of female identity (namely, motherhood, heterosexuality, romantic longing, sexual desire, friendship, marriage and career) the New German Comedy films and their female protagonists engender a subversive laughter which represents their true *locus* of textual politics. It is this popular reformulation of the romantic comedy genre that I would argue facilitates the socio-psychological extension of our original textual analysis; and it is within this laughter and the ultimate denial of the 'vicarious nurturance and enjoyment' of romantic narrative consummation, that we can ultimately find the true discourse of resistance of these contemporary failed romances.

THE FAILED ROMANCE

> The after-effects of the women's movement are dealt with in the singles comedies – and this includes that original prototype, *Making Up* – but only on the superficial level of entertainment.[70]

As Caprio implies, it would be difficult to argue that Claire Johnston's vision of a cinema which combines both 'the notion of film as political tool and as entertainment' has been realized in these New German Comedies.[71] *Making Up, Talk of the Town, A Man for Every Situation, Workaholic*, and *The Superwife* all clearly embody elements of the struggle between the forces of incorporation and resistance, negotiation and play, which critics such as John Fiske and Christine Gledhill perceive in all marginal social groups 'emerging into new public self-identity' and becoming incorporated, as they do so, into the cultural mainstream.[72] Through their exploration of the themes of patriarchal inadequacy and female homosociality the films toy with the generic conventions of the romantic comedy. I would argue, however, that the questions they raise as to the nature of female sexuality and self-determination produce little more than a certain ambiguity. In this respect, they truly offer food for reflection upon the 'limits of political film-making in the nineties'.[73]

However, in the process these failed romances also negotiate a mainstream imaginary space in which a male-centred female reality is problematized and a female-centred alternative is explored. This interpretation of ideal romances as an 'exploration of the meaning of patriarchy for women'[74] can represent a more positive and useful starting point from which to approach these mainstream, woman-centred entertainment films and the ideological implications of their resonance with their female audiences. In their subversion of the romance and their exploration of a specifically female desire the woman-centred New German Comedies can be seen as contributing to a 'rewriting of the romance in an effort to articulate its founding fantasy to a more relevant politics'.[75]

Notes

1   All statistics from *FFA: German Federal Film Board*, http://www.ffa.de.

2   A reference to the mainstream melodramas, musicals and *Heimatfilme* which dominated the 1950s. Until the more recent revisionist work of Marc Silberman and Heide Fehrenbach these films had been largely ignored within histories of German film, labelled as escapist and reactionary populism for the masses. See Heide Fehrenbach, *Cinema in Democratizing Germany: Reconstructing National Identity after Hitler* (Chapel Hill and London: University of North Carolina, 1995); Jan-Christopher Horak, 'Die Tradition des deutschen Films' in Heike Amend and Michael Bütow (eds.), *Der bewegte Film* (Berlin: Vistas, 1997), pp. 13–24; Mark Silberman, *German Cinema: Texts in Context* (Detroit, Michigan: Wayne State University Press, 1995).

3   See David N. Coury, 'From Aesthetics to Commercialism: Narration and the New German Comedy', *Seminar*, 33.4 (1997), 356–73.

4   This term has come to represent a body of films which centre their slapstick narrative trajectories around the misadventures of uncouth, lower-class males, as typified by Tom Gerhardt's popular successes *Totally Normal* (*Voll Normaal*, 1994) and its sequel *Ballermann 6* (1997). See Georg Seeßlen, 'Warum das neue deutsche Komödienkino dem alten so furchtbar ähnlich ist', *Die Zeit*, 12 December 1997, p. 59.

5   According to Sabine Hake these films are typical of the mainstream cinematic output of the 1990s, relying on the 'adaptation of generic conventions to contemporary sensibilities' and, as we shall see, 'including an acute awareness of identity as a construction and a performance'. Hake, *German National Cinema* (London: Routledge, 2002), p. 182.

6   Originally cited by Andreas Kilb, 'Ein allerletzter Versuch, die neue deutsche Filmkomödie zu verstehen', *Die Zeit*, 26 April 1996, p. 49.

7   See Brad Hagen, 'Women control pic picks', *Variety*, 19–25 August 1996, p. 20.

8   See Claudia Lenssen, 'Departure from the "Women's Corner" – Women Filmmakers in Germany Today', *Kino Magazine*, 4 (2001), http://www.german-cinema.de/magazine/2001/04/focus/womens corner.html.

9   Hagen, 'Women control pic picks', p. 20.

10   Interviewed by Hagen, Anatol Nitschke, sales manager of independent film distributor Filmwelt-Prokino states that, 'all our marketing campaigns for films that could appeal to women are directed at them first'. See Hagen, 'Women control pic picks', p. 20.

11   For a more detailed discussion of the importance of female audiences throughout the history of German film see Janice Petro, *Joyless Streets: Women and Melodramatic Representation in Weimar Germany* (Princeton: Princeton University Press, 1989).

12   The term 'female-centred' – or, as I shall consequently refer to it, 'woman-centred' – implies a meta-genre of mainstream cultural texts, which focus on women and thematic concerns of direct relevance to women as the primary subjects of representation. In my understanding, the term carries with it no preconceptions as to the relative progressive or regressive nature of this representation. For a more detailed discussion see Toril Moi, 'Feminist, Female, Feminine' in Catherine Belsey and Jane Moore (eds.), *The Feminist Reader: Essays in Gender and the Politics of Literary Criticism* (London: Macmillan, 1989), pp. 117–32.

13   Coury, 'From Aesthetics to Commercialism', p. 356.

14   Janice Radway, *Reading the Romance* (London: Verso, 1987).

15   *ibid.*, p. 176.

16   In the German context, it is interesting to note the substantial percentage of the new relationship comedies which have been adapted from works of woman-centred popular fiction. Peter Timm's *A Man for Every Situation* and Sönke Wortmann's *The Superwife* both started out as best-sellers for women's author Hera Lind. More recently, Ingrid Noll's darker and more critical fictional explorations of women's relationship to the heterosexual norm, *The Pharmacist* (*Die Apothekerin*, 1997) and *The Heads of My Loved Ones* (*Die Häupter meiner Lieben*, 1999) have also been adapted for film by directors Rainer Kaufmann and Hans-Günther Bücking respectively.

17   Radway, *Reading the Romance*, p. 173.

18   Temby Caprio, 'Women's Cinema in the Nineties: *Abgeschminkt!* and Happy Ends?', *Seminar*, 33.4 (1997), 374–87 (p. 385).

19   See Claire Johnston, 'Women's Cinema as Counter Cinema', *Notes on Women's Cinema*, (Society for Education in Film and Television: London, 1973), pp. 24–31.

20   Julia Knight, *Women and the New German Cinema* (London: Verso, 1992), p. 87.

21   'Es gibt jetzt so viel Komisches und Ironisches über Frauen zu erzählen. Witzige Frauenfilme – klingt schon wie ein Widerspruch in sich – sind ja in Deutschland bisher selten. Alles war so entzetzlich schwerblütig.' 'Tempo, Tempo, Tempo: Die Regisseurin Katja von Garnier über ihren Überaschungserfolg *Abgeschminkt*', *Der Spiegel*, 6 September 1993, p. 214.

22   See Lenssen, 'Departure from the "Women's Corner"'.

23   'Frauen erkennen sich wieder, Männer können was lernen.' 'Tempo, Tempo, Tempo'.

24   For a more detailed discussion of *Making Up* in relation to a German tradition of feminist filmmaking see Caprio, 'Women's Cinema in the Nineties'.

25   See 'Das Lachen macht's', *Der Spiegel*, 16 September 1996, pp. 214–25 (p.223).

26   I draw here upon Pierre Bourdieu's term 'cultural capital', which refers to the significance of distinctions of cultural taste to the struggle between subordinate and dominant social groups. See Pierre Bourdieu, *Distinction: A Social Critique of the Judgement of Taste*, tr. Richard Nice (London: Routledge & Kegan Paul, 1984).

27   Gaye Tuchman, 'The Symbolic Annihilation of Women by the Mass Media' in Stanley Cohen and Jock Young (eds.), *The Manufacture of News: Social Problems, Deviance and the Mass Media*, revised edn (London: Constable, 1981), pp. 169–83 (p.183).

28   'eine biologische Zeitbombe'.

29   'Ein Mann ist wirklich das letzte, was ich brauche'.

30   'unverschämter mieser arroganter Angeber'.

31   Radway, *Reading the Romance*, p. 301.

32   *ibid.*, p. 74

33   Barbara Klinger, '"Cinema/Ideology/Criticism" Revisited: The Progressive Genre' in by Barry Keith Grant (ed.), *Film Genre Reader II* (Austin: University of Texas Press, 1995), pp. 74–90 (p. 79).

34   Steve Neale and Frank Krutnik, *Popular Film and Television Comedy* (London: Routledge, 1990), p. 136.

35   David R. Shumway, 'Screwball Comedies' in Grant (ed.), *Film Genre Reader II*, pp. 382–99 (p. 383).

36   The exception to the rule within the romantic comedy genre is where the male characters are coded as either feminized (as in the case of the gay characters René in *Talk of the Town* and Norbert in *Maybe, Maybe Not*) or desexualized (as with Enno in *The Superwife*).

37   Angela McRobbie, *Feminism and Youth Culture* (Basingstoke: Macmillan, 1991), pp. 98–9.

38   As Dwight Macdonald has argued, this process of *dis*empowerment in which 'the whole competitive struggle is presented as a lottery in which a few winners, no more talented or energetic than anyone else, drew the lucky tickets' is enacted in all products of mass culture. Macdonald, 'A Theory of Mass Culture' in Bernhard Rosenberg and David Manning White (eds.), *Mass Culture: The Popular Arts in America* (New York: Macmillan, 1957), pp. 59–73.

39   'This brand of "Girl Power" really is a kind of ad-agency version of what nineties feminism has become: a safe form of self-expression that has more to do with changing your hairstyle than changing the world. It is a strange combination of superficial bolshiness and girlier-than-girliness, of shocking appearance and utter conservatism [...] it is no real threat to anybody.' Betty Dodson, 'Girl Power: Safe Spice', *Living Marxism*, 100 (1996).

40   Clearly, Veronica Ferres's widespread media dissemination as a glamorized and sexualized star persona adds depth and authenticity to Franziska's glamorous transformation in *The Superwife*.

41   Naomi Wolf, *The Beauty Myth: How Images of Beauty Are Used Against Women* (London: Vintage, 1990), p. 10.

42   'Die Frauen sind alleinstehend, berufstätig und fast immer kinderlos. Das seelische Gleichgewicht hält kein Traummann aufrecht, sondern die Freundin, die Mutter oder der gleichgesinnte beste Freund.' 'Das Lachen macht's', p. 224.

43   Nancy Chodorow, *The Reproduction of Mothering: Psychoanalysis and the Sociology of Gender* (Berkeley: University of California, 1978).

44   'daß es im Leben um mehr geht als nur Männer!'.

45   For a discussion of the threat of female sexuality within German film see Andreas Huyssen, 'Technology and Sexuality in Fritz Lang's *Metropolis*', *New German Critique*, 24–25 (1981–1982), 221–37.

46   According to Radway, in the failed romance the narrative has not only emphasized 'the hero's extraordinary cruelty' but has also stressed 'the purely sexual nature of the attraction exerted by the heroine upon the hero'. Radway, *Reading the Romance*, p.169.

47   'heiraten, Kinder kriegen und so'.

48   'Also, ich finde deinen Busen wunderschön'.

49   'Du hast sicher keine Zeit'.

50   'Das war jetzt schön mit dir'.

51 Christine Gledhill, 'Pleasurable Negotiations' in Frances Bonner *et al.* (eds,), *Imagining Women: Cultural Representations and Gender*, 2nd edn (Cambridge: Polity Press, 1995), pp. 193–209.

52 Shumway, 'Screwball Comedies', p. 398.

53 See Radway, *Reading the Romance*, p. 146.

54 Eve Sedgwick, *Between Men: English Literature and Male Homosocial Desire* (New York: Columbia University Press, 1985).

55 Klinger, '"Cinema/Ideology/Criticism" Revisited', p. 77.

56 Radway, *Reading the Romance*, p. 151.

57 *ibid.*, p. 147.

58 Shumway, 'Screwball Comedies', p. 393.

59 Klinger, '"Cinema/Ideology/Criticism" Revisited', p. 79.

60 Radway, *Reading the Romance*, p. 304.

61 Shumway, 'Screwball Comedies', p. 395.

62 Klinger, '"Cinema/Ideology/Criticism" Revisited', p. 83.

63 Shumway, 'Screwball Comedies', p. 393.

64 Norman Denzin, *Theory, Culture & Society* (London: Sage, 1991), p. viii.

65 Gledhill, 'Pleasurable Negotiations', p. 193.

66 *ibid.*

67 Neale and Krutnik, *Popular Film and Television Comedy*, p. 135.

68 *ibid.*, p.139.

69 Radway, *Reading the Romance*, p. 300.

70 'Auf flachem Unterhaltungsniveau werden in vielen der Junggesellinnen-Farcen – auch hier gilt das Vorbild *Abgeschminkt* – die Nachwirkungen der Frauenbewegung verhandelt.' 'Das Lachen macht's', p. 222.

71 See Johnston, 'Women's Cinema as Counter Cinema'.

72 John Fiske, *Cultural Studies and the Study of Popular Culture* (Edinburgh: Edinburgh University Press, 1996), p. 4; Gledhill, 'Pleasurable Negotiations', p. 199.

73 Caprio, 'Women's Cinema in the Nineties', p. 385.

74 Radway, *Reading the Romance*, p. 75.

75 *ibid.*, p. 306.

Chapter 8

From perverse to queer: Rosa von Praunheim's films in the liberation movements of the Federal Republic

Randall Halle

In 1994 Rosa von Praunheim was out with his cameras to film the celebrations surrounding the repeal of §175. After over a century of existence in the German penal code, the government struck this paragraph, which had specifically criminalized male–male sexuality, from its books. §175 had ruined many lives in its long and infamous history and had passed through many forms – the most severe of which appeared during the Third Reich. However, historically the struggle against it had also sparked the formation in Germany of the world's first homosexual emancipation organization, Magnus Hirschfeld's Scientific–Humanitarian Committee. Thus it was very appropriate that von Praunheim should include the footage of the celebrations in his film *Gay Courage – 100 Years of the Gay Liberation Movement* (*Schwuler Mut – 100 Jahre Schwulenbewegung*, 1998). In over thirty years as an engaged filmmaker, von Praunheim has made more than fifty films, most of which address social transformations like the events of 1994. From the early gay liberation movement, through the AIDS crisis, to the outing scandals of the 1990s and the emergence of queer culture, von Praunheim the activist, filmmaker, media critic, author and personality has been a central figure. As a result of his engagement, von Praunheim could actually claim a special role in this victory. His film *Not the Homosexual Is Perverse, but the Situation in Which He Lives* (*Nicht der Homosexuelle ist pervers, sondern die Situation in der er lebt*) is commonly credited with setting off the modern gay liberation movement in Germany. The film premiered at the Berlinale in 1971 and sparked such controversy among both heterosexuals and homosexuals that the debates led directly to the formation of homosexual action groups. If with *Not the Homosexual* von Praunheim set a movement in motion, in *Gay Courage* he sought critically to document its emergence into political emancipation.

In his work it is possible to distinguish between documentary films that study and attend to social transformations and more socially satirical fiction films which seek to provoke transformation. *Not the Homosexual* was followed by documentaries like *Homosexuals in New York* (*Homosexuelle in New York*, 1971) and *Army of Lovers or Revolution of the Perverts* (*Armee der Liebenden oder Revolte der Perversen*, 1979). After the biting AIDS farce *A Virus Knows No Morals* (*Ein Virus kennt keine Moral*, 1985) he produced the *AIDS Trilogy* (1990). Likewise the documentaries *Transsexual Menace* (*Vor Transsexuellen wird gewarnt*, 1996) and *Queens Don't Cry* (*Tunten lügen nicht*, 2002) followed from *I Am My Own Woman* (*Ich bin meine eigene Frau*, 1992). *The Einstein of Sex: Life and Work of Dr M. Hirschfeld* (*Der Einstein des Sex – Leben und Werk des Dr. Hirschfeld*, 1999) followed *Gay Courage*. If we review this impressive body of films, comparing an earlier film like *Not the Homosexual* to von Praunheim's more recent productions, we recognize a dramatic transformation. The shifts in the titles of films alone, 'Homosexual', 'Pervert', 'Gay/*Schwul*', 'Queens/*Tunten*' gives some indication of the extent and parameters of this transformation. In his work of the 1990s in particular, we recognize von Praunheim's new participation in and contributions to the then emergent queer political movement.

If we step back from von Praunheim and survey the context of his film productions, we also recognize that politically, socially and philo-sophically the 1990s proved a decade of transformation in the overall discourse of gender and sexuality in the Federal Republic. After a century, §175 was, of course, repealed as part of the unification process. The Unification Treaty required that disparities in the penal codes of the GDR and the FRG had to be resolved; §175 did not exist in the East. At the same time, while gay men literally had cause to dance in the streets, we also should recall that the Bundestag of the new Federal Republic upheld §218, the West German anti-abortion paragraph, in the context of the same legislative review of the penal code. Although the legislature did retain a 'liberalized' form of §218 which allowed abortions, a heated debate driven by conservative and religious opinion mobilized opposition. Abortions can now only take place in the first trimester with a doctor's permission, and three days after a counselling session that urges the woman to change her mind. Women in the eastern federal states of the new Germany suddenly confronted the criminaliz- ation of a former right, and throughout Germany the struggle for women's self-determination had to continue. Of course conservative and religious figures also opposed the repeal of §175. However, the majority of the members of parliament no longer understood homosexuality as an illegal state, out of which other forms of criminal behaviour flowed. The state no longer sought to intervene in the private lives and choices of gay men even as it asserted its right to do so *vis-à-vis* women. These two decisions indicate a clear and gendered difference in the social phil- osophy around the regulation of sexuality.

Parallel to these transformations, heated debates erupted within the German academy about the status of research on gender and sexuality. The *Historikerinnenstreit* ('female historians debate'), as Atina Grossman characterized it, erupted among feminist historians in the 1990s.[1] This debate challenged assessments of the patriarchal structure of Nazi culture that viewed women as an oppressed class and, therefore, as exempt from culpability. The 'Butler Debate' resulted from the German reception of the work of Judith Butler in the 1990s, and incited partici- pants from the humanities and social sciences. I will come back later in the chapter to address the specifics of these debates. At this point it is important to recognize that although much of the debates might appear to the outsider as a matter of dense philosophy, the participants were engaged in a questioning of the terms of gender, sex and sexuality that materially shape institutional structures, as well as structure practically research orientations and curricula. These debates corresponded to attempts to carve out a space for the investigation of sexuality distinct from gender, and marked a strain between the related but institutionally more established Women's Studies and the newly emergent direction of Queer Studies.

The term queer/*quer* emerged in Germany at this time as a new descriptor not only of academic research but also of social organization and self-identification. Adapting the term from English, queer/*quer* emerged to compete with and even replace older designations like, homosexual, *Schwul*, gay and lesbian. The emergence of the new term marked a transformation in social organization, much like the emergence of Schwul in the context of the radical sexual liberation movements of the 1970s once competed with the clinical and pathologizing term 'homosexual'. Gay pride (*schwuler Stolz*) competed with queer consciousness (*queres Denken*). Queer contested the normalizing and integrating aspects of existing models of liberation, not only in the gay movement but also in the women's and lesbian movements. It opened up significant new possibilities of organization between and among once disparate communities: women, men, homosexuals, heterosexuals, gays, lesbians, bisexuals, transgendered, S/M activists, fetishists, AIDS activists, sex workers and so on. Beginning with common bars and clubs, this new social and political space has proven highly significant given that since the 1970s (or even, one might add, since the 1870s) there has been little co-ordination even between gay men and lesbians. Queer theoretical discussions of the interconnections in the social regulation of gender, sex and sexuality countered precisely the dominant social philosophy that isolated the women's and the gay liberation movements, and served to offer a new invigoration of political activism. Yet this new activism was not without debate or contention.

The emergence of queer had a profound effect on von Praunheim's film work, the central object of this chapter. Through von Praunheim's work we can both recognize the queer shift of the 1990s and what was at stake in the surrounding debates. In a birthday gift to himself, von Praunheim filmed *Neurosia: 50 Years of Perversion* (*Neurosia – 50 Jahre pevers*, 1995), a biting satire both of his own autobiography but also of the dynamics of sexual liberation. The title's positive evaluation of a lifetime of perversion stands in direct contrast to *Not the Homosexual Is Perverse*. Both films rely on satire and pseudo-documentary style, yet if we conduct a closer examination we will recognize that the earlier film presents a negative filmic portrayal of the gay male's self-incurred immaturity and tutelage to perversion, whereas the later film celebrates the perverse 'nature' of the gay man as precisely the site of his revolutionary potential. The next section of this chapter takes up *Not the Homosexual* as an example of the possibilities and limitations of gay liberation in order to clearly present a contrast with von Praunheim's contemporary work.

This pseudo-documentary *Not the Homosexual Is Perverse, but the Situation in which he Lives* presents a travelogue into the twilight world of the homosexual.[2] The film's narrative centers on Daniel, a country boy who comes to Berlin and begins a *Bildungsreise* more of the order of Alice in Wonderland than Wilhelm Meister. He meets Clemens in the opening sequence and quickly falls in love. This 'eternal love', however, proves confining and their relationship quickly succumbs to Daniel's desire for new experiences. Separating from Clemens, Daniel travels further through the homosexual subculture or, better phrased, underworld (*Unterwelt*). While the film relentlessly exposes all of the perversions of the situation in which 'he', the homosexual Daniel, lives, it also portrays homosexuals as pathological types. Following Daniel on his adventures the spectator meets characters such as 'the old queen', 'the queer', 'the fag' and 'the leather freak' along the way. The spectator also sees, however, that the more Daniel familiarizes himself with the subculture, the more sexually addicted the once-innocent boy from the country becomes. The pathology of the homosexuals' situation pulls Daniel in. He searches out sexual encounters everywhere, from the mansions of the *haute bourgeoisie* to parks and public toilets, and becomes like the types with whom he spends his time. Yet the film ends with Daniel visiting a gay male commune and here, stretched out on a sort of large communal bed with a number of naked men, Daniel participates in a consciousness-raising session. The activists confront him with a critique of existing sexual politics and his own behaviour. Daniel openly asks questions and seems to accept their judgments. In effect this commune presents a social, political and philosophical hope for the future situation of gay men. The film cuts to a final drawn image of a rose as the soundtrack escalates into a crescendo of slogans for active political rebellion: 'out of the toilets and into the streets'.

The film stands out in relationship to its postwar precursors like infamous Nazi-propagandist Veit Harlan's 1957 contribution *The Third Sex* (*Anders als du und ich*) with its clear and insidious attack on homosexuals as 'predators'. Likewise it distinguishes itself from its contemporaries, for example Fassbinder's art-house film of lesbian decadence *The Bitter Tears of Petra von Kant* (*Die bitteren Tränen der Petra von Kant*, 1972) or the more exploitative examination of the antics of a homosexual serial-killer in Uli Lommel's 1973 film *The Tenderness of Wolves* (*Die Zärtlichkeit der Wölfe*). While none of these films seeks to provide positive images of homosexuality, von Praunheim's film clearly engages in a critical relationship with the dominant social philosophy of the period, and seeks to push forward new discursive paradigms.

The film relied on counter-cinema practices drawn from Brechtian techniques. There is an episodic quality such that the elapsing of film time is unclear. Daniel's shift to new circles clearly takes place over time, but there are no markers of the passing of time – short of changes in Daniel's sideburns, which become, in good 1970s style, ever 'modder' as the film progresses. Indeed the film begins suddenly with the camera tracking in front of two men walking down the street. An alienating non-synchronized voice-over dialogue replicates a discussion between the two that stands in no immediate relationship to their action of simply walking. The spectator eventually associates the dialogue with the characters. The film cuts to a static frame of them in a room where they proceed to embrace. They are, then, in a romantic relationship.

The opening voice-over dialogue between Clemens and Daniel quickly gives way to the voices of two commentators who provide various observations on the unfolding episodes. These voices dominate the film. One commentator is a darker, more critical voice; the other provides more neutral clinical observations. This narrative ultimately replaces dialogue. The Daniel voice is rarely heard and then usually only to ask questions. About two-thirds of the way through, while focusing on a leather scene, the film drops sound entirely. The camera observes a staged cruising scene in silence, which lends it an eerie ritualistic feel. Daniel's style of dress does not match the leather men, covered in chains, and biker and police paraphernalia. He is excluded from the hands that play with the chains and the fetishization of leather-clad body parts. Thus while we focus repeatedly on Daniel, the film's use of such alienation techniques does not establish an affective relationship. The film rejects Aristotelian identification, and instead constructs Daniel as a character outside of our sympathy.

These techniques all confront the audience and reject the viewing practices of Hollywood-style narrative film as well as positive image aesthetics. However, although the film seeks to present its characters through a provocative typification that forecloses easy identification, its satirical representations of the subculture rely on tropes of deviance, masks, ritualism and exoticism. Without a narrative that establishes identification or sympathy, this descent into the milieu has an exposé quality to it, not unlike a product of the tabloid press. Because of its focus on the subculture, the perverse 'situation in which [the homosexual] lives' is not a result of social oppression, heterosexism, patriarchy, or any other outside repressive forces that could bear responsibility for the unhappy conditions of the homosexual. It does not allow for any easy adoption of a victim status. For example, one of the few scenes in which (presumably) heterosexuals play a role is a gay-bashing scene in which an older man, 'an old queen', is accosted and roughed up at a toilet where he has been cruising for sex. The relentless critical language of the film actually continues at this point, expressing no sympathy or outrage over the attack, rather the language assesses it as a predictable result of a particular form of perverse behaviour. Here the film proves particularly incapable of approaching the very real threat of violence present in heteronormative society. The aspect of the film that we could identify as victim blaming comes into full relief in this particular scene. We can note further that the film ignores the devastation of political organizing wrought by the Nazi era. In fact the film's relentless concentration on 'the situation' allowed only for a focus on immediate subcultural conditions.

Within the analysis of the film, the homosexual existed in self-created perversion and bore sole responsibility for the transformation of his own conditions.[3] Many viewers experienced the film as promoting stereotypes and weaknesses, and they became angry with von Praunheim for betraying his community. Even if they understood that the film was about gays for gays, they knew that he still screened it in front of heterosexuals. Von Praunheim readily accepted the recrimination, yet argued that his strategy had been productive for a wider understanding of the situation of gay men:

People – and especially gay men – feel that the gay film [i.e. *Not the Homosexual Is Perverse*] is an incredibly biting satire. Gays hid underneath their seats and were very embarrassed that every single one of their weaknesses was being attacked in the film, and they kept thinking that the result of this method would be that the heteros would point a finger at them and say: into the gas chamber with you, hide yourself, you're so unpleasant, because they [i.e. gay men] don't have the confidence to admit to their own weaknesses. And suddenly afterwards there was a huge wave of sympathy above all from heteros, who said, it's on account of your weaknesses that we like you so much, its precisely the fact that its okay to show weaknesses which makes us like the film much more than a conventional, liberal film.[4]

The encoded message of the film allowed for a very limited number of responses. It primarily provoked the spectator into adopting a critical position *vis-à-vis* the portrayals of homosexuals. Given that the spectator could not easily enter into an identification with any of the characters, he was encouraged rather to identify as a homosexual of a different, politically engaged type. This type appeared only at the end when the men of the commune sit naked together yet speak against the sexually addicted 'fag'. Their nakedness acts as a sign of their nonconformity, their comfort with their bodies and with each other. However, in their critique the film only vaguely hints at the exact nature of the political engagement toward which it strives. We could say that von Praunheim's film undertakes an expansion of Simone de Beauvoir's now classic statement: one is born *neither* a woman *nor* a pervert. Central to overcoming socially constructed perversion was an *identification as Schwul* and further, the film advocates more than a *liberation* of sexuality, but rather its sublimation into communal politics.

In regard to the further practicalities of political organization, von Praunheim readily acknowledges that he quickly got bored with such considerations. In an interview he described the ensuing meetings as 'too theoretical for me as an artist' especially as an artist who treats provocation as art.[5] Von Praunheim had already turned to Martin Dannecker for assistance with the theoretical foundation of the film. At the time, Dannecker was engaged in the influential study that would be published three years later in 1974 under the title *The Ordinary Homosexual (Der gewöhnliche Homosexuelle)*. This study, an undertaking in quantitative sociology, exhibits the same trajectory we observe in the film.[6] The result of this collaboration was a stance which opposed the assimilation to what von Praunheim and Dannecker identified as bourgeois values: the search for romantic love, the desire for marriage-like conditions, the participation in consumerist behaviour. They approached homosexuality as a potential site of revolutionary activity, basing these ideas on a modified reading of Reich, Marcuse and the Frankfurt School. (Alluding to Walter Benjamin's essay, von Praunheim once described the film as 'sex in the age of mechanical reproduction'.)[7] They hoped that the film would lead to solidarity within a group that was presumed to have some a priori political commonality formed in this case by a shared sexual desire.

The film draws from this theoretical work and narrowly focuses on gay male sexuality. If gender appeared at all in the film as part of its analysis, it was only to comment on the perversion of either hyper-masculinization of the leather scene, or the hyper-feminization of figures like 'the old queen'. According to the logic of the film, these perversely gendered characters exist situationally, are superstructurally determined and can be resolved with a transformation of the base of sexuality. Transgendered existence is covered only in relation to transvestitism and bisexuality. The possibility that heterosexual practices might also pursue queer radical aims is not addressed.

In the theoretical background of the film, then, we recognize a *proper* identity relationship to a sexual predisposition, which provides the basis of emancipatory strivings or political practice. The failure of this identity relationship, when homosexuals collaborate in the values of bourgeois society, results in a 'counter-revolutionary' perversion. However an alignment of identity and predisposition presents the further possibility of homosexual solidarity and political agency.[8] Indeed, while the film primarily undertakes a description of how the aims of a repressive society can be pursued in homosexual practice, *Not the Homosexual* ends with a series of programmatic declarations that allude to the possibility of positive homosexual agency. In the slogans of the final sequence and the credits homosexuals appear as the vanguard in the general struggle against repressive desublimation.

The homosexual vanguard requires a radical transformation, involving not only a rejection of the closet and cruising in public toilets and parks, but also a rejection of bourgeois monogamy. Thus transformed homosexuals are able to create the kind of gay community called for:

organizations like gay-owned bars, general self-help and cooperation between 'butches' and 'queens', as well as an alignment with blacks, women and workers. These final slogans come quickly and, upon reflection, seem to contrast with the fact that the film excludes women, workers, blacks and so on from its analysis. In its strict orientation to gay men, the model of political action here, based in this proper alignment, must necessarily exclude questions of gender, class or ethnicity. In fact, this social philosophy corresponds to positions *vis-à-vis* race, gender and sex found in other contemporary movements: minority, women's, lesbian or bisexual liberation movements and the more recent transgendered movement. Each of these movements establishes their understanding of community and communal politics as deriving from a proper identity relationship to an essential racial, gender, sexed or even class predisposition. A more complex system of gender and sexuality functioned in the case of the lesbian movement, but likewise the contemporary emergence of a distinct transgendered movement is based on a similar structure deriving from body sex.

These social philosophies based on this structure strove for the transformation of an essentialist gender or sexuality *in itself* to a self-transforming movement oriented toward gender or sexuality *for itself*. If gays could overthrow the shackles of internalized homophobia and behave like homosexuals, if women could overthrow the deformations of patriarchy and behave like women, the gay or the women's liberation movements would experience success. In keeping with this understanding, each movement produced its own tagline to define its essence: women shared a 'universal sisterhood', gays emphasized that they were 'born this way', contemporary transgendered narrative includes a statement of having 'always known I was the other sex', and so on.

Such social philosophy, however, ultimately resulted first in a self-interested minority politics, which, on the one hand, succeeded in establishing institutions and community support structures, while on the other, also established homogenizing and normativizing tendencies in those institutions. The reality of the gay, women's, bisexual and transgendered communities therefore fails to meet the demands of the slogans at the end of *Not the Homosexual*. Those slogans, in calling for a wider transformation of a repressive society, would have required that the communities exceed their own minority status. To do so the participants in the movement would have had to go beyond precisely their self-interests and form coalitions to support other movements. In practice, such coalition politics between self-interested minority groups proved much more than difficult, such that gay men and lesbians, two groups that would seem to share a common ground of same-sex desire, could not find a basis of shared interest upon which they could organize together. In retrospect, von Praunheim himself acknowledges that the conscious exclusion of lesbians from the film was problematic: 'We were egotistical men, but we also knew too little about lesbians and could only hope that they would be inspired to organize themselves. Which then did happen.'[9]

As if already aware of this inherent failure in the possibility of gay community politics, the camera in Not the Homosexual spends the majority of the time focused on the queers and perverts. The penultimate scene, set in a gay bar, establishes a foil to the hippie commune and also trumps the lengthy leather scene already mentioned for a kind of engaged camerawork. The bar is filled with transvestites, clones, cigar smokers, leather types and a single black man. Daniel sits at a table with outrageous muttonchops, smokes distractedly and observes in a cool Brechtian fashion what the aggressive commentator identifies as a 'fantastic theatre of freaks'. Those gathered variously dance, kiss and even yodel facing a fairly static camera. Given that the commentator frames this environment with such a negative description, and that this bar serves as final foil to the commune, the fact that the camera remains proximate to the characters becomes all the more significant, as the proximity makes the cinematic space seem crowded but also intimate. The scene is fairly protracted; like the earlier leather scene it lasts much longer than is necessary to present Daniel's narrative motivation. Indeed, as in that scene Daniel fades into the background and the film has a sort of revue quality, showing a talent night at the bar. The shots in this scene have an almost familiar home movie quality to them as the lay actors, dressed in their regalia, periodically recognize the camera with a straight-on gaze. Indeed it is hard not to recognize that this fantastic theatre consists of friends who turned out to be in 'Rosa's movie' and it is these 'freaks' who will feel provoked by the film. Importantly, however, the scene indicates precisely the direction von Praunheim will take in later films. Von Praunheim here gives an indication of his future distance from totalizing identities. The diversity portrayed here already represents the impossibility of a gay essence, or a homogeneous gay identity, and it represents moreover the limits to models of health and perversion, as well as of self-interested coalition politics. The bar's theatre of fantastic diversity presents a more realistic vision of (queer) community than the staged utopian gay family bed of the final scene. Ultimately in the course of his work it is not to the gay liberationist commune but to the fantastic theatre that von Praunheim will continually return his camera.

In 1998 von Praunheim's film *Gay Courage* premiered. Funded by the German television stations Hessischer Rundfunk and Arte, and co-ordinated with the momentous exhibition of gay history at the Academy of the Arts in Berlin, *Goodbye to Berlin? 100 Years of Gay Liberation*, the docudrama tries to pack one hundred years of gay activism into ninety minutes of footage. For this reason, many of the choices of included material seem idiosyncratic, but the film follows a logic of past struggle and persecution, contemporary emancipation and utopic future. Two-thirds of the film, persecution to emancipation, focuses on Germany, with a time frame from Magnus Hirschfeld's founding of the Scientific–Humanitarian Committee through to the 1994 repeal of §175, but the camera then suddenly travels to San Francisco to find the utopic future. At this point the film takes on a very different quality. Fictionalized history gives way to more traditional documentary footage, which reserves realism for utopia and represents historical reality through fictionalized film.

A longer and transitional sequence concentrates on the celebrations surrounding the striking of §175 from the legal code. Here von Praunheim's camera pans over thousands of people celebrating, many decked out in splendid drag and festive costume. After surveying the scene, the film moves over into 'man on the street' interviews with some of the celebrants and asks them for their vision of the future. The film does not rely on information from politicians or the official spokespeople of the movement; rather it goes into the community and onto the streets seeking to interrogate the homosexual celebrant as political subject. The interviewer is heard to ask, 'Do you think the gay movement is over? […] Is there any further direction for gay rights?' to which various revellers simply reply with 'yes' or laugh giddily and say, 'I don't know'. The repeal of this paragraph and the transformation of the political conditions of gays also calls for a transformation of gay politics and von Praunheim seems here to search for signs of what that might look like. We could object that it was unfair to expect well-articulated responses from people at that time and place, randomly solicited. However, from out of von Praunheim's critical perspective, the spectator is left to observe a dulling impact on queerness by its 'emancipation'.

Typical of the trope of all utopias, San Francisco contrasts with Germany, the former appearing as a centre of dynamic cultural diversity, a *queer* community of experimentation, as it has overcome the AIDS crisis and the commercialization of gay culture. From the perspective of von Praunheim's camera, San Francisco's queers do not rely on totalizing identity politics or succumb to normative exclusionary tendencies. Rather they expand the diversity of community, which in their heterogeneous inclusion obviates coalition politics and counters heterosexual moralizing. San Francisco queers do not seek a place at the table, instead they invite everyone to their picnic. In other words, von Praunheim establishes San Francisco as a utopic foil to the German gay rights movement, and thus celebrates its great success. We could question whether he accurately portrays San Francisco, but I would rather focus on the fact that in *Gay Courage* von Praunheim inverts the ending of *Not the Homosexual*, which places the commune as a foil to the queer community. This inversion marks a significant shift in von Praunheim's representation of the gay community. Significantly it also corresponds to a greater shift in the general relationship to identity politics of activists and theorists involved in social movements, a shift toward queer politics.

Robert Tobin has noted the explosion in the use of the term queer/ *quer* in German. This started with the appearance in 1992 of a Queer Nation group and expanded within a few years to use in academic publications, conferences, social and cultural organizations, parties, clubs, publications, television and radio programs, film series and so on.[10] Queer here marked first an opening up of a social and political space that crossed the gender barriers of the gay and lesbian community. In doing so, however, it also marked a shift away from homogenizing identity politics. But it must be underscored that this shift away from identity to queer politics and queer organizing reached far beyond the German gay community. The relationship between identity and political practice was questioned in the women's liberation movements before the emergence of Queer Theory. In the 1980s, women of colour and feminists in the developing world challenged 'universal sisterhood' and the ability of white Western bourgeois feminists' to speak on behalf of all women.[11] Likewise just as Turkish–German and Afro-German feminists confronted the racist and xenophobic bias of the women's movement, the gay community in the 1990s witnessed the rapid formation of Turkish, black and Asian minority groups as a response to experiences of discrimination, exoticization and isolation. Thus queer, as a simple term, opened up space for heterogeneous social and political organizing that was not available within the parameters of identity politics. There is no doubt that it was easier for queer social events to accommodate gays, lesbian, bisexuals, transgendered people and fetishists, or to cut across class, ethnic and racial difference, than it was for queer politics to identify a common goal or platform. Everyone can show up at a dance or a potluck, but when the work of articulating a common political platform or goal begins, queer organizers immediately recognize how difficult it is to find common interests.

Queer opened up not only new social and political space, but also intellectual and academic space. During the 1990s Queer Theory undertook what I would describe as a further extension and radicalization of de Beauvoir's dictum 'one is not born a woman but becomes such' to include the social construction of gender and sexuality and even of the sexed body itself: i.e. one is not born a woman or a man, nor hetero- or homosexual, nor male or female, but becomes such. As mentioned in the opening of the chapter, a series of academic debates emerged in Germany in the early 1990s around the status of gender research. Ostensibly focused on the reception of Judith Butler's work, Barbara Duden's suggestively titled 1993 article 'Woman without a Lower Body' set off the debate, attacking the queer theoretical recognition of the social construction of the body, its gender and sex as epistemologically produced artefacts.[12] For Women's Studies such a position meant that if the female body did not exist in itself, it could not offer an immutable object of historical objectification. Thus women's bodies as such could no longer contain an essential truth which could offer women a unified political direction. Moreover, we should underscore that Queer Theory has presented a similar challenge to the various 'Queer Studies' that also derive from identity politics: Gay Studies, Lesbian Studies, Transgendered Studies, Bisexual Studies, Fetish Studies and so on.[13]

The transgendered and intersexed movements, even though they might have emerged during the decade as identity-based movements, lived out this extended dictum to its fullest extent and in doing so actually presented significant challenges to other identity-based groups. The transgendered movement in seeking to take individual control over the social construction of the sexed body, or the intersexed in rejecting the interventions of the medical establishment on the polymorphous human body, confronted the essentialist presumptions of the gender and sexual liberation movements – presumptions that these movements actually share with heteronormative society – that the world divides into two essential different sexes.[14] While the transgendered and intersexed movements do counter a bipolar model of sex with a continuum of difference, such a position does not of course necessarily challenge an essentializing empirical approach to the body. The transgendered and intersexed body certainly presents itself for measurement to the calipers of the scientists, and a continuum can still leave polar opposites intact as ideals. However, attention to transgendered and intersexed people has supported a theoretical shift from understanding the body as an empirical object to approaching it as an epistemological subject. Rather than inquiring what percentage of births display 'abnormal' sex characteristics, Queer Theory might question what socially defined sex ideals compel the paediatric establishment to undertake drastic sexual reassignment surgery on newborns. We might summarize the difference in the essentializing and the queer positions as the difference between an exploration of, on the one hand, what it means to *be* a woman and, on the other, what it means to *become* a woman; what it means to be a homosexual versus to become gay.

Von Praunheim's docudrama *I Am My Own Woman* (1992) takes up this shift and not only illustrates this new direction in social philosophy, but also represents a milestone in the radical potential for new modes of representation, which the body as epistemological subject makes possible for film and the filmmaker. The film focuses on the life of Charlotte von Mahlsdorff, a transgendered woman born in 1928 as Lothar Berfelde. She grew up in the Third Reich, and in spite of the social pressure and extreme danger was nevertheless able to live part of her life as a young girl on the estate of her aunt. There she was introduced to sexological literature and learned to describe herself as a woman trapped in a man's body. Lothar took the name Charlotte von Mahlsdorff and after the war began a new life in the GDR first as a *Trümmerfrau* (literally, 'rubble woman') working to rebuild bombed-out Berlin, then as self-appointed restorer and curator of first the Friedrichsfelde Palace, before becoming curator of her own museum of Victoriana (*Gründerzeitmuseum*). Over time her independence and resilience in the face of the authorities of the GDR propelled her to the centre of the East German gay community. The film chronicles her development to the point after the fall of the Wall when Charlotte received the Cross of the Federal Order of Merit (*Bundesverdienstkreuz*).

In passing through the episodes of Charlotte's life, the film almost sets up a fairy tale narrative – although other elements such as the awarding of the medal at the end propel the story into the realm of the nineteenth-century moral narrative – with Charlotte as the finally triumphant hero. Such heroizing of Charlotte is remarkable in a von Praunheim film, precisely because Charlotte's often bawdy story contains episodes of the type explicitly denounced in *Not the Homosexual*: from the very fact that she is transgendered, to her cruising of public toilets and parks, her romantic S/M relationships or the scenes of Charlotte dressed in her characteristic matron outfit tending to her bourgeois household museum. What von Praunheim earlier denounced as a perversion of the social and political potential of the homosexual appears here as the individual's potential for social and political liberation. It is not Charlotte who is perverse, rather the totalitarian situations in which she lives. Indeed the film's celebration of Charlotte's life actually contravenes much of the programme of *Not the Homosexual*. Its very title, *I Am My Own Woman*, presents an individualistic orientation not easily reconciled with collective identity-based movements. The absence of satire also indicates a significant moment in von Praunheim's filmwork, perhaps it would be more correct to say that by focusing on the perverse exploits of Charlotte, the film does not need to create satire. Von Praunheim has produced a small number of films that have a loving quality, a heroizing relationship to their subjects, and this is one of them.

The film's visual technique takes a direction directly opposite to *Not the Homosexual*. We can distinguish that the film is not pseudo-documentary, like *Not the Homosexual*, nor mockumentary, like *Neurosia* or *A Virus Knows No Morals*, but a docudrama. It is, furthermore, a docudrama whose visual techniques rely fully on the art of self-fashioning and transformation inherent in its transgendered subject. Jens Taschner plays Charlotte in her adolescence and the Berlin drag queen Ichgola Androgyn plays her in her adult years; however, the characters are introduced in a particular fashion. The film begins with Charlotte meeting a young boy (Jens Taschner) in an *S-Bahn* train. The boy accompanies her and listens to her descriptions of her childhood, but then somewhat seamlessly transitions into her character, enacting the story she was recounting. The film seems to open up into a straightforward narrative as he acts out her conflicts with her father and the discovery of the pleasures of cross-dressing, until Charlotte, the character, receives a beating from her father, at which point the adult Charlotte enters into the scene and discusses the father with the boy actor. She gives him instructions and then withdraws as he returns to acting. This disruption reminds the audience that a dramatization is unfolding and that visual narrative can set in motion a form of play; the spectator is made aware that a boy can play a boy who plays at being a girl, or that a drag queen can leave her typical camp play on the stage to appear playing a passing transgendered woman. In foregrounding such play in its own visuals, it opens up the possibility of the recognition of a greater possibility of social form in quotidian life.

Such disruption does reveal the apparatus of the film and thus allows for a dynamic questioning of the facticity of the narrative, although the film does not distance itself necessarily from the facticity of Charlotte's remembrances. Charlotte is continually given a commentating and directorial status in this remembrance of things past, and in staging her interruptions the film documents its own dramatization of a life worth emulating. This technique, as a central aspect of the heroizing of Charlotte, allows the film repeatedly to construct, in its own diegesis, relations of identification that the spectator can occupy. The entry of the real Charlotte has an alienating effect from the unfolding narrative of her life, yet it ultimately serves to assert Charlotte as storyteller and diegetic director; this film is Charlotte's story told by Charlotte. While it might alienate the spectator from a straightforward unfolding of a linear re-enactment, this technique does not distance the spectator from the action of the film, rather it establishes a position almost as if we, the spectators, were comfortably sitting at 'Auntie Charlotte's' feet as she tells her life story. While the film does not easily allow us to occupy a position in the narrative *as* Charlotte, it does encourage the viewers, the beneficiaries of this history, to occupy a position within an unfolding genealogy, to be *like* Charlotte in their own lives.

If in von Praunheim's counter-cinematic practice we still witness a form of alienation technique, in *I Am My Own Woman* the distance actually assists in the documentation of lifeworlds and life-forms that cannot be articulated through identity politics; von Prauenheim actually undertakes the sympathetic documentation outside or in opposition to paradigms of counter-revolutionary perversion. The vanguardism of *Not the Homosexual* established an obscuring distance from the artefacts of queer culture, while a film like *I Am My Own Woman* begins by examining what *is* there, rather than what *should be* there. The film thus reveals the filmmaker's rapid retreat from the aesthetic and political purity of the radical gay commune to a fascination with and reliance on precisely what appeared as perverse elements in *Not the Homosexual*. The leather scene or the final bar scene of *Not the Homosexual* becomes a primary subject of von Praunheim's subsequent films. Indeed *I Am My Own Woman* contains a scene in the *Bier-Bar* that almost replicates that earlier bar. However, here the bar appears as a positive part of a historical legacy, with Charlotte first instructing friends about how things used to be. As in most of von Praunheim's subsequent films, in *I Am My Own Woman*, the character types such as 'the leather queen', 'the fag' and so on, appear not as perverts but as queer and disruptive. In his films he does not draw an explicit political programme from them, or a simply more interesting provocative visual object, but rather a broader more flexible and developing community. Typically, *I Am My Own Woman* portrays queer disruptions of sexual, gender, sex and class norms; in addition to Charlotte and her elaborate erotic experiences, it positively features lesbians, gays and heterosexuals.

Indeed the film takes the disruptions of lived practice as the structuring principle of its narrative, yet the film also displays the interaction of lived practice with discourse, for example in the scene in which

Charlotte describes herself as a woman trapped in a man's body. Similarly, in an elaborate sequence in the Friedrichsfelde Palace, Charlotte breaks out of an interview setting to act as a quasi tour guide. Charlotte reflects on the architecture and the queer history of the building, it being the site of the famous transvestite balls organized by its earlier owner, Kuno von Moltke. Here Charlotte turns to aesthetic discourse and remarks that art makes good nature's failure, an observation that is directed to the body of the transvestite as much as to the architecture. Periodically Charlotte offers up such observations, which the film does not represent as the truth of transgendered essence but rather as Charlotte's truth of her existence. These statements are not so much explanations or justifications for her cross-dressing, rather they act as assertions of a queer social philosophy. In these statements and throughout the film, we witness how the interaction of individual practice and social discourse generates gender, sex and sexuality.

As a queer film, it concentrates on Charlotte, much like *Not the Homosexual* concentrated on Daniel, but this focus on the individual ultimately creates an uneasy relationship to the larger political history. Although it is clear that the Third Reich is filled with danger for her, Charlotte avoids persecution under the Nazis in part because of her youth, but in part because she spent the last years in prison for killing her father. The subsequent portrayal of her relationship with the state security of the GDR takes on a mixture of, at times, heroic resolution and, at other times, naïve fantasy. In 1973, Charlotte offers her museum as a safe haven for the meetings of the newly formed Berlin Homosexual Common Interest Group (*Homosexuelle Interessengemeinschaft Berlin* or HIB), but as it concentrates on Charlotte, the film gives little insight into this movement. Toward the end, the film recounts a horrific event in which a group of neo-Nazi skinheads attack a party that Charlotte has organized at her house. The film thus touches on the rise of neo-Nazis, and the general xenophobia and violence against queers that surfaced in post-unification Germany. However, once again the film's concentration on Charlotte limits this event to a personal experience and does not give insight into collective practices that were undertaken to counter this violence. The film does not end with any equivalent to the gay commune. Indeed, von Praunheim seems to distance himself from such proscription and instead relies on description. We may recall how in *Gay*

Courage gay politics gives way to a queer culture that likewise seems to exist distinctly from gay politics.

What the film also illustrates is an uneasy connection between such individual lived practice, collective emancipatory politics and queer theoretical analysis. In contrast to the gay rights movement of earlier decades, the queer movement of the 1990s drew no direct connection between identity and politics. If gay politics sought direction from an immanent gay interest, in Queer Theory the direct connection between identity and political practice is gone, as is an essential base of sexuality, gender or even sex; instead there is a gap between the actual practice of individual queerness and Queer Theory. It is much like the gap between the life of Charlotte and the film.

In the diegesis of the film, the spectator witnesses Charlotte's idiosyncratic production of gender, sex and sexuality. The portrayal of Charlotte presents a practice of queerness. As described earlier, in the representation of her life we also find a relationship between discourse and practice; her various moments of self-description, her interactions with state authorities of the Third Reich, the GDR and the FRG, her relationship to the gay liberation movement of the GDR and the FRG, each scene is played out across cultural space and time with the individual Charlotte at its centre. In this equation a direct relationship between gender, sex or sexual identity and politics drops out entirely. Instead gender, sex and sexuality appear as produced by discourse and practice, rather than as their a priori presuppositions.

However, this paradigm does not produce practice or politics, rather it suggests that, in the relationship of practice and discourse, gender, sex and sexuality are performed politically but not, however, voluntarily. The film plays out this dynamic repeatedly. The confrontation between Charlotte and the authorities of the Communist Party takes place because her transgendered existence conflicts with the heteronormative presumptions of the state. As she appears in the same frame with the director of the museum in which she works, her refusal to dress as a man makes her gender transgression clear. Yet Charlotte dresses conservatively, matronly, and in other contexts simply passes as an elderly German woman. Her gender transgression is obscured by her success at passing in her social setting. When the camera pans around the room to show the members of the HIB, the matronly lady stands out from the gathering of gay men and lesbians, because her transgression fades when surrounded by people portraying the iconography of hippie counter-culture.

There is ultimately a lack of individual voluntarism vis-à-vis the social constructions of gender, sex and sexuality. One is not born female, but becomes such, in a social context. The film plays out this dynamic perhaps nowhere more poignantly than in a scene in which Charlotte living as a woman, as a *Trümmerfrau* in postwar Berlin, meets a group of drunken Soviet soldiers on the streets one night. She confronts the sex and gender politics of the occupation as the soldiers begin to harass her and the threat of rape becomes imminent. The commenting voice of Charlotte is absent at this moment in the film and thus the tension mounts further as the spectator, aware of what the soldiers will find, awaits a continued unfolding of the violence. However, the soldiers, upon discovering Charlotte's penis simply laugh and move off: the threat is over. It could have gone differently, and the spectator is confronted with a residual awareness of what a female person would have experienced. Although the body might be a social construction, there is no outside to that construction. Humans may engage in self-fashioning, but not according to circumstances entirely of their own choice nor fully under their control.

Yet we also recognize that for all the foregrounding of Charlotte as diegetic director, there is an apparatus that constructs the film of which Charlotte is only a part. If the representation of Charlotte belongs to the film, behind this world we find von Praunheim as the director, Valentin Passoni credited with the script, Renée Gundelach and René Perraudin with production, Lorenz Haarmann with cinematography and so on. This apparatus is distinct from the practice of queerness proper and it is where the work of Queer Theory takes place. If we move away from the narrative of Charlotte told by the film and focus on how the camera frames her in its projected image, and how the general apparatus of the film is distinct from this story, then we glimpse a similarity to the function of Queer Theory. Like the distance of the camera, queer theorists rely on a willed alienation from their subjects. Sabine Hark pointedly stated in the midst of the Butler Debates that '"*Queer* science" [*Queere Wissenschaft*] is accordingly a science that is exactly not defined through "queer objects", but rather through its reflexive practice'.[15] Hark adopted this position to counter those occupying an identity political paradigm or a Queer Studies model. Although it might serve this purpose, the position, while highlighting reflexive practice or willed alienation as achieving a distance from the object, is perhaps too polemical a position. Obviously without Charlotte there could be no film, without the queer object, theory would exist in a vacuum, yet *I Am My Own Woman* is a representation of Charlotte organized by a critical apparatus. Thus the relationship of Queer Theory to its objects does indeed take place across a gap, but this does not mean that the object is on one side and the 'reflexive practice' on the other, rather 'reflexive practice', or willed alienation, fills the gap between the filmic apparatus and the film's representations, this makes possible the critical social philosophy of Queer Theory. It is in taking a step of distance from identity movements and the appearance of gender, sex and sexuality that Queer Theory becomes possible. Such distance made *I Am My Own Woman* possible.

For activists, academics, cultural critics and so on this paradigm created a new relationship to politics, and this new relationship generated the tension of the debates of the 1990s. It should be clear that because there is a gap does not mean that there is no relationship between the politics of queerness and the practice of Queer Theory, however, the problem of Queer Theory's relationship to the political movement should be clear. Ultimately the film presents its images to spectators who, compelled by it, move its representations into political discourse. In turn the production of political discourse leads back to practice. Thus we acknowledge *I Am My Own Woman* as a document of Queer Theory producing political discourse as much as we acknowledge the texts of the Butler Debate. Academic Queer Theorists might understand the success of this model as deriving from their ability to occupy the almost impossible position von Praunheim sometimes holds of acknowledged public intellectual in a mediatized public democracy. However, just as it seems to have humbled von Praunheim, such a model of social philosophy ultimately humbles academic theorists with vanguardist aspirations as they seek to engage with the movements of a pluralist society. En route to political discourse, Queer theorizing must be recognized as an expansive and inclusive activity, which acknowledges the contributions of a community of organic intellectuals.

If one peruses the listings for cities like Berlin or Cologne, one will recognize a vibrant colourful mix of new organizations that have emerged which rely on a notion of queerness for their self-description. Such organisations include *Queer Christ* for queer Christians, *Queer gegen Rechts* for queer anti-fascists or *queerSchlag* for queer rowers. These groups exist alongside the more venerable institutions of the liberation movements and this should indicate a certain waning of the tensions of the 1990s. However, it also indicates new questions and challenges to Queer Theory on the horizon. In this steady expansion of community, queerness comes to take on a different meaning, which must impact Queer Theory. How do we identify queer objects to analyze? The formation of spaces like Gayhenna (a monthly Turkish–German queer cultural gathering in Berlin), Christopher Street Day (the German version of Gay Pride marches) or Schöneberg's Street Festival in Berlin positively allow for gays and lesbians, heteros, homos, bis, trannies, immigrants and non-immigrants to gather together, but this means that we cannot define queer as that which is disruptive or outside. To rely on such an understanding, as some have done, is to condemn Queer Theory to the generation of only negative politics, which would soon diverge from lived experience. Yet how does one row or play table tennis queerly? How do we avoid placing lived practice into the position that sex/gender essentialism once occupied: queer is as queer does? And certainly not all that is queer is positive or heroic. Although we should like to attend generally to the type of politics generated here, such an examination would prove too broad for the scope of this chapter. However, I can conclude by drawing some final observations on the general tendency of von Praunheim's films and politics today.

Von Praunheim responded to these dilemmas with a historical turn in his films of the 1990s. *I Am My Own Woman* and *Gay Courage*, of course, but likewise *The Einstein of Sex* turned to history by taking up the life of Magnus Hirschfeld. In *Neurosia* von Praunheim historicized his own life and, moreover, in more traditional documentaries like *Queens Don't Cry* or even *Wonderful Wrodow* (*Wunderbares Wrodow*, 1999), which respectively concentrate on a Berlin drag queen community and an eastern German village, he approached his living subjects from a historical perspective similar to that through which he framed Charlotte. These films survey history and the viewers, the beneficiaries of this history, are led to occupy a position within an unfolding gene-alogy, filled with past heroes responsible for the gains in the present. From this position we find in Charlotte a positive character whose heroism is represented at the end of the film through the medal of honour pinned to her smock. The camera lingers on this image of the elderly lady whose life the film has just reviewed, wearing the medal on her very traditional dress surrounded by functionaries of the federal and local government. This scene is produced as a queer moment yet clearly the film presents her as an emulatable practical model for the spectator, even though it does not end with a manifesto and does not provide a specific direction. Of course its concentration on an individual story does not mean that it is impossible to portray broader movements. San Francisco offers a final utopic model in *Gay Courage*, yet clearly the images represented in this queer film do not operate in and on behalf of a liberation movement and, in all these cases, emulatable models exist only at a distance and do not allow for an easy translation into proximate political or social practice. San Francisco is not Germany, Wrodow is not Hoyerswerda, I am not a transgendered woman.

Given the break with past models of the gay liberation movement I am seeking to document here, it is remarkable and poignant that the 1970s are not vilified. Rather, in this turn to history, von Praunheim's films challenge the spectator in the contemporary moment to appreciate the investment in their present and to continue the progress. However, guidelines remain vague and I would point out that the single most significant sign of the distance between *Not the Homosexual* and *I Am My Own Woman*, between Daniel and Charlotte, is precisely the fact that Charlotte's story does belong to the past whereas Daniel's belonged to the present. With Charlotte, after emancipation from §175 and from the queer utopia of San Francisco, we look back from a position at the end of history, whereas with Daniel we looked forward filled with an awareness that we are making our future.

Notes

1   Participants included Gisela Bock, Angelika Ebbinghaus, Lerke Gravenhorst, Frigga Haug, Claudia Koonz, Annette Kuhn, Marianne Lehker, Dorothea Schmidt, Christina Thürmer-Rohr, Annemarie Tröger and Karin Windaus-Walser. See Atina Grossmann, 'Feminist Debates about Women and National Socialism', Gender & History, 3.3 (1991), 350–8; Lerke Gravenhorst and Carmen Tatschmurat (eds.), Töchter Fragen NS-Frauen Geschichte, ed. by (Freiburg: Kore, 1990).

2   For further discussions of von Praunheim's work see Alice A. Kuzniar, The Queer German Cinema (Stanford: Stanford University Press, 2000); Wolfgang Jacobsen (ed.), Rosa von Praunheim (Munich: Carl Hanser Verlag, 1984); Robert Tobin 'Okzidentalismus: Der verquerte Orientalismus im schwul-lesbischen deutschen Film', Forum Homosexualität und Literatur, 41 (2002), 75–89.

3   Kuzniar reads the film differently, finding in the commentators' voices an exterior commentary that is the 'symbolic dominant order'. Kuzniar, The Queer German Cinema, p. 98. However, I understand the commentators as part of the interior. I read an earlier version of this chapter at a conference organized by Kuzniar before the publication of her book where we discussed this point. I would continue to position the commentators in the interior of the homosexual subculture because they become silent as we arrive at the final scene where the voices of the gay commune replicate some of their observations. In this position the commune members seem to subsume and exceed the commentators' discourse. See also the role of Martin Dannecker in the theoretical apparatus of the film, discussed below in note 7.

4   'Der Schwulen-Film wird ja als wahnsinnig beißende Satire empfunden – gerade von Schwulen. Die Schwulen haben sich ja unter den Sitzen verkrochen und sich wahnsinnig geniert, daß plötzlich ihre Schwächen im Film von vorn bis hinten attakiert worden sind, und sie haben immer gedacht, diese Methode führt dazu, daß die Heteros mit den Fingern auf sie zeigen und sagen: ab in die Gaskammer, versteck dich, du bist so unangenehm, weil sie sich selber nicht zutrauen, zu ihren Schwächen zu stehen. Und es ist plötzlich hinterher eine unheimliche Welle der Sympathie gerade von den Heteros gekommen, die sagten, gerade durch eure Schwäche seid ihr uns so lieb geworden, gerade daß man Schwächen zeigen darf, ist uns tausendmal lieber als ein angepaßter liberaler Film.' Rosa von Praunheim, 50 Jahre pevers: Die sentimentalen Memoiren des Rosa von Praunhem (Cologne: Kiepenheuer & Witsch, 1993), p. 120.

5   Jacobsen (ed.), Rosa von Praunheim, p. 61.

6   Dannecker's book, co-authored with Reimut Reiche, begins with das coming out and then moves on to examine 'the homosexual subculture' where we find different chapters like 'The Subculture as Sex Market' or 'The Different Bar Types'; then we go on to examine 'Homosexual Friendships', 'Promiscuity', 'Sexuality', 'Perversions' and 'The Collective Neuroses of the Homosexuals'. See Martin Dannecker and Reimut Reiche, Der gewöhnliche Homosexuelle (Frankfurt/Main: Fischer, 1974). In these chapters it is easy to recognize the trajectory that Daniel follows in the film. Here also we find a conscious exclusion of women and lesbians from the study (p. 10).

7   Jacobsen (ed.), Rosa von Praunheim, p. 61.

8   In Dannecker's case in particular, identity like sexuality is a latent psychic state. See his discussion in Der gewöhnliche Homosexuelle, especially pp. 11–12.

9   'Die Lesben hatten wir in unserem Film bewußt ausgeklammert. Wir waren egoistische Männer, wußten auch zu wenig von Lesben und konnten nur hoffen, daß sie sich, angeregt durch uns, selbst organisierten. Was ja dann auch passierte' (von Praunheim, 50 Jahre pevers, p.119). For further discussion of the relationship of lesbians to the gay movement, see Susanna Jäger, Doppelaxt oder Regenbogen?: Zur Genealogie lesbisch-feministischer Identität (Tübingen: Edition Diskord, 1998); Ursula Linnhoff, Weibliche Homosexualität: Zwischen Anpassung und Emanzipation (Cologne: Kiepenheur & Witsch,

1976); Ina Kuckuc (pseud. Ilse Kokula), *Der Kampf gegen Unterdrückung: Materialien aus der deutschen Lesbierinnenbewegung* (Munich: Verlag Frauenoffensive, 1975). Finally an issue devoted to articles on the history of the lesbian movement can be found in *Ihrsinn*, 10 (1994).

10 See Robert Tobin, 'Queer in Germany: Sexual Culture and National Discourses', paper given at the conference '50 Years of the Federal Republic of Germany through a Gendered Lens', University of North Carolina – Chapel Hill, 24 September 1999.

11 This challenge came out of positions of race, ethnicity and class. For discussions of the transformations in Germany see the issue *Beiträge zur feministischen Theorie und Praxis*, 27 (1990), which was devoted to the topic, 'Rassismus, Antisemitismus, Fremdenhaß: Geteilter Feminismus' ('Racism, Antisemitism, Xenophobia: Divided Feminism').

12 Barbara Duden, 'Die Frau ohne Unterleib: Zu Judith Butlers Entkörperung. Ein Zeitdokument', *Feministische Studien*, 2 (1993), 24–34. For a discussion of the academic debate and the institutional tensions which resulted see Sabine Hark 'Umstrittene Wissensterritorien: Feminismus und *Queer Theory* – Reflexivität als Programm' in by Ursula Ferdinand, Andreas Pretzel, Andreas Seeck (eds.), *Verqueerte Wissenschaft: Zum Verhältnis von Sexualwissenschaft und Sexualreformbewegung in Geschichte und Gegenwart* (Münster: LIT, 1998). Of course in the 'post-feminist' era, Women's Studies finds itself in productive tension not only with Queer Studies, but with various directions in Women's Studies as well as between various generations of Women's Studies researchers and students. An excellent volume for an overview of these tensions is by Ilse Modelmog and Ulrike Gräßel (eds.), *Konkurrenz und Kooperation: Frauen in Zwiespalt?* (Hamburg and Münster: LIT, 1994).

13 Queer Studies, or *Queerstudien*, should be understood as distinct from but related to Queer Theory. Queer Studies represents projects larger than Gay and/or Lesbian Studies, going beyond these two identity positions to include others such as bisexuals and gender radicals. In an examination of the history of these developments, it is noteworthy that many of the first Gay Studies courses in Germany were set up and taught by US academics, and significantly by one person in particular, Prof. James Steakley. We will have to wait for him to write on his own experiences with these programmes, but for reflections on the establishment of *Homo-Studien* in Bremen see Rüdiger Lautmann, *Der Homosexuelle und sein Publikum* (Hamburg: Männerschwarm, 1997). Queer movements likewise began in the US and have now emerged in Germany taking on their own particular form.

14 Transgendered persons, however, also contain the potential to counter the existing model with a new form of empiricism. As noted above this movement is emerging along similar trajectories as the gender and sexuality movements where sex comes to relate to identity as the structural source of a political practice. There are many voices within the transgendered movement especially that base themselves on essentialist models that emerged in the nineteenth century, e.g. a woman's soul trapped in a man's body. Psychological diagnoses of gender disphoria disorder, the contemporary version of the nineteenth century discourse are necessary in most countries to acquire a sex change operation. For an insightful discussion of transsexuality in the German context see Gesa Lindemann, *Das paradoxe Geschlecht: Transsexualität im Spannungsfeld von Körper, Leib und Gefühl* (Frankfurt/Main: Fischer, 1993). Lindemann evidences a conscious desire to work within Feminist and Queer Theory and uses ethnomethodological interviews to mediate. This results in a complicated argument that might not always succeed but provides a great deal of interesting material. For a discussion of the problematic relationship of transsexuality to feminism – especially male-to-female transsexuals – see Rita Kronauer, 'Transsexualität', *Ihrsinn*, 7 (1993), 78–99. For a self-portrait of the experience of a male-to-female transsexual in Germany see Waltraud Schiffel, *Frau werden – Von Walter zu Waltraud* (Dortmund: eFeF-Verlag, 1992).

15 '"Queere Wissenschaft" ist demnach eine Wissenschaft, die gerade nicht definiert ist über "queere Gegenstände" sondern durch ihre reflexive Praxis.' Hark, 'Umstrittene Wissensterritorien', p. 22.

Index

*Film directors are listed below.
Individual films can be found
in the 'index of films'.*

INDEX OF DIRECTORS

INDEX OF FILMS